JAPAN
BETWEEN
ASIA
AND THE
WEST

JAPAN
BETWEEN
ASIA
AND THE
WEST

Economic Power
and Strategic Balance

MING WAN

AN EAST GATE BOOK

M.E. Sharpe
Armonk, New York
London, England

An East Gate Book

Serialized in the *Japanese Economy: Translations and Studies*,
vol. 26, no. 5; vol. 26, no. 6; and vol. 27, no. 1.

Library of Congress Cataloging-in-Publication Data

Wan, Ming, 1960–
  Japan between Asia and the West : economic power and strategic balance / Ming Wan.
    p. cm.
  Includes bibliographical references and index.
  ISBN 0-7656-0777-8 (alk. paper); 0-7656-0778-6 (pbk.)
    1. Japan—Foreign economic relations. 2. Japan—Foreign relations.
  3. Japan—Strategic aspects. I. Title.

  HF1601.W36 2001
  337.52—dc21
                                           2001049148

Printed in the United States of America

BM (c) 10   9   8   7   6   5   4   3   2   1
BM (p) 10   9   8   7   6   5   4   3   2   1

To Laolao

Contents

List of Tables and Figures

Tables

Figures

Acknowledgments

As this book took a long time to complete, I am indebted to many individuals and institutions for assistance in various stages of research and writing. Unfortunately, I can only name a few here, knowing well that I will not do justice to many others.

This book originated from my dissertation research. I want to thank the Department of Government of Harvard University for a Mellon Dissertation Research Fellowship in 1991–92 and a Mellon Dissertation Completion Fellowship in 1992–93, both administered through the Department. My special thanks go to Robert O. Keohane, Susan J. Pharr, and Lisa L. Martin, who served on my dissertation committee. Bob provided invaluable advice and guidance. Susan offered very useful comments and involved me in numerous Japan-related activities. I would also like to thank the U.S.–Japan Program, headed by Susan, for awarding me a postdoctoral fellowship in 1993–94, which enabled me to further my research. In addition, I appreciate the award of a Graduate Summer Travel Grant from the Edwin O. Reischauer Institute of Harvard, which supported my research at Tsukuba University in the summer of 1992. I am grateful to the late Professor Hideo Sato and many others at Tsukuba for their hospitality and advice.

While taking the basic question of my dissertation as a foundation, this book adopts a different theoretical framework, different arguments, and different organization, based on subsequent research on Japan's leadership in Asia and its relations with the United States. Besides my own research for the book, I have benefited from two related research projects. In 1994–96 I participated in a project on Global Leadership Sharing sponsored by the Social Science Research Council and the Japan Society for the Promotion of Science. I want to express my gratitude to Hideo Sato and I.M. Destler for inviting me to the project. I coauthored a chapter on Japan's unique leadership in Asia with Susan Pharr. In addition, as a member of the China Project of the Harvard Committee on Environment in 1995–98, I coauthored a chapter with Susan on Japan's environmental aid to China. I am deeply indebted to Susan for involving me and sharing her knowledge of Japan and Asia with me in these projects from which my research interest in Japan's two-track foreign policy evolved.

George Mason University kindly offered me a Summer Research Award in the summer of 1998 to work on this book. I would also like to thank Scott Keeter, the chair of the department, for commenting on my book proposal and for general encouragement for my teaching and research.

Pacific Affairs kindly allows me to use my article "Japan and the Asian Development Bank (vol. 68, no. 4, 1995/96, pp. 509–528) in Chapter 4.

Last but not the least, I cannot thank my wife Anne enough. She offered support and understanding and patiently read and commented on all the chapters.

Conventions

In this book I list Japanese and Chinese surnames first, as is the custom in Japan and China. However, Japanese and Chinese names are presented in Western order if authors choose to do so when writing in English.

Acronyms

ADB	Asian Development Bank
ADF	Asian Development Fund
AFTA	ASEAN Free Trade Area
AMF	Asian Monetary Fund
APEC	Asia-Pacific Economic Cooperation Forum
ARF	ASEAN Regional Forum
ASEAN	Association of Southeast Asian Nations
CHINCOM	China Committee of COCOM
COCOM	Coordination Committee for Multilateral Export Controls
COMECON	Council for Mutual Economic Assistance
DAC	Development Assistance Committee
EAEG	East Asia Economic Group
ECAFE	Economic Commission for Asia and the Far East
ESAF	Enhanced Structural Adjustment Facility
FDI	Foreign Direct Investment
FSX	Fighter Support Experimental project
GCI	General Capital Increase
GNP	Gross National Product
GoJ	Government of Japan
HNS	Host Nation Support
IBRD	International Bank for Reconstruction and Development
IDA	International Development Agency
IFB	International Finance Bureau

IMF	International Monetary Fund
JBIC	Japan Bank for International Cooperation
JExIm	Japan Export-Import Bank
JICA	Japan International Cooperation Agency
JSF	Japan Special Fund
KEDO	Korean Peninsula Energy Development Organization
LDCs	Less Developed Countries
LDP	Liberal Democratic Party
MDBs	Multilateral Development Banks
MITI	Ministry of International Trade and Industry
MOF	Ministry of Finance
OCR	Ordinary Capital Resources
ODA	Official Development Assistance
OECD	Organization of Economic Cooperation and Development
OECF	Overseas Economic Cooperation Fund
OOF	Other Official Flows
PKO	Peacekeeping Operation
SCI	Special Capital Increase
SDRs	Special Drawing Rights
SFR	Special Fund Resources
TMD	Theater Missile Defense
WTO	World Trade Organization

JAPAN
BETWEEN
ASIA
AND THE
WEST

1
Introduction

Two competing visions of Japan prevail in academic research and policy analysis. On the global level, Japan is often seen as a power that knows how to achieve economic success but does not know what to do in foreign policy. By contrast, on the regional level the country is viewed, with both awe and suspicion, as dominating the East Asian regional economic order with a strong sense of purpose, resourcefulness, and determination. Japan itself has adopted a two-track foreign policy—one track for the West and one track for East Asia. Japan's prolonged economic stagnation in the 1990s has drastically changed the world's view of the country. Japan is now seen as stuck in a system that has outlived its usefulness. But this recent development highlights rather than negates the importance of critically examining the cleavage between Asia and the West in Japan's foreign policy to shed light on Tokyo's motivation and strategic behavior. In fact, while retreating to some extent in the world, Japan has become more active, relative to its past behavior, in East Asia in recent years.

This topic has theoretical implications. Japan is often considered a one-dimensional power. Different from the United States, which possesses a wide range of resources, Japan's main instrument of foreign policy is economic power. Japan is thus a good case for studying the effects and limitations of economic leverage. Also, Japan joined major international organizations well after they were established, thus allow-ing us to test the impact of international institutions on a latecoming economic power. In addition, the fact that Japan has behaved differently from what international relations theory predicts a "normal power" would have done illustrates the importance of ideas and learning in shaping a country's foreign policy behavior.

The topic also has practical implications. A study of how Japan has used economic power is essential for determining whether Tokyo in-tends to act as a regional or world leader and how it will proceed if it does so. This is important because shifts in power distributions among major powers in the past have threatened international stability. In addi-tion, whether and how Japan assists one region at the expense of another affects global balance of power.

This book focuses on Japan's use of economic power. Economic state-craft has been Japan's main instrument of foreign policy since the end of World War II. Japan has used economic power to advance its political and strategic interests as well as economic and commercial ones. Spe-cifically, the discussion covers the three basic ways in which Japan may use its economic power: (1) defense spending, (2) consumption, and (3) in-vestment. Japan's direct use of economic resources—namely, whether it rewards or punishes other countries—is also explored.

This book discusses Japan's relations with the United States and East Asia, the two most important policy areas for the country. In addition, it touches on Japan's relations with the World Bank, the International Mon-etary Fund (IMF), and the Asian Development Bank (ADB). These cases place Japan's dealings with Asia and the United States in a multilateral context, allowing a contrast with its bilateral and regional relations.

The following arguments are made: Japan has used cooperative spend-ing to alleviate U.S. criticism of its massive accumulation of wealth and rapid overseas economic expansion and to protect its security arrange-ments with the United States. Toward other Asian nations, Japan has used cooperative spending to alleviate historical distrust and to facili-tate economic exchange. There are three important qualifiers for this general assessment. First, Japan's dealings with Asia and the West some-times come into conflict when the relationship between the United States and some East Asian nations becomes contentious and when Japan's cooperative spending for Asia or the West is seen as uncooperative or even harmful by the other party. Second, Japan's relationships with the United States and East Asia have become more competitive. Third, there has been a moderate increase in noncooperative or even conflictual use of economic power in Japanese foreign policy in recent years.

Japan has been largely successful in achieving what *it wants to achieve* in its use of economic power. Japan has not only survived but also thrived. Japan has used its economic power to secure markets and stable supplies of natural resources, to win friends, and to ease its rise in the world. And, the Asia we see today is much closer to what the Japanese envisioned four decades ago than it is to the U.S., Soviet, or Chinese visions. communist visions have completely failed; Asia is not a communist bloc controlled by Moscow, nor one with "Chinese characteristics." Despite America's triumph over the Soviet Union in the cold war, few in the United States can say with confidence that this is the Asia they were hoping for. Capitalism has indeed flourished in the region, but in a manner that enables Asia to compete "unfairly" with the West and threaten U.S. supremacy in the global economy. In addition, Asia as a whole has not embraced Western ideas of human rights and democracy. This is not simply a historical coincidence. The Japanese have articulated their visions and committed economic resources to facilitate realization of their objective of leading a prosperous Asia. More important, based on its own success, Japan has altered the incentive structure faced by other Asian countries.[1]

At the same time, there are limits to Japan's success. Use of economic power mitigates but does not eliminate sources of conflict and disputes. Japan's financial support has alleviated American concerns for a Japan turning against the United States but has not done away with U.S. economic grievances. Also, Japan can no longer simply rely on economic instruments in the post–cold war era when the United States expects Japan to do more in security areas. Furthermore, Japan's choice of limited forms of cooperation—namely, official development assistance (ODA) and private investments—restricts its influence in the world. Japan could have acquired far greater influence in global and regional political economy if it had been willing to lead by example, which includes, in the first instance, opening its market to foreign goods and services.

Four factors explain the pattern and dynamic of Japan's relations with the United States and East Asia: Japan's bargaining power, its norms and ideas, its position and roles in international organizations, and its domestic politics. Japan behaves the way it does because it is at the same time a latecoming power, a status quo power, and a changed power. It is well known that Japan was a rising power until recently as measured by economic, financial, and technological indicators, and this has enhanced its bargaining position. But it is less recognized that Japan is also a status quo power in its attitudes toward both formal international organizations and informal norms and rules. Japan has not attempted to restructure international institutions; it is mainly interested in higher status and greater prestige in them. This is in part because Japan is a much changed power in its norms and ideas—I focus on "instrumental" rather than "fundamental" norms and ideas in this book—based on its learning from World War II and its patterns of interaction with other nations after the war.

This chapter includes three sections. The first section makes the case that Japan has behaved strategically in international relations, which is reflected in its two-track foreign policy toward the West and Asia. The next section conceptualizes and operationalizes the key concepts used in the book to describe and explain use of economic power. The last section lays out the design of the book.

Japan's Strategic Behavior

A country uses a strategy in setting goals and seeking to accomplish these goals by employing its available resources given both external and internal constraints and opportunities. As Kenneth B. Pyle argued, "in the post–World War II era, Japan had a more clearly defined national strategy than any other major power."[2] Chalmers Johnson went further: "[T]he Japanese, like the Venetians before them, might be master strategists" if we recognize "the essence of all strategies—indirect approach . . . and the disguise of intent."[3]

The conventional wisdom in Japan and the United States is that Japan is passive. Sassa Atsuyuki, a former cabinet official, argued that "[w]aiting for demands from the Americans and then responding to them . . . is the single basic theme running through Japan's post-war foreign relations."[4] "Without its own strategic vision for international order," Noda Nobuo, a former Kyoto University professor, offered a gloomy prediction that "the Japan of the twenty-first century will probably be like a soccer ball kicked back and forth between the Americans and Chinese players."[5] Foreign observers often share this view. Kent E. Calder argued that Japan, as a "reactive state," adjusts its foreign policy in response to external pressure.[6] Michael Blaker saw Japan's foreign policy as "coping"—assessing carefully external environments and adopting minimum adjustments.[7]

However, being "passive" is a strategic choice that has benefited Japan. Pyle maintains that the reactive nature of Japan's foreign policy is "the product of a carefully constructed and shrewdly implemented foreign policy."[8] Susan J. Pharr argued that Japan is not "reactive" but "defensive" in that it pursues a "low-cost, low-risk, benefit-maximizing strategy."[9] Chinese scholars, who are generally more concerned than Americans about Japan's rising power, believe that Japan has clear strategies to become the leader in Asia and one of the three poles in the world by "winning without victories"—gaining influence without alarming potential opponents.[10]

What are Japan's strategic objectives? Japan's long-term goal is creation of a situation in which the nation is safe and prosperous. This is certainly not unique to Japan. What is unique about Japan is the way it has pursued this goal. For the first twenty years after Japan recovered its sovereignty from the United States in 1952, it concentrated on economic growth while relying on the United States for security protection and political leadership. Japan's single-mindedness in mobilizing resources to achieve economic growth could be compared to the U.S. preoccupation with competing with the Soviet Union during the cold war. Since the 1970s, Japan has become more active in foreign relations. The end of the cold war, in particular, has affected Japan's external environment. But Japan's basic mission remains unchanged. What has changed is Japan's realization that it has to depend more on its own efforts for a higher status and greater respect in an international system that it is basically happy with.[11]

Few people, including those who see no clear Japanese foreign policy strategies, dispute that Japan has adopted explicit strategies for economic growth: a single-minded desire to catch up with and surpass the West. For example, Chalmers Johnson argued that "in modern times Japan has always put emphasis on an overarching, nationally supported goal for its economy rather than on the particular procedures that are to govern economic activity."[12] Although we may debate whether Japan is a successful "developmental state," the Japanese government has actively designed and implemented economic development strategies.[13] The view that Japan is passive originates from its perceived "timidity" in using its tremendous economic power for well-defined, discrete foreign policy goals. But this book shows that Japan has behaved strategically in its use of economic power vis-à-vis the United States and East Asia, although not always as coherently or explicitly as the term "strategy" indicates. As in its guidance of domestic political economy, the Japanese government combines market forces and interventions to achieve long-term strategic objectives abroad. Japan's policy is shaped through trial and error, bargaining, and consensus-building between various players facing domestic and external constraints and opportunities. But this does not suggest that Japan lacks strategic actions. In securing an external environment for its survival and prosperity, Japan has been remarkably strategic and successful.

Japan's strategic use of economic power is indicated in its varying degree of cooperation between regions and over time depending on its competitive needs, its bargaining positions, and the rules of the game. Conversely, how cooperative one evaluates Japan's use of economic resources to be depends on one's own objectives. To understand Japan's use of economic power, therefore, we need to study regional differences in its foreign policy.

Japan has extended its global reach since the 1980s, but it still follows a two-track foreign policy: one track for Asia and the other for the West. Saito Shiro used the term "twin-track diplomacy" to characterize Japan's balancing between Asia and the West, focusing on Japan's participation at Group of Seven (G-7) summits and its dialogues with the Association of Southeast Asian Nations (ASEAN) at the group's annual ministerial meetings. He reasoned that "without an assured political and security relationship with the West, especially with the United States, Japan could not safely pursue its economic interests in the Asian Pacific region; without roots in Asia, it would not count for much in the Western world."[14] "In non-Asian regions Japan, even today, basically follows U.S. leadership," as Susan J. Pharr and Ming Wan argued. "Within Asia, however, Japan has a long postwar track-record of greater independence from the Unites States and today increasingly pursues an independent course."[15] It is a prevailing theme in studies on Japanese foreign policy by Chinese scholars that Japan is torn between Asia and the West and that to play a significant global role Japan needs support and understanding of its East Asia neighbors, particularly China.[16]

Japan seeks competitive advantage over the West and Asia, but mainly through cooperative means that facilitate the realization of the goals of those nations. The pattern and dynamic of Japan's cooperation differ between the West and Asia. More important, what is cooperative for East Asia may not be cooperative for the United States and vice versa.

How cooperative one evaluates Japan's use of economic power to be depends on whose objectives such spending facilitates or impedes.

In addition to Japan's relations with Asia and the West, this book investigates Japan's approach toward international financial organizations. If we want to label Japan's foreign relations, we may classify its relations with the United States as "bilateralism," its relations with Asia as "regionalism," and its relations with international organizations as "multilateralism." As Dennis T. Yasutomo argued, Japan has displayed activism in multilateral development banks (MDBs) such as the World Bank, the ADB, and the European Bank for Reconstruction and Development (EBRD) in the 1990s. This new multilateralism cannot be explained simply as reaction to American demands.[17] Japan's use of economic power in international financial organizations displays unique features. International institutions offer opportunities for Japan as well as imposing restrictions on the country. Nevertheless, Japan's multilateralism has not yet become important enough to use the term "three-track" to describe its foreign policy. As Yasutomo recognized, two of Japan's policy objectives in the MDBs are taking care of Asian interests and cooperating with the United States on management and operations without being submissive.[18]

Concepts and Theories

Describing Use of Economic Power

Cooperation and conflicts are the key concepts used in this book to describe Japan's use of economic power. Robert O. Keohane has defined cooperation as a process that requires that "the actions of separate individuals or organizations—which are not in pre-existent harmony—be brought into conformity with one another through a process of negotiation."[19] Conflict is a self-evident concept, with its academic and vernacular meanings virtually indistinguishable: It refers to a clash or confrontation over divergent interests. Theories of both cooperation and conflict assume a lack of harmony between nations, the main difference between the two being whether players are willing to adjust their behavior to each other.

How do we know that cooperation actually occurs? I adopt Keohane's operational definition of cooperation: "*Intergovernmental cooperation takes place when the policies actually followed by one government are regarded by its partners as facilitating realization of their own objectives, as the result of a process of policy coordination.*"[20] This operational definition focuses on two key elements—that is, whether Country A *intends* to cooperate with Country B and whether Country B itself *agrees* that Country A has indeed been cooperative. Based on this definition, actions of Country A that may unintentionally facilitate the realization of Country B's goals are not considered to be cooperative here. Actions of Country A that are meant to facilitate the realization of Country B's goals but are not recognized by Country B as such are not considered to be cooperative either. This points to the importance of coordination and communications, since cooperation is deliberate behavior. Conversely, conflict takes place when countries follow policies regarded by other states as hindering realization of their objectives.

How cooperative a country is in its use of economic power is reflected in its choices for spending. There are basically three ways in which a country can use its financial resources: (1) defense expenditure, (2) consumption, and (3) investment. Defense expenditure translates economic power into military capabilities. It includes not only the cost of maintaining a national military force but also the cost of supporting security alliances. Such use of economic power either reduces or contributes to international conflict, depending on whose security objectives it facilitates or impedes. A country may simply consume its wealth, which stimulates greater demand for goods and services at home and often leads to increased imports. Investment channels economic resources into production both at home and abroad to generate greater wealth. In a global economy, a country's consumption and investment patterns may be cooperative for another country if they facilitate realization of the latter's objectives.

A country may engage in economic statecraft—a direct use of economic resources to advance its policy objectives. David Baldwin defined economic statecraft as "influence attempts relying primarily on resources which have a reasonable semblance of a market price in terms of money."[21] He saw economic statecraft coming in different forms, such as embargoes, boycotts, aid suspensions, export controls, direct purchases, and provision of aid and investment guarantees. Depending on the policy intent, a country may punish or reward other countries with its economic resources. Economic sanctions punish the target country: They aim at denying realization of other countries' objectives.[22] In contrast, a country may provide financial assistance to facilitate realization of other countries' goals.

Cooperation is therefore measured by degrees of cooperation in investment, consumption, defense expenditure, and economic statecraft, and by the ratio of financial assistance to sanctions. A completely cooperative Japan would (a) spend as much or as little on defense as desired by its partners, (b) consume and invest both at home and abroad in a way that facilitates the political and economic objectives of its partners, (c) avoid imposing economic sanctions on its partners or impose sanctions on third nations at the urgings of the partners, and (d) provide financial assistance to its partners or third nations as they desire. An extremely uncooperative Japan would do the opposite. Japan's actual behavior falls somewhere in between and varies between different regions and periods.

Besides cooperation and conflict, I examine how competitive Japan has been. Competition is defined here as a process in which players try to do better than each other.[23] Recognizing explicitly the competitive intent of Japan's use of economic power avoids confusion in assessing its foreign policy behavior. Japan's cooperation is often dismissed because of the country's perceived gains from its own actions. International relations theories tend to see cooperation only in the cases where countries do things for others "against their own interests," which is a difficult standard. Since national interests are broad and vague, one may always point out some self-interests that a country's "altruistic" behavior actually serves or dispute the claim that the country's actions indeed deny its interests. I emphasize that *cooperation is not about what Country A gains from its actions but about facilitating realization of Country B's goals.* Furthermore, cooperation based on self-denial may not even be desirable because there are no clear incentives for continuation. Recognizing Japan's competitive intent allows a focus on how cooperative Japan is in its use of economic power judged by its own intent and by the assessment of target nations. It also facilitates analysis of why Japan, on the balance, has chosen cooperative means to advance its competitive aims.

Explaining Use of Economic Power

Japan's bargaining power, its norms, and its role and position in international institutions explain how cooperative it has been in its use of economic power. This book does not suggest that all three are equally important. Rather, the variation in Japan's cooperation over time and across regions helps us understand the relevance of each factor.

Of my three independent variables, bargaining position and international institutions are systemic variables that condition a state's general approach. Bargaining power arguments draw heavily from realism, while emphasis on international institutions is largely based on the institutionalist theories. Based on a reading of representative realist and institutionalist works, I have listed some core realist and institutionalist expectations of state behavior in use of economic power even though there are different views within each approach.[24]

Realist explanations: For realists, a country's rising power improves its bargaining position, except when such a development causes suspicion from other countries, which may respond by strengthening their own capabilities or forming defensive alliances. A rising power adopts more assertive strategies due to greater interests and higher stakes. If a country's power grows to the point where it becomes a hegemon—a country with a dominant economic and military position—it may become cooperative in spending by providing public goods for the international system. However, cooperative spending is only one use of economic power by a hegemon, security spending and economic sanctions being others. And a country's bargaining position is issue-specific and may not translate easily from one issue area to another.

Bargaining position here refers mainly to relative power position. It recognizes that power is issue-specific and not always convertible.[25] Bargaining position itself is determined by a variety of factors depending on the circumstances. Japan's structural power factors in its bargaining position. I measure Japan's structural economic power as a percentage of global or regional gross domestic product (GDP), supplemented at times by Japan's share of global or regional trade and investments. I use bargaining position rather than structural power as an independent variable in this book. It is true that structural power tells us a few big and important things about international relations, but structural power alone does not explain state choices or outcomes of state interactions.

This book includes a chapter on Japan's participation in three international financial institutions—namely the World Bank, the IMF, and the ADB. Besides institutionalist arguments, we should also examine how power of member states, especially powerful ones, affects institutions and what interests states pursue.[26] To study power and institutions, I investigate distributions of power, positions, influence, and benefits. I also examine the overall power distribution underlying an institution and the specific power distribution within it. The overall and specific power distributions are not necessarily congruent. A state may be "poorly endowed" with the power element relevant for the issue, but its overall power still has an effect in the issue area through issue linkage. The specific power distribution is often reflected in the distribution of voting shares. The institutional position of a state refers to how many important positions its nationals occupy and where they are placed along strategic command chains. The distribution of positions is a crucial indicator of the distribution of influence, although they may not overlap because a member may exercise informal influence. A nation's influence is reflected in roles of "initiator," "vetoer," "controller," or "broker."[27]

Some states enjoy "institutional advantages"—a favorable position that allows them to play their strong suit in the game and, consequently, exert greater influence. The founder usually enjoys institutional advantages because it is in a position to define the criteria for power relevant for the institution—a power formula that suits its own circumstances. In addition, it shapes the institutional construct and occupies central organizational positions. As a result, a nation's initial institutional advantages often allow it to enjoy more benefits later. The founder can use its voting power and organizational positions to shape the future development of the institution. Once established, institutional advantages are difficult to eliminate. The nation itself is also likely to maintain its commitment to the institution due to the "institutional investments" it has already made. Institutional structures—positional distributions in particular—do not change easily. The states on the top will try to guard their positions. They may also use their institutional advantage for more rewards. For the distribution of benefits, I consider mainly tangible rewards that an institution is established to provide. I will also consider possible intangible benefits a state may be seeking in a case.

Institutionalist explanations: Institutionalists focus on the constraints and incentives of international institutions, which are broadly defined as principles, norms, rules, and decision-making procedures. For institutionalists, power distribution and bargaining positions are only the first cut (and a crude one at that) for explaining interstate interaction. The nature of the international system is interdependence rather than anarchy. Institutional participation affects how a state calculates its transaction costs by allowing long-term perspectives and providing useful information. Institutional impact mitigates the effects of changing power distribution if not rendering them inconsequential.

Keohane defines international institutions as "persistent and connected sets of rules (formal and informal) that prescribe behavioral roles, constrain activity, and shape expectations."[28] International institutions include international regimes, which refer to "principles, norms, rules, and decision-making procedures around which actor expectations converge in a given issue-area."[29] The extent of institutional establishment or entrenchment in an issue area is "institutionalization." Ernst B. Haas defines institutionalization as "the development of new organs, subunits, and administrative practices that are designed to improve the performance of the organization in the wake of some major disappointment with earlier outputs."[30] Institutionalization also applies to the international system in terms of the extent of behavior "recognized by participants as reflecting established rules, norms, and conventions."[31] For an individual state, institutionalization is reflected in the degree of its involvement in and commitment to an international institution. In order to understand how an international institution affects Japan's strategic choice, we need to investigate how Japan participates in the institution, its calculations, and its definition of interests.

Ideationalist explanations: Structural realist and institutionalist approaches derive preferences from structural or institutional constraints and opportunities. But a state's preferences are not simply reduced to its structural position and institutional participation. Ideas and norms also shape preferences.[32] Ideas, as defined by Judith Goldstein and Robert Keohane as "beliefs beheld by individuals," consist of three categories: world views, principled beliefs, and causal beliefs.[33] Norms are "shared expectations about appropriate behavior held by a community of actors."[34] Simply put, nations act differently given their norms and ideas even if their bargaining positions and the institutional constraints and incentives remain the same. Norms and ideas change because nations, like all social and political entities, learn from past experience or from friends and adversaries.[35]

It is more difficult to conceptualize and operationalize norms and ideas than bargaining power and institutions. As scholars of this approach recognize, it is difficult to construct a research program that establishes cause–effect relationships between certain ideas or norms and state actions. The realist and institutionalist approaches face such difficulties as well. While it is relatively easy to identify power distributions and presence or absence of institutions, we need to know, in the final analysis, whether such structural or institutional factors indeed motivate or drive state actions. This is difficult. Self-declaration may distort true intentions. Revealed intentions from actions cause circular thinking about what motivates the very actions in the first place. This is indeed a methodological challenge. I will discuss my partial solution in the next section.

The Design of the Book

Methodology

I use a combination of methods to make descriptive and causal inferences in this book.[36] First, to determine Japan's cooperation, I use two kinds of information. Public information is readily available for Japan's use of economic power in investment, security expenditure, sanctions, and foreign assistance. It is more difficult to determine Japan's intent for its actions and the assessment of these actions by the countries Japan deals with. To judge Japan's intent to cooperate we certainly should listen to what the Japanese government says about its intention. However, the Japanese government, like other governments, often labels its actions as cooperation no matter the intent or impact. To minimize this problem, I check government statements against interviews with government officials and policy analysts and studies of well-informed scholars and observers. In addition, I provide my own assessment of Japan's actions.

Second, I compare critical cases to examine the relevance of different causal factors based on observable events predicted by different approaches. If power arguments are correct, we should see Japan being more assertive and successful based on its rising power and, where it has greater relative power, providing for the reactions of other nations. The gap between realist arguments and realities points to alternative explanations, such as institutionalist and ideationalist ones. To test the relevance of institutionalist and ideationalist approaches, I examine how different institutions or norms explain different Japanese responses given similar structural constraints and how similar institutional arrangements or norms explain similar Japanese behavior despite different structural circumstances. In addition to these "actual case" studies, counterfactual arguments are made in this book.[37] The methods discussed so far point to the inadequacy of certain approaches and suggest probable causal factors. They are supplemented by "process tracing" to track how ideas and norms lead to policy choice, and "causal mechanism," which focuses on the process by which A causes B.[38]

Japan's foreign policy, like any country's foreign policy behavior, is explained by multiple causes. I consider bargaining power, institutions, norms, and ideas as three important causal factors, but not the only ones. My approach is to consider different "packages of causal factors" for Japan's behavior in different regions and over different time periods. The varying content of these packages indicates the relevance of different approaches. One shortcut for both decision-makers and analysts is to view Japan's role in a certain situation.[39] Role conception refers to "the policy makers' definitions of the general kinds of decisions, commitments, rules, and actions suitable to their state and of the functions their state should perform in a variety of geographic and issue setting."[40] Used as a road map for decision-makers to determine what is expected of them, role identification indicates what goals a state is likely to pursue in a given situation. One's role identification and role conception is therefore based on its power, its expectations about appropriate behavior, and the institutional constraints and incentives it faces—the three independent variables in this book.

Chapters of the Book

This book includes five chapters. Chapter 2 shows that Japan has served as a supporter in use of economic power for the West, in part to compensate for its fierce economic competition. This is not that surprising. Despite its rising economic power, Japan remains dependent on the United States for security protection, leadership in global free trade, assurance of flow of oil, and access to the U.S. market and technologies. Japan is also enmeshed in international institutions largely created and dominated by the United States, which affects its calculation of national interests and facilitates support for the West. Moreover, Japan has learned a hard lesson from its confrontation with the West in World War II. What is surprising then is mainly the way Japan chooses to support the West. Tokyo consistently searches for less costly substitution to weather "relationship crises" rather than addressing Western concerns head-on; it prefers economic contributions to security ones, investment to consumption, and assistance to sanctions. This is due to Japan's neo-mercantilist preferences for economic gains and learning the best way to manage relations with the United States.

Chapter 3 examines Japan's relations with East Asia. While its economic relations with its Asian neighbors are largely complementary, Japan seeks to enhance its competitiveness versus the West and maintain a structural lead over other Asian nations. Japan has acted as a unique leader in Asia, providing massive financial resources and affecting the incentive structures for the countries in the region. But it has avoided taking up costly leadership responsibilities, such as access to its market for distress goods and acting as lender of last resort. In addition, Tokyo prefers economic cooperation to economic sanctions and use of military force. The main reason for Japan's cautious and nonconfrontational approach is that Japan has learned that an aggressive and high-profile approach would backfire by causing suspicion and hostility among its neighbors and a cooperative and low-profile approach has enabled the country to accomplish its goals without straining its relations with them.

Chapter 4 discusses Japan's relations with the World Bank, the IMF, and the ADB. Japan has cooperated with these three financial institutions as a generous financier, demonstrating its willingness to contribute public goods. Japan does not compete with the institutions per se but with other member states for benefits, positions, power ranking, and voice in agenda-setting. In recent years, Japan has also become more assertive in affecting the policy agenda of the institutions and offering an alternative development model. Much of Japan's behavior in the institutions is explained by its policies toward the United States and Asia. Japan tries to represent Asian interests in the global institutions and has been active in the ADB because it serves the interests of the region. At the same time, Japan treats its relations with the United States as a priority when it considers policies toward both global and regional institutions. However, compared to its bilateral and regional policies, Japan's policy toward international organizations has been more cooperative, seeking less direct economic gains in return for its contributions. Japan's behavior in international institutions is best explained by institutionalist arguments.

Chapter 5 summarizes the main arguments developed in the book and highlights Japan's balancing between Asia and the West. In addition, the chapter discusses Japan's current foreign relations and contemplates its future foreign orientations. The dominant feature of Japan at present is that of a stagnant economic power stuck in its once successful but now ineffective system. Although there are hopeful signs that Japan may indeed start serious reforms thanks to a combination of domestic and international pressure, its past failure in living up to reform promises calls for caution. At the same time, the current Japanese government has shown "signs of adopting a self-directed stance in foreign affairs—an unusual development for a country whose foreign policy has tended to consist of passive responses to actions by others."[41] Japan has taken on more security responsibilities in the Asia-Pacific region in cooperation with the United States and acted more firmly against China than before. However, Japan's preference for cooperation with the United States, East Asia, and international institutions is unlikely to experience fundamental change. Japan will continue to seek balance between Asia and the West and economic tools will remain its most important foreign policy instrument.

Notes

1. For a more extensive discussion on this issue, see Susan J. Pharr and Ming Wan, "Japan's Leadership: Shaping a New Asia," in Hideo Sato and I.M. Destler, eds., *Leadership Sharing in the New International System: Japan and the United States,* Special Research Project on the New International System, University of Tsukuba, Japan, September 1996, pp. 133–70.

2. Kenneth B. Pyle, *The Japanese Question: Power and Purpose in a New Era,* 2d ed. (Washington: AEI Press, 1996), p. ix.

3. Chalmers Johnson, "The State and Japanese Grand Strategy," in Richard Rosecrance and Arthur Stein, eds., *The Domestic Bases of Grand Strategy* (Ithaca: Cornell University Press, 1993), p. 223.

4. Quoted in Robert Delfs, "Carrying the Can," *Far Eastern Economic Review,* July 18, 1991, p. 18.

5. Noda Nobuo, "Japan in a World of Rival Empires," *Japan Echo* 26, no. 3 (June 1999), p. 11.

6. Kent E. Calder, "Japanese Foreign Economic Policy Formation," *World Politics* 40, no. 4 (July 1988), pp. 517–41.

7. Michael Blaker, "Evaluating Japanese Diplomatic Performance," in Gerald Curtis, ed., *Japan's Foreign Policy After the Cold War: Coping with Change* (Armonk, NY: M.E. Sharpe, 1993), pp. 1–42.

8. Kenneth B. Pyle, "In Pursuit of a Grand Design: Nakasone Betwixt the Past and the Future," in Pyle, ed., *The Trade Crisis: How Will Japan Respond?* (Seattle: Society for Japanese Studies, 1987), p. 7.

9. Susan J. Pharr, "Japan's Defensive Foreign Policy and the Politics of Burden Sharing," in Curtis, ed., *Japan's Foreign Policy After the Cold War,* p. 235.

10. Institute of Japanese Studies, Chinese Academy of Social Sciences, *Gaojishu yu riben de guojia zhanlue* [High-tech and Japan's state strategies] (Beijing: Institute of Japanese Studies, internal publication, 1991); Xi Runchang, *Hehou shidai de jianglin: Dazhanlue yu lieguo fenzheng* [The coming of the post-nuclear age: the great strategy and the various countries' dispute] (Changsha, Hunan: Hunan chubanshe, 1992), pp. 221–25. Chinese analysts and officials tend to see Japanese

as shrewd strategists. This was reconfirmed by my interviews in Beijing and Shanghai in May and June 1999.

11. Ozawa Ichiro, a key figure in the Liberal Democratic Party (LDP) until 1993 and now the head of the conservative Liberal Party, pointed out that Japan's mission today is "to ensure that we maintain and enhance the affluence and stability that we now enjoy." To accomplish this mission, he argued that Japan needs "peace and stability in the international environment and the free trade that flourishes as a result." Ozawa, *Blueprint for a New Japan: The Rethinking of a Nation* (Tokyo: Kodansha International, 1994), p. 93. His view is not different from that held by the ruling LDP. "While it is axiomatic that the basic objective of Japanese foreign policy is to ensure Japan's security and prosperity, today's heightening international interdependence means that this cannot possibly be done independent of the international community's stability and prosperity," stated Foreign Minister Ikeda Yukihiko in his speech to the Diet on January 20, 1997.

12. Chalmers Johnson, *MITI and the Japanese Miracles* (Stanford: Stanford University Press, 1982), p. 20.

13. Some studies have challenged Johnson's view of Japan as a successful command capitalist system. See David Friedman, *The Misunderstood Miracle: Industrial Development and Political Change in Japan* (Ithaca: Cornell University Press, 1988). Economists tend to see Japan's industrial policy as residual rather than being the principal reason for Japan's rapid economic growth. See Ryoshi Minami, *The Economic Development of Japan: A Quantitative Study,* 2d ed. (London: Macmillan Press, 1994) and Hugh Patrick and Henry Rosovsky, eds., *Asia's New Giant: How the Japanese Economy Works* (Washington: The Brookings Institution, 1976). Other scholars offer a more complex picture of the government–private sector relationship in Japan. See Daniel I. Okimoto, *Between MITI and the Market: Japanese Industrial Policy for High Technology* (Stanford: Stanford University Press, 1989); Richard J. Samuels, *The Business of the Japanese State: Energy Markets in Comparative and Historical Perspective* (Ithaca: Cornell University Press, 1987); and Kent E. Calder, *Strategic Capitalism: Private Business and Public Purpose in Japanese Industrial Finance* (Princeton: Princeton University Press, 1993).

14. Shiro Saito, *Japan at the Summit: Its Role in the Western Alliance and in Asian Pacific Co-operation* (London: Routledge, 1990), p. 23.

15. Pharr and Wan, "Japan's Leadership," p. 134.

16. For example, see Wang Yizhou, *Dangdai guoji zhengzhi* [International politics] (Shanghai: Shanghai renmin chubanshe, 1995), p. 325; Lu Zhongwei, *Xinjiu jiaoti de dongya geju* [East Asia in transition] (Beijing: Shishi chubanshe, 1993), p. 58; Zhang Biqing, "Riben jiasu tuixing zhengzhi waijiao de xindongxiang" [The new trends in Japan's push for political diplomacy], *Riben wenti* 6 (1990), p. 16.

17. Dennis J. Yasutomo, *The New Multilateralism in Japan's Foreign Policy* (New York: St. Martin's Press, 1995), p. 120.

18. Ibid., pp. 128–30.

19. Robert O. Keohane, *After Hegemony: Cooperation and Discord in the World Political Economy* (Princeton: Princeton University Press, 1984), p. 51.

20. Ibid., pp. 51–52.

21. David Baldwin, *Economic Statecraft* (Princeton: Princeton University Press, 1985), pp. 13–14.

22. Gary Hufbauer, Jeffrey Schott, and Kimberley Elliott define economic sanc-

tions as "the deliberate, government-inspired withdrawal, or threat of withdrawal, of customary trade or financial relations." Hufbauer, Schott, and Elliott, *Economic Sanctions Reconsidered: History and Current Policy,* vol. 1, 2d ed. (Washington: Institute of International Economics, 1990), p. 2.

23. The term "competition" here is different from the term used in economics. For economists, competition—used in contrast to oligopoly and monopoly—means that a large number of well-informed players, who can freely move in and out of an industry, compete with each other by offering better products and prices in a market where they are price takers.

24. See Robert Keohane, ed., *Neorealism and Its Critics* (New York: Columbia University Press, 1986); Joseph Nye, "Neorealism and Neoliberalism," *World Politics* 40, no. 2 (January 1988), pp. 237–51; David Baldwin, ed., *Neorealism and Neoliberalism: The Contemporary Debate* (New York: Columbia University Press, 1993); Kenneth N. Waltz, *Theory of International Politics* (Reading, MA: Addison-Wesley, 1979); Hans J. Morgenthau, *Politics Among Nations,* 5th ed., revised (New York: Alfred A. Knopf, 1978); Morton Kaplan, *System and Process in International Politics* (New York: Wiley, 1957); Richard Rosecrance, *Action and Reaction in World Politics: International Systems in Perspective* (Boston: Little, Brown, 1963); Charles P. Kindleberger, *The World in Depression, 1929–1939* (Berkeley: University of California Press, 1986); Stephen Krasner, "State Power and the Structure of International Trade," *World Politics* 28, no. 3 (April 1976), pp. 317–47; Stephen Walt, *The Origins of Alliances* (Ithaca: Cornell University Press, 1987); Robert O. Keohane, *After Hegemony* and *International Institutions and State Power: Essays in International Relations Theory* (Boulder: Westview Press, 1989); Stephen D. Krasner, ed. *International Regimes* (Ithaca: Cornell University Press, 1981); Robert Keohane and Joseph S. Nye, Jr., *Power and Interdependence* (Boston: Little, Brown, 1977); Richard N. Cooper, "Economic Interdependence and Foreign Policies in the Seventies," *World Politics* 24, no. 2 (January 1972), pp. 159–81.

25. David A. Baldwin, "Power Analysis and World Politics: New Trends Versus Old Tendencies," *World Politics* 31, no. 2 (January 1979), pp. 161–94.

26. For works using the realist approach in studying institutions or regimes, see Joanne Gowa, "Bipolarity, Multipolarity, and Free Trade," *American Political Science Review* 83, no. 4 (December 1989), pp. 1245–56; Stephen D. Krasner, "Global Communications and National Power," *World Politics* 43, no. 3 (April 1991), pp. 336–66.

27. For a discussion of these roles, see Robert Cox and Harold Jacobson, "The Framework for Inquiry," in Cox and Jacobson, eds., *The Anatomy of Influence: Decision Making in International Organization* (New Haven: Yale University Press, 1974), pp. 12–13.

28. Keohane, *International Institutions and State Power,* p. 3.

29. Stephen D. Krasner, "Structural Causes and Regime Consequences," in Krasner, ed., *International Regimes* (Ithaca: Cornell University Press, 1983), p. 1.

30. Ernst B. Haas, *When Knowledge Is Power* (Berkeley: University of California Press, 1990), pp. 85–86.

31. Keohane, *International Institutions and State Power,* p. 1.

32. See Judith Goldstein and Robert Keohane, eds., *Ideas and Foreign Policy: Beliefs, Institutions and Political Change* (Ithaca: Cornell University Press, 1993); Henry R. Nau, "Identity and International Politics: An Alternative to Neorealism"

(paper presented at the 1993 annual meeting of the American Political Science Association in Washington, DC, September 1993); Martha Finnemore, *National Interests in International Society* (Ithaca: Cornell University Press, 1996); Alexander Wendt, "Collective Identity Formation and the International State," *American Political Science Review* 88, no. 2 (June 1994), pp. 384–96.

33. Goldstein and Keohane, "Ideas and Foreign Policy: An Analytical Framework," in Goldstein and Keohane, *Ideas and Foreign Policy,* pp. 3–30.

34. Finnemore, *National Interests in International Society,* p. 22.

35. For the studies on learning, see Joseph S. Nye, Jr., "Nuclear Learning and U.S.–Soviet Security Regimes," *International Organization* 41, no. 3 (Summer 1987), pp. 371–402; George Modelski, "Is World Politics Evolutionary Learning?" *International Organization* 44, no. 1 (Winter 1990), pp. 1–24.

36. For a useful guide on how to make descriptive and causal inferences, see Gary King, Robert O. Keohane, and Sidney Verba, *Designing Social Inquiry: Scientific Inference in Qualitative Research* (Princeton: Princeton University Press, 1994).

37. See James D. Fearon, "Counterfactuals and Hypothesis Testing in Political Science," *World Politics* 43, no. 2 (January 1991), pp. 169–95.

38. Albert S. Yee, "The Effects of Ideas on Policies," *International Organization* 50, no. 1 (Winter 1996), pp. 69–108.

39. For national role conceptions, see Stephen G. Walker, ed., *Role Theory and Foreign Policy Analysis* (Durham: Duke University Press, 1987); Naomi Bailin Wish, "Foreign Policy Makers and Their National Role Conceptions," *International Studies Quarterly* 24, no. 4 (December 1980), pp. 532–54; Shih Chih-yu, "National Role Conception as Foreign Policy Motivation," *Political Psychology* 9, no. 4 (December 1988), pp. 599–629.

40. K.J. Holsti, *International Politics: A Framework for Analysis,* 4th ed. (Englewood Cliffs: Prentice Hall, 1983), p. 116.

41. Tanaka Akihito, "Obuchi Diplomacy: How to Follow a Successful Start," *Japan Echo* 26, no. 2 (April 1999), p. 8.

2

Competitor and Supporter for the United States

Japan competes with the United States economically while acting as a supporter, not a challenger, in world politics. Japan is America's number one ally in Asia. It has made economically based contributions. How cooperative has Japan been in the use of economic power for the United States? The answer to this question depends on three questions. First, does Japan intend to facilitate realization of U.S. policy objectives? Second, what does the United States want from Japan? Does Washington believe that Tokyo has been cooperative? Third, how should researchers assess Japan's cooperation based on "objective" evidence? This chapter examines these questions.

The Japanese policy community has expressed willingness to support the West. Takashi Inoguchi, a noted Japanese international relations specialist, argued that as a supporter "Japan's course is thus to contribute to U.S. policy as much as possible with its abundant economic resources."[1] *The Japan That Can Say "No,"* a 1989 best-seller, received wide attention precisely because bold statements about standing up to Washington are rarely heard from influential Japanese.[2] Japanese also argue that Japan has indeed been a good supporter for the West and resent U.S. criticism of their alleged free-riding.

In contrast, Washington has criticized Japan's efforts in virtually all areas. Focusing on Japan's economic expansion, the revisionists argued in the late 1980s and early 1990s that Japan aimed at economic superiority at the expense of its partners. They saw Japan as a free-rider and challenger.[3] A more extreme view even saw Japan as a potential enemy.[4] Japan's economic clout was also a concern for those who wanted closer cooperation with Japan because Japan "will become powerful enough to play a spoiler's role in international politics."[5] The revisionist views strongly influenced the Clinton administration's tough policy toward Japan. Japan's economic recession and Asia's financial crisis put the revisionists on the defensive.[6] Ironically, while revisionists and their critics disagree on the nature and merit of the Japanese system, they were both critical of Japan's lack of cooperation for resolving the Asian financial crisis.

To provide my own evaluation, I examine Japan's use of economic power in defense, consumption, investment, development assistance, and sanctions. To be a perfect partner, Japan would spend as much on defense as the United States desires and for missions consistent with U.S. preferences. Japan would primarily spend at home to stimulate consumption and boost imports, which would reduce its huge foreign earnings. Japan would provide foreign aid to countries that Americans prefer and withhold assistance to those that Americans dislike. And the country would change its approach corresponding to changing U.S. priorities. Ideally, Tokyo would take the initiative to assist its Western allies rather than come forward only under pressure. This is an impossible task for Japan—indeed, for any self-respecting sovereign nation.

Japan is not as cooperative as it claims but is considerably more so than the West gives it credit for. Japan is basically cooperative because it uses economic power to facilitate rather than hinder the realization of the policy objectives of the United States. But the Government of Japan (GoJ) consistently searches for substitution rather than addressing Western concerns head on; it prefers economic contributions to security contributions, investment to consumption, and assistance to sanctions. Tokyo's strategic objective is to maintain its competitiveness abroad and minimize adjustment costs at home through self-serving means. As a result, although Japan is cooperative in selective areas, it is not sufficiently so for the West in the larger scheme of things.

The fact that Japan seeks competitive gains is not an issue here. The basic premise of this book is that countries seek to advance their interests in the world. The issue here is why Tokyo chooses to support the West. To a large extent, Japan's support for the West is not surprising and can be explained by a confluence of realist, liberalist, and ideationalist factors. First, despite its rising economic power, Japan remains dependent on the United States for security protection, leadership in global free trade, assurance of flow of oil, and access to the U.S. market and technologies. And there are no clear viable alternatives to the United States. Second, Japan is enmeshed in international institutions largely created and dominated by the United States—a fact that affects Tokyo's calculation of national interests and facilitates support for the West. Third, Japan has learned a lesson from its folly in confronting the West before and during World War II. On a fundamental level, Japan has become a functional democracy, which pulls the country toward the United States as a fellow democracy. On an instrumental level, Japan has learned how to "manage" the West since the end of the war.

Japan's support for the United States would be surprising only if the country would have fared better by offering no support or even opposition to the West. This counterfactual reasoning obviously does not hold. What is surprising then is mainly the way Japan chooses to support the West: a strategic choice of arenas and degrees of support. Japan prefers to use less costly substitutes to weather "relationship crises." An explanation that addresses not whether but how much Japan supports the United States is not unimportant. In an interdependent world, the chance for developed nations to make drastic strategic realignment is slim. On this level, Japan's behavior is actually unusual if one considers what the United States or Europe would do in a similar situation.

This chapter includes four sections. The first section examines Japan's substitution of economic for security contributions. The second section discusses Japan's preference to invest abroad rather than to consume at home. The third section studies the country's choice of carrots over sticks. The fourth section concludes the chapter.

Security Versus Economic Contributions

Japan wants to ensure U.S. protection while minimizing its military spending and, more important, its defense responsibilities. Put another way, Japan does not want to be trapped in conflicts that do not affect its direct interests but also wants to avoid abandonment by the United States.[7] Tokyo has made substantial contributions directly to the alliance. But Japan has more often used economic contributions, such as official development assistance (ODA) and foreign direct investments (FDI) as substitution, which is less costly financially and politically while yielding side benefits.

Free-Riding Through the 1960s

After Japan's defeat in 1945, the U.S. government initially wanted to demilitarize the country and prevent it from becoming a military power ever again. But the start of the cold war produced a shift in Washington's objectives to rearming Japan. Prime Minister Yoshida Shigeru succeeded in ensuring U.S. protection while limiting Japan's defense efforts. Based on realist calculations, he advocated alliance with the United States for Japan's revival.[8] Japan did not have many options under the occupation; Yoshida described Japan as a "carp on the chopping board."[9] Japan's strategic thinking was also based on the regional power distribution; the Japanese knew that a shift of the U.S. focus from China to Japan would help their cause.[10]

The realist considerations of leading Japanese politicians were influenced by their ideas and learning from past experience. Yoshida's thinking best illustrates this. Yoshida supported alliance with the United States based on his belief from the prewar period that Japan needed to form an alliance with the dominant Western power to advance its cause in Asia. He learned a lesson from World War II: Without the Anglo–Japanese Alliance, which allowed Japan to expand successfully in Asia but ended in 1922 to Yoshida's great disappointment. Japanese military officers attacked Manchuria and China, which led to the war with the United States and Japan's defeat.[11] Yoshida was the most influential figure in Japanese politics in the postwar period, leading five cabinets between 1946 and 1954. His legacy influenced subsequent Japanese politics and foreign policy, especially through his disciples, such as prime ministers Ikeda Hayato and Sato Eisaku.

Until the 1970s Japan supported the United States by providing bases and hosting U.S. troops. Consistent with the Yoshida doctrine, Japan was slow in increasing its defense expenditure. Indeed, although the absolute volume of military spending rose from ¥134.9 billion ($374 million) in 1955 to ¥301.4 billion ($837.2 million) in 1965 and ¥1,327.3 billion ($4,472.2 million) in 1975, defense expenditure as a share of gross national product (GNP) actually decreased over the same period from 1.78 percent to 1.07 percent and 0.84 percent (Table 2.1). In fact, GoJ adopted a 1 percent GNP ceiling for defense spending in 1976 and has since only exceeded the ceiling barely in 1987–89.

Table 2.1

Japan's Defense Expenditure—Original Budget (units: ¥100 million, %)

FY	GNP (Initial Forecast) (A)	General Account (B)	Growth from Previous Year	Defense Budget (C)	Growth from Previous Year	Defense Budget to GNP (C/A)	Defense Budget to General Account (C/B)
1955	75,590	9,915	-0.8	1,349	-3.3	1.78	13.61
1965	281,600	36,581	12.4	3,014	9.6	1.07	8.24
1975	1,585,000	212,888	24.5	13,273	21.4	0.84	6.23
1976	1,681,000	242,960	14.1	15,124	13.9	0.90	6.22
1977	1,928,500	285,143	17.4	16,906	11.8	0.88	5.93
1978	2,106,000	342,950	20.3	19,010	12.4	0.90	5.54
1979	2,320,000	386,001	12.6	20,945	10.2	0.90	5.43
1980	2,478,000	425,888	10.3	22,302	6.5	0.90	5.24
1981	2,648,000	467,881	9.9	24,000	7.6	0.91	5.13
1982	2,772,000	496,808	6.2	25,861	7.8	0.93	5.21
1983	2,817,000	503,796	1.4	27,542	6.5	0.98	5.47
1984	2,960,000	506,272	0.5	29,346	6.55	0.99	5.80
1985	3,146,000	524,996	3.7	31,371	6.9	0.997	5.98
1986	3,367,000	540,886	3.0	33,435	6.58	0.993	6.18
1987	3,504,000	541,010	0.0	35,174	5.2	1.004	6.50

1988	3,652,000	4.8	37,003	5.2	1.013	6.53
1989	3,897,000	6.6	39,198	5.9	1.006	6.49
1990	4,172,000	9.6	41,593	6.1	0.997	6.28
1991	4,596,000	6.2	43,860	5.45	0.954	6.23
1992	4,837,000	2.7	45,518	3.8	0.941	6.30
1993	4,953,000	0.2	46,406	1.95	0.937	6.41
1994	4,885,000	1.0	46,835	0.9	0.959	6.41
1995	4,928,000	-2.9	47,236	0.86	0.959	6.65
1996	4,960,000	5.8	48,455	2.58	0.977	6.45
1997	5,158,000	3.0	49,475	2.1	0.959	6.39
1998	5,197,000	0.4	49,397	-0.2	0.950	6.36

Source: Japan Defense Agency, *Defense of Japan,* various years.

Note: FY 1997 and FY 1998 budgets included the cost for projects related to the Special Action Committee on Okinawa (¥6.1 billion for FY 1997 and ¥10.7 billion for FY 1998).

Japan benefited from its security arrangement with the United States. With U.S. protection, Japanese concentrated on economic development. Hugh Patrick and Henry Rosovsky calculated that Japan's annual growth rate would have dropped from 10 percent to 8 percent in 1954–74 if it had spent 6 or 7 percent of GNP on defense.[12] Tokyo's success in minimizing defense contributions was due to the circumstances of the cold war. Washington could not force Tokyo to increase defense spending when it was in the United States' own strategic interest to defend Japan against the Soviet Union.

However, as its economic power grew, Japan faced higher U.S. expectations for contributions. To support its war in Vietnam, Washington urged Tokyo in the 1960s to increase economic aid to noncommunist countries in Asia, namely Taiwan, South Korea, Indonesia, and the countries involved in the Mekong River project.[13] Japanese gladly portrayed its growing aid to the region as an indication of support for the United States.

Burden Sharing in the 1970s and 1980s

U.S. pressure on Japan for defense contributions intensified in the late seventies. Defense Secretary Harold Brown in the Carter administration publicly urged Japan to increase defense spending. In response, Tokyo adopted the "Guidelines for Japan–U.S. Defense Cooperation" in November 1978, which specified U.S.–Japan joint military training and intelligence exchange. Japan's defense spending grew from ¥1,691 billion ($6.3 billion) in 1977 to ¥2,230 billion ($9.8 billion) in 1980. In addition, in 1978 Japan began Host Nation Support, which came to cover around 70 percent of all U.S. direct costs of stationing troops in Japan in the nineties. In the eighties the Reagan administration saw burden sharing as a central concern in U.S. policy toward Japan and other allies. Defense Secretary Caspar Weinberger stated in December 1981 that Japan had not done enough for defense. In December 1982 the Senate passed a unanimous resolution demanding that Japan enhance its defense efforts. The Reagan administration also urged Tokyo to take on more defense missions.

By agreeing to assume responsibilities for monitoring and defending sea-lanes within one thousand nautical miles south of Tokyo and then for monitoring Soviet submarines in the Sea of Okhotsk and blocking the sea in the time of war, Japan acquired advanced U.S. weapons.

Nakasone Yasuhiro, who became prime minister in November 1982, called for "unity and cooperation with the United States and the free nations of Europe" in security issues. Japan's defense spending increased by about 6 percent a year in the decade, reaching ¥3,137 billion ($13.2 billion) in 1985 and ¥4,159 billion ($28.7 billion) in 1990. But Japan's military spending remained around 1 percent of GNP, much lower than that of its Western allies. GoJ's priority was fiscal restraint rather than defense spending.[14]

Japan preferred not to use defense spending as its principal form of international contribution. A report to the prime minister by the Foreign Economic Policy Study Group in April 1980 suggested that to meet international expectations for more contributions Japan should focus on economics, diplomacy, culture, science, and technology rather than "hasty expansion of direct military cooperation."[15] As Pharr noted, in the late seventies Japan used the concept of "comprehensive security" to legitimize "substitution" of development aid, strategic aid, and debt relief for defense spending.[16] "Military power plays a critical role in maintaining the global balance of power," Masahiro Sakamoto argued, "but defense costs cannot be shared in proportion to the economic size of nations. International commitments must be shared by major countries in a more comprehensive way, which includes economic as well as military costs."[17] Besides increasing the volume of development assistance, Japan offered "strategic aid" to "countries bordering on areas of conflict," such as Turkey, Pakistan, and Thailand, which were strategically important to the West in the wake of the Soviet invasion of Afghanistan and the Vietnamese invasion of Cambodia. Japan's strategic aid was meant to support U.S. strategic objectives.[18]

Washington accepted, to some degree, Tokyo's use of nonmilitary contributions, a development noticed and welcomed by the Japanese.[19] The cold war was an important reason for the U.S. position, especially during the first term of the Reagan administration, which engaged in an arms race with the "evil empire." The Soviet invasion of Afghanistan and the military buildup in the Far East meant greater need for Japanese cooperation with the United States.

The substitution of economic aid for defense contributions was a good deal for Japan. As Table 2.2 indicates, Japan's combined defense and ODA expenditure as a share of GNP was significantly lower than those of its Western allies—a mere 1.29 percent in 1986 compared to 6.83 percent for the United States, 3.53 percent for Germany, 5.11 percent for Britain,

Table 2.2
Defense and ODA of the United States, Japan, Germany, Britain, and France

Nation/Years	Defense Spending (Budget)			ODA (Disbursement)			Defense and ODA
	$ million	% of GNP	% of West*	$ million	% of GNP	% of DAC**	% of GNP
United States							
1961	62,008	9.1	72.6	2,943	0.49	56.6	9.59
1970	77,854	7.9	73.3	3,046	0.31	59.3	8.21
1980	143,981	5.6	54.1	7,318	0.27	26.1	5.87
1986	335,048	6.6	60.7	9,564	0.23	26.1	6.83
1990	306,170	5.5	57.5	11,366	0.21	21.0	5.71
1996	263,727	3.6	51.8	9,377	0.12	16.9	3.72
1997	262,159	3.4	51.5	6,878	0.09	14.2	3.49
1998	251,836	—	50.9	8,786	0.10	16.9	—
Japan							
1961	827	0.9	1.0	108	0.20	2.1	1.10
1970	1,595	0.8	1.5	458	0.23	6.7	1.03
1980	9,768	0.9	3.7	3,353	0.32	12.3	1.22
1986	24,811	1.0	4.5	5,634	0.29	15.4	1.29
1990	28,524	1.0	5.4	9,069	0.31	16.8	1.31
1996	51,095	1.0	10.0	9,439	0.20	17.0	1.20
1997	51,320	1.0	10.2	9,358	0.22	19.4	1.22
1998	51,285	—	10.4	10,640	0.28	20.4	—
Germany							
1961	4,612	4.0	5.4	366	0.44	7.0	4.44
1970	6,188	3.3	5.8	599	0.32	8.8	3.62
1980	26,692	3.3	10.0	3,567	0.44	13.1	3.74
1986	39,889	3.1	7.2	3,832	0.43	10.5	3.53
1990	42,320	2.8	7.9	6,320	0.42	11.7	3.22
1996	40,343	1.7	7.9	7,601	0.33	13.7	2.03
1997	38,906	1.6	7.8	5,857	0.28	12.1	1.88
1998	38,878	—	7.9	5,581	0.26	10.7	—

Britain

1961	5,886	6.3	6.9	457	0.59	8.8	6.89
1970	5,850	4.9	5.5	447	0.36	6.6	5.26
1980	26,749	5.1	10.1	1,854	0.35	6.8	5.45
1986	42,867	4.8	7.8	1,737	0.31	4.7	5.11
1990	39,776	4.0	7.5	2,647	0.27	4.9	4.27
1996	34,404	3.0	6.7	3,199	0.27	5.8	3.27
1997	32,201	2.7	6.5	3,433	0.26	7.1	2.96
1998	32,320	—	6.5	3,864	0.27	7.4	—

France

1961	5,316	6.2	6.2	903	1.35	17.4	7.55
1970	6,014	4.1	5.7	971	0.66	14.3	4.76
1980	26,425	4.0	9.9	4,162	0.63	15.2	4.63
1986	41,081	3.9	7.4	5,105	0.70	13.9	4.60
1990	42,589	3.6	8.0	9,380	0.79	17.3	4.39
1996	46,596	3.0	9.2	7,451	0.48	13.4	3.48
1997	47,037	3.0	9.4	6,307	0.45	13.1	3.45
1998	45,978	—	9.3	5,742	0.40	11.0	—

Source: Defence data are at 1970 constant prices and exchange rates for 1961–1970, at 1980 prices for 1980, and at 1995 prices for 1996, 1997, and 1998 from Stockholm International Peace Research Institute, *SIPRI Yearbook.* ODA data are based on current dollars, calculated from OECD, *Development Cooperation* and http://www.oecd.org/dac.

*The West here refers to NATO members plus Japan; **Increasing DAC membership tends to somewhat depress the percentage of all five nations included here.

and 4.60 percent for France. A true substitution would have had Japan contribute more than ten times its actual ODA to be on par with other major developed nations.

Japan came under U.S. pressure for burden sharing because of the shifting economic balance between the two nations. By the late eighties Japan produced almost 15 percent of the world GNP, compared to around 25 percent each by the United States and the European Community.[20] Japan also acquired massive surplus capital, as indicated in trade and current account surpluses, foreign reserves, and domestic savings. Its spending power received a major boost after the 1985 Plaza Accord when the yen appreciated sharply against the U.S. dollar, from ¥238.54 in 1985 to ¥128.15 in 1988. To Washington, it thus seemed only fair for Japan to make greater contributions to the international system from which it had benefited so much.

The Japanese were aware of their increased power. Kuriyama Takakazu, a former vice foreign minister and ambassador to Washington, characterized the balance of power between the United States, Europe, and Japan in a ratio of five (the United States, with a GNP of $5 trillion), five (Europe with $5 trillion), and three (Japan with $3 trillion) based on the 1988 data; together, the three powers account for 65 percent of the world GNP (about $20 trillion).[21] Both internationalists and realists supported cooperation with the West and differed only in reasons for cooperation and in degrees and arenas of cooperation. Internationalists wanted greater Japanese contributions to the international community. Realists knew that Japan remained dependent on the United States; a realistic government should therefore do more, but not too much more, to secure U.S. support and to continue maximizing gains in changing domestic and international environments. As a compromise, substitution of economic contributions for defense contributions could satisfy a wide range of constituencies. Nonmilitary contributions appealed to a strong pacifist sentiment among Japanese. Such a strong sentiment was certainly utilized by those policy elites who did not see wisdom in military contributions to the alliance.

Japan's possession of advanced technologies became a contentious issue in this period. On the one hand, as Japan became a technological power on par with the United States, its dual-use technologies could enhance U.S. defense capabilities.[22] The Pentagon asked the Japanese government for technologies. The Nakasone government agreed in January 1983, but only a few minor cases of transfer actually took place in the 1980s. Japan's plan to develop its own fighters in the Fighter Support Experimental project (FSX) in the early 1980s led to intense negotiations with the Americans, resulting in its decision in 1987 to cooperate with the United States.[23] On the other hand, Japan could compromise the U.S. strategic position if it transferred technologies to U.S. adversaries. In a rare but dramatic case, Japan's Toshiba Machine Company in the 1980s sold the Soviet Union sophisticated milling machines, which were used to manufacture quieter Soviet submarines. In response to strong U.S. criticism, the Japanese government decided in May 1987 to ban Toshiba from selling anything to the Soviet Union and thirteen other Communist countries for one year.

The limited technological cooperation between Japan and the United States highlighted the competitive nature of the bilateral economic relationship. In the eighties Washington became highly protective of its advanced technologies and preferred to "black box" sensitive components rather than licensing them to the Japanese. For their part, Japanese exhibited strong nationalism, a version Richard J. Samuels calls "technonationalism." He argued that "indigenization, diffusion, and nurturing of technology define the core of Japanese technonationalism," which "evolved from nineteenth-century mercantilism and survived twentieth-century militarism."[24] This nationalist ideology explains Japan's reluctance to share its technologies with foreigners.

Responsibility Sharing in the Post–Cold War Era

As the Soviet threat began diminishing, the Bush administration eased pressure on Japan to increase military spending and shoulder more responsibility. Michael H. Armacost, the U.S. ambassador to Japan under Bush, was not instructed to pressure the Japanese government in this regard. The U.S. interest in enhancing Japanese military capacity further decreased when the cold war ended. A Pentagon document leaked to the press in 1992 suggested that the United States should now discourage countries such as Japan and Germany from becoming major military powers by acquiring nuclear and power projection capabilities.[25]

The Gulf War strained the U.S.–Japan alliance. Under heavy pressure Tokyo grudgingly contributed $13 billion to the U.S.-led coalition. Japan's financial support was important. Kitaoka Shinichi calculated that the war cost $500 million a day, totaling $45 billion in three months. Therefore, the $9 billion Japan initially committed accounted for 20 percent of the total—higher than Japan's share of the world total GNP (15 percent).[26] "Had it not been for the Japanese, Desert Shield would have gone broke in August," General H. Norman Schwarzkopf, the commander of the coalition forces, recalled. "While western newspapers were complaining about Tokyo's reluctance to increase its pledge of one billion dollars to safeguard Saudi Arabia, the Japanese embassy in Riyadh quietly transferred tens of millions of dollars into Central Command's accounts."[27]

However, Japan's huge financial contribution won little praise. While resentful about the "respect deficit," one lesson Japanese drew from the Gulf War is that "in times of military crisis, the banker does not get nearly as much respect as the soldier."[28] Realizing that respect required a contribution of personnel as well as money, the Diet passed a law in June 1992 to allow Japanese military personnel to participate in UN peacekeeping operations (PKO). Japanese soldiers have served with PKO missions in Cambodia, but personnel contributions are still the exception for Japan rather than the rule in the security arena.

After the cold war ended, Japan alone among the developed nations expanded rather than shrank military spending. Its defense expenditure grew steadily on a yen basis in the 1990s (Table 2.1). But Japan still spent only 1 percent of GDP on defense in the 1990s compared to 4–5 percent for the United States (Table 2.2).[29] But more than defense expenditure, the United States in the 1990s wanted from Japan a clearer sense of mission and obligation for maintaining regional stability. Japan can no longer meet U.S. expectations by substituting economic cooperation for defense cooperation. In particular, the Americans were critical of Japan's lack of support during the nuclear crisis in the Korean Peninsula in early 1994. After intense discussions to strengthen bilateral security cooperation between U.S. and Japanese defense officials starting from mid 1994, President Bill Clinton and Prime Minister Hashimoto Ryutaro reaffirmed the U.S.–Japan Security Treaty in April 1996. After further discussions, the two governments signed a new "Guidelines for U.S.–Japan Defense Cooperation" in New York in September 1997.[30] Japan accepts responsibility for search-and-rescue missions, evacuation operations, inspection of ships in case of a UN-imposed embargo, and agrees to allow U.S. forces to use Japanese military and civilian airports, ports, and hospitals in the event of military conflicts in Japan or in areas surrounding Japan. The Japanese Self-Defense Force is also to conduct activities such as intelligence gathering, surveillance, and minesweeping. The Diet passed laws putting the guidelines into place in May 1999, but Tokyo has yet to develop a clear strategy to implement the guidelines.

Another area where Washington wants Tokyo to cooperate is a joint Theater Missile Defense (TMD) program in and around Japan against a conventional missile attack. Deputy Defense Secretary William Perry first raised the issue during his visit to Tokyo in May 1993. Japanese initially showed little enthusiasm for the program because of its high costs and uncertain effectiveness, as well as China's criticism. Under American pressure, Japan reluctantly agreed to participate in the program. However, North Korea's test launch of a ballistic missile over Japan in May 1998 drastically changed Japanese calculations. The Japanese government has committed $280 million over the next six years on TMD in collaboration with the United States. While American plans to build a national missile defense system have invited strong international criticism, Japan has quietly pursued its own plan. However, if a Japanese system can ever be successfully deployed, it may create tension between Japan and the United States over command and control. Tokyo will be unlikely to let Americans control launch decisions, but an independent Japanese chain of command will surely cause concern in the region.[31]

Two issues currently strain the Japanese–U.S. alliance. First, the rape of a twelve-year-old schoolgirl by three U.S. soldiers in 1995 sparked large demonstrations in Okinawa demanding removal of U.S. bases in the island. To appease local residents in Okinawa, the Japanese and U.S. governments agreed in 1996 to return in phases 21 percent of land used by the U.S. military, including the relocation of Marine Corps Air Station Futenma. But the Japanese side has yet to come up with a plan to implement the relocation. To buy off local opposition, Tokyo staged the G-8 summit in Okinawa in June 2000. But local opposition to U.S. bases remains. To make things worse, the alleged fondling of a fourteen-year-old girl by a U.S. marine in June 2000 led to renewed protests.

Second, in an unprecedented move, the Japanese Ministry of Finance (MOF) reviewed the Host Nation Support (HNS) budget in December 1999 and recommended a reduction of 2.8 percent for the fiscal year 2000 budget. Until that shocking announcement, Tokyo's financial support for the 47,000 U.S. troops based in Japan was a good area of cooperation for the Americans. Japan's HNS now costs over $4 billion a year,[32] amounting to three-quarters of the total cost of maintaining U.S. troops. Joseph Nye, Jr., former assistant secretary of defense for international security, notes that it is cheaper to base troops in Japan than in the United States.[33] As Armacost commented, Japan accepted "the most generous offset agreement the United States had ever concluded with any ally."[34] MOF justified its decision to reduce financial support based on Japan's economic difficulties and America's strong economy. But Washington strongly opposed MOF's plan, seeing it also as indicative of Japan's weaker commitment to the alliance.

Investment Versus Consumption

While trying to substitute economic for security contributions, Japan again picks and chooses areas for cooperation. One pattern to its choices is a clear preference for investment over consumption.

Catching Up in the 1950s and 1960s

How Japan achieved an economic miracle is a familiar story. Japan was a beneficiary of the U.S. hegemony. The United States provided military protection, foreign aid, technology transfer, access to its market, and persuasion for other nations to accept Japan back into the international community. In return, Japan followed U.S. leadership and provided military bases. The government adopted a consistent approach to enhance the competitiveness of Japanese companies in the global market while protecting the Japanese domestic market.

Washington supported Japan's economic development because "economic progress seemed a prerequisite to Japan's remaining democratic and aligned against the Soviet Union."[35] In fact, the United States, with its clear economic dominance, had virtually no leverage over Japan for market access. Washington considered an open U.S. market consistent with its fundamental interests while it saw little value in the Japanese market. The United States did not threaten to close its market to Japanese goods in this period. If it had done so, Japan would have called its bluff.[36]

From Exporter to Investor in the 1970s and 1980s

By the early 1970s, the Japan–U.S. economic relationship had become competitive. The textile dispute in 1969–71 created the most serious crisis in Japan–U.S. relations since 1952.[37] Since then the two nations have engaged in ever more intensive trade disputes. Japan's trade and current account surpluses grew rapidly since the late 1960s. As Figure 2.1 shows, after experiencing current account and trade deficits during the second oil crisis at the end of the 1970s, Japan entered a period of chronic surpluses on both accounts in the 1980s.[38] U.S. strategies toward Japan shifted from restrictions on Japanese exports to pursuing macroeconomic policy coordination, such as foreign exchange adjustment, Japanese market opening, and sectoral agreements. However, despite important changes since the mid 1980s, Japan imported few manufactured goods and lacked intra-industry trade with other developed nations.[39] While its share of world total exports increased from 6.79 percent in 1980 to 8.51 percent in 1990, its share of world imports decreased from 7.06 percent in 1980 to 6.79 percent in 1990.[40] Japan's strategy was to give in as little as possible and make vague promises.[41]

Japan preferred overseas investment to domestic consumption. T.J. Pempel noted a major shift in Japanese foreign economic policy from export promotion to greater integration with the world market through overseas investment after the first oil crisis in 1973–74.[42] Japanese FDI increased after 1980 when the government liberalized capital controls on investments abroad, with an annual average outflow of $32.1 billion in 1986–90.[43] Most Japanese FDI went to the United States—45.5 percent in 1987 and 45.9 percent in 1990.[44] Japan's investment facilitated the U.S. objective of creating jobs, which explains why most state governments opened office in Tokyo to attract Japanese investment to their regions. But, as acknowledged by Kiyohiko Fukushima, a senior economist of the Nomura Research Institute, Japan's investment strategy for advanced nations "is designed to secure markets previously acquired through exports and to avoid protectionism."[45] As Dennis J. Encarnation showed, Japan's freedom to invest in the United States and the impediments to U.S. investments in Japan explains why Japan sold so much more to the United States than the other way around.[46] Japanese discouraged inward foreign investments despite recognized efficiency gains because they were interested in protecting Japanese firms from competition in their home turf.

More than FDI, Japan's portfolio investments in the 1980s were seen as a contribution to the United States. Japanese purchases of U.S. Treasury bills, amounting to $138 billion by April 1986, "subsidized" U.S. hegemony, recycling surplus Japanese savings to the United States to fund excess consumption. Japanese financing enabled the Reagan administration to engage in an arms race with the Soviet Union and conduct major tax cuts without reducing government expenditures.[47] But again, Japan's portfolio investments were not simply driven by co-operative strategic concerns. There were market forces at work and Japan's investment served its own economic interests: Japanese investors believed they would receive better returns in the United States than in Japan.

Some Japanese officials took to arguing that the country's trade and current account surpluses were actually good for the world. "Among the industrial countries some should remain capital suppliers," commented Okita Saburo in an interview in 1986. "Japan has contributed to the creation of employment in the United States." Conversely, "if we were to eliminate all of our current account surplus, it would cause serious repercussions in the world economy."[48] A finance ministry advisory group, headed by former vice finance minister Oba Tomomitsu, issued a report in 1990 recommending that Japan maintain moderate trade surpluses to finance its international objectives, a position shared by some top economic officials in the country. They maintained that "the nation's current account surplus is serving to support stable world economic growth rather than causing confusion in the global economy."[49]

Such reasoning did not convince the Americans. In response to Japan's claim that it needed surpluses to provide reconstruction capital for Eastern Europe, Treasury Secretary Nicholas F. Brady commented that Europe's need for capital "should not be confused with the need for surplus countries to continue to bring down their external surpluses by increasing investment relative to savings" at home.[50] Washington made several attempts through the 1980s, without much success, to pressure Tokyo to contribute to global economic growth and reduction of U.S. trade deficits by stimulating domestic consumption and increasing imports.

At the G-7 summits of 1977 and 1978, Japan and Germany were asked to serve as "locomotives" for the world economy with explicit growth targets and stimulation packages to address the imbalance in current account payments. Japan pledged a 7 percent growth rate for 1978 based on a domestic-led growth strategy. But Tokyo dropped the locomotive theory in favor of neoclassical, anti-inflation policies after the 1979 summit.[51] At the 1985 Plaza Conference, Japan promised to shift from its traditional emphasis on exports to domestic consumption by lowering interest rates. In the following years, Tokyo announced domestic stimulus packages to appease Washington, often as "souvenirs" when the prime minister met the president. But there was much packaging in Japanese proposals, and Japan's trade and current account surpluses shot up again in 1991 after dipping in 1989–90 (Figure 2.1).

Few in the West were satisfied with Japan's cooperation in trade. By the mid 1980s, Japan was seen as engaging in comprehensive competition with the United States, with far-reaching strategic significance. James Fallows wrote that "America doesn't have a chance to stop declining if it must keep competing with both the Russians and the Japanese."[52] American concerns about the United States losing its great power status to Japan received an intellectual boost when Paul Kennedy published *The Rise and Fall of the Great Power* in 1987, which in effect argued that the United States, like great powers before it, had reached a stage of imperial overstretch and was beginning to decline.[53] The U.S. government sought to reduce its trade deficits with Japan through sectoral agreements as well as macroeconomic measures to bring down Japan's massive trade and current account surpluses. Their failure in achieving this goal led to far greater trade frictions when Bill Clinton became president in 1992.

Muddling Through the Recession in the 1990s

Continuing the trend in the previous period, the main objective of U.S. economic policy in the early 1990s was "increasing access to Japan's markets, stimulating demand-led growth in the Japanese economy, and raising the standard of living in both the U.S. and Japan."[54] But U.S. officials lost patience in trade negotiations with the Japanese. "The process has simply not gone as well as we had hoped," pointed out J. Michael Farren, undersecretary of commerce for international trade in the Bush administration. "We'll make incremental progress, but it's not going to put us in the position where the trade frictions are eliminated."[55] To maintain U.S. competitive advantages, particularly in high-technology industries, some influential American analysts proposed "activist" or "cautious activist" strategies toward Japan and other advanced nations in the early 1990s.[56]

Unlike previous administrations, the first-term Clinton administration wanted to enhance U.S. competitiveness by reducing federal deficits and by training and education. In addition, the administration pushed for a comprehensive bilateral framework with Japan, which included sectoral agreements that gave greater attention to results. The intellectual foundation of Clinton's Japan policy in his first term was revisionism, a school of thought that had emerged in the late 1980s. Despite

40

Figure 2.1 **Japan's Current Account and Trade Balances in 1977–98**

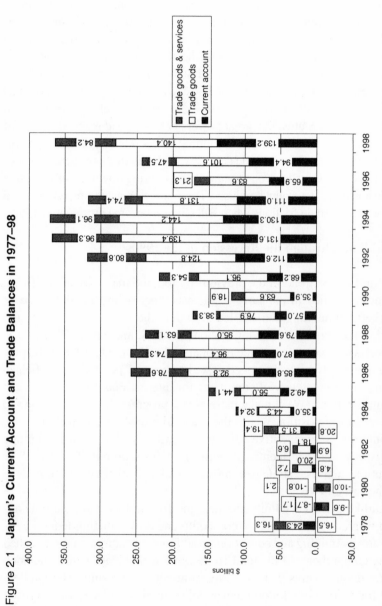

Source: International Monetary Fund (IMF), *International Financial Statistics Yearbook*, 1998, pp. 522–23. The data for 1998 are from the Ministry of Finance of Japan, February 15, 1999, and Associated Press, February 15, 1999.

differences in opinions, revisionists generally agreed that Japan was fundamentally different from the United States and used unfair practices to advance its economic interests at the expense of the United States. As a result, they argued Washington had to adopt an unconventional results-oriented approach in trade negotiations. The economic policy team of the first Clinton administration, which included many with revisionist views, designed a tough trade policy toward Japan. In fact, trade people dominated U.S. policy toward Japan until 1994. The United States and Japan signed the "Framework for a New Economic Partnership" in June 1993. Twenty-three trade agreements, most of which came under the Framework, were reached between January 1993 and May 1997. But the United States achieved only limited success. The American Chamber of Commerce in Japan concluded in a report released in January 1997 that only thirteen of the forty-five trade agreements reached between 1980 and 1996 were successful.[57] For some American analysts, the U.S. government did not engage in a tough and persistent strategy to force Japan to comply. But the main reason was that Washington was not ready to sacrifice its security interests in Asia by damaging its relations with its number one ally in the region. The so-called Nye Initiative, named after then assistant secretary of defense Joseph Nye, was launched in 1994 and resulted in a highly publicized Pentagon report on U.S. security strategy for the Asia-Pacific region in February 1995. The report paved the way for reaffirmation of the U.S.–Japan Security Treaty in April 1996. Nye argued elsewhere that "linking security to trade as a tactic for short-term gain risks the overall relationship" with Japan.[58]

For the past few years, while continuing to complain about Japan's trade practices, Washington has shifted its principal focus to Japanese macroeconomic policy and urging the Japanese government to revive its own economy through greater domestic demand stimulus and banking sector reform. Americans believe that Japan's economic revival is central to regional economic revival and to preserving U.S. economic growth as well.[59] To increase pressure on Japan, Clinton and senior U.S. government officials have made public demands on the Japanese government to take resolute action to revive Japan's economy with permanent tax cuts and serious economic restructuring.

Under repeated U.S. pressure, the Japanese government announced ten stimulus packages in the 1990s, totaling $1,135 billion, with the latest package coming in November 1999 at ¥18,000 billion.[60] Japanese leaders have often announced stimulus packages right before G-7 summits, Asia-Pacific Economic Cooperation (APEC) forum summits or meetings with American leaders. As a result of much counting manipulation, these packages have been grossly exaggerated, with little real money committed for economic stimulus. Adam Posen of the Institute for International Economics calculated that of seven stimulus packages totaling $511 billion announced between March 1992 and September 1995, only $197 billion (38.5 percent) was real stimulus money. The rest was largely front-loading prior budgetary commitments. A real sizable package would have had real impact.[61] After Hashimoto announced the 1998 package, Clinton commented to the media that the package "will be a plus," he said, "if it's real—that is, if it's real money and it's implemented rapidly and vigorously."[62] During Prime Minister Obuchi Keizo's visit to Washington in May 1999, Clinton praised Obuchi for implementing measures that are showing some results but still pressed Japanese to do more to open the market.[63]

Washington has high stakes here: Unless Japan absorbs some excess Asian goods, other Asian nations will turn to the United States to export out of their financial difficulties. Japan is also exporting its way out of its economic recession. As C. Fred Bergsten argues, Japan sees export surpluses as the path to recovery since its stimulus measures have all failed.[64] Indeed, Japan's current accounts were $120.7 billion in 1998 and $106.9 billion in 1999, close to its historic high of $131.6 billion in 1993. Japan's trade surpluses in goods were $122.4 billion in 1998 and $123.3 billion in 1999, trailing closely its historical high of $144.2 billion in 1994.[65] Japan's politically sensitive trade surplus with the United States grew from $42.4 billion in 1997 to $52.2 billion in 1998, an increase of 23.1 percent.[66] In fact, on a yen basis, Japan's surplus with the United States accounted for 50.3 percent of its total surplus in 1997, 47.8 percent in 1998, and 56.7 percent in 1999.[67]

GoJ responds to U.S. criticism and pressure despite strong resentment. But it is striking that the Japanese so consistently use much-padded packages to appease Americans while avoiding what the Americans really want—a permanent tax cut, deregulation of the economy, and opening their markets—even when Americans have clearly become tired of Japan's maneuver. Because of its preferences, trade is where Japan compromises as little as possible and where almost all serious conflicts with the United States have taken place.[68] Any cooperation in Japan's use of economic power, therefore, has to be balanced against its earning behavior: In 1991–99, Japan's export surplus in goods totaled $1,067.1 billion and its current account surplus amounted to $941.5 billion.[69]

Japanese have not given up on mercantilist tendencies despite much rhetoric and some actions to liberalize the economy. Due to entrenched neomercantilist ideas and institutions, GoJ has been reluctant to conduct fundamental reform of the system even though neomercantilism outlived its usefulness once Japan caught up with the West. Ideas and habits do not die easily, especially when Japanese policy elites have vested interests in preserving their status quo or still consider these ideas beneficial to the nation or are simply at a loss as to how they can resolve the serious problems facing the nation.

Foreign Assistance Versus Sanctions

Given its massive financial power, Japan's direct use of economic power, as carrots or sticks, has important implications for U.S. foreign policy. How cooperative Japan is with the United States in this regard depends on the nature of U.S. relations with the target nations and the benefits and costs for Washington resulting from Japan's choice of instruments. For the United States, Japan's cooperation in economic assistance is indicated in channeling development capital to the types of projects and the nations preferred by Washington based on its national interests or development philosophy. In addition, GoJ's aid to a particular country should not give Japanese companies competitive advantages over U.S. firms in that country and U.S. firms should gain a fair share of project procurements. Japan's support for the United States in economic sanctions is judged in three ways: whether Japan supports U.S.-led sanctions; whether it compromises U.S. efforts by assisting countries targeted for American sanctions; and whether it sanctions countries against U.S. wishes.

Tokyo prefers carrots to sticks. Japan became the world's number one ODA donor in the late 1980s. In addition to ODA, Japan's Export-Import Bank (JExIm) provided untied loans for development and economic adjustment with international contribution in mind in 1986.[70] In contrast, Japan has seldom taken the lead in punishing other countries economically, as opposed to the United States and other major nations. Japan adopts an incremental approach: Adjustments in allocation usually come at the margins. And Japan has cooperated less with the United States in sanctions than in development assistance.

Growing Importance of Aid Through the 1980s

Japan became an aid donor in 1954 as a participant in the Colombo Plan and provided its first bilateral official loan to India in 1957. Through the 1960s Tokyo used its war reparations programs as "aid" to re-enter Asian markets and promote exports. Japanese ODA grew steadily from $159.2 million in 1960 to $1,147.7 million in 1975 (Table 2.3). In March 1960 Japan became a founding member of the Development Assistance Group, which became the Development Assistance Committee (DAC) of the Organization for Economic Cooperation and Development (OECD) in October 1961. By joining the group of rich and powerful states, Japan acquired better knowledge of aid policies of other developed nations. The DAC also became a forum for international pressure. The United States wanted a group target for aid at 1 percent of GNP at the DAC meeting in London in March 1961. Japan resisted setting its ODA target beyond its capacity. Although Japan pledged giving ODA at 1 percent of GNP at the second meeting of the United Nations Conference on Trade and Development in 1968 and agreed to a 0.7 percent of GNP target in 1970, it did not set an explicit target date.[71] In fact, Japan has not lived up to that pledge to this day, with its ODA below 0.30 percent of GNP.

In the early 1970s, Japan's ODA aimed at securing supplies of food, energy, and natural resources. Okita Saburo, president of the Overseas Economic Cooperation Fund (OECF) from 1973 to 1977, stated that while the Soviet and U.S. aid programs were tied to cold war foreign policy objectives, Japan had to follow a different path.

> Because Japan is dependent on other countries for food, energy, and natural resources, and about half of our trade is with developing nations, it is imperative for Japan that these developing nations increase their food production and become wealthier, in case the world food situation worsens, as it did in 1972 when there was a worldwide scramble to purchase soya beans and grains from the United States, the only major producer with any surplus. In that respect, Japan's aid to developing countries can be said to be related to the nation's comprehensive security, and Japanese trade and aid can be thought of as twin pillars sustaining the State.[72]

Japan did not initiate any economic sanctions through the 1970s. But Tokyo participated in U.S.-led sanctions against communist countries. In 1952 Japan joined the Coordinating Committee on Multilateral Export Controls (COCOM), which was formed in November 1949 to con-

Table 2.3

Japan's Net Flow of Financial Resources to Less Developed Countries (LDCs) and Multilateral Agencies ($ million)

	1960	1965	1970	1975	1980	1986	1991	1995	1997
Total official and private	259.3	485.5	1823.9	2890.1	6765.9	14579	24883	42295	29509
1. ODA	159.2	243.7	458.0	1147.7	3303.7	5634	10952	14489	9358
(a) Bilateral	117.9	226.3	371.5	850.4	1960.8	3846	8860	10419	6552
(i) Grants, including technology	66.9	82.2	121.2	201.7	652.6	1703	3383	6298	4985
technology	NA	6.0	21.6	87.2	277.8	599	1374	2398	1956
(ii) loans	57.5	144.1	250.3	648.7	1308.2	2143	5477	4120	1568
(b) Multilateral	41.3	17.4	86.5	297.3	1342.9	1788	2092	4071	2806
2. OOF, net*	—	—	693.6	1369.4	1478.0	-724	2582	5544	3975
3. Private, at market terms	100.1	241.8	669.4	362.9	1957.8	9586	11182	22046	15953
Total/GNP	0.57	0.55	0.93	0.59	0.65	1.09	0.74	0.82	0.70
DAC Average	0.89	0.77	0.74	1.05	1.04	0.73	NA	0.76	0.86
ODA/GNP	0.24	0.28	0.23	0.24	0.32	0.29	0.32	0.28	0.22
DAC Average	0.52	0.44	0.34	0.36	0.37	0.35	0.33	0.27	0.22

Source: OECD, *Development Assistance* (later called *Development Cooperation*), various years.

Note: NA = Not available; OOF, net* refers to "Other Official Flow," a category introduced in 1968—mainly official export credits. Multilateral: Grants to UN agencies and other institutions; capital subscription payments to the World Bank, International Finance Corporation (IFC), International Development Agency (IDA), regional development banks and others; and concessional lending.

trol exports of strategic goods to the Soviet bloc. Japan also joined the China Committee of COCOM (CHINCOM) (1952–58), which imposed even tougher sanctions on China than on the former Soviet Union. But Japanese were not enthusiastic about embargoes on China, their largest trading partner before the war. This issue will be discussed in greater detail in Chapter 3.

Since 1978 Japan drastically increased ODA in a series of five medium-term aid-doubling plans. Its annual ODA grew from $1.4 billion in 1977 to $8.9 billion in 1989, the year Japan became the world's largest ODA donor for the first time. The first medium-term target, announced at the Bonn G-7 Summit in 1978, doubled ODA over the 1977 level of $1.4 billion in three years. The second target (1981–85) aimed at doubling ODA from 1976–80 to $21.4 billion. The third target (1986–92) set quantity and quality goals, pledging $40 billion for the period. The fourth target (1988–92), for $50 billion, announced at the G-7 Toronto Summit in 1988, was to double the performance of 1983–87. The fifth target (1993–97) promised $70–75 billion. Japan presented its massive ODA as a shining example of contributions to the international community, which explains why Japanese leaders often chose G-7 summits as platforms for announcing the plans.

In addition, Japan announced three "capital recycling plans" between 1986 and 1989 to channel a total of $65 billion worth of surpluses to developing nations and multilateral institutions. The recycling plans, which included ODA, other official flows, and private flows, involved much repackaging and double counting—the disbursements from OECF were counted toward both the recycling plan and the fourth medium-term ODA target. Apart from ODA, Japan's other official flows included principally JExIm trade and investment credits and untied loans. In the end, Japan's net flow of capital to developing nations and multilateral institutions was $95.6 billion in 1987–91, compared to $70.1 billion from the United States.[73]

Japan's recycling plans were meant as contributions to international public goods at a time when the Latin American debt crisis created a severe capital shortage in developing countries. The principal mission of the expanded recycling program, announced in July 1989, was to contribute to the debt strategy proposed by Treasury Secretary Nicholas Brady in March 1989 mainly for Latin American countries. Japan saw its financial contribution to the Brady Plan as a good example of its contribution to the United States since Latin America is far more important to Washington than to Tokyo. Hosono Akio, Japan's leading Latin American expert, pointed out that Japan's assistance to Latin America's economic recovery benefited U.S. exports to the region. U.S. export to Mexico was $33.3 billion in 1992 as compared to $2.8 billion for Japanese exports. And 38 percent of the untied loans from the JExIm was spent on purchases from the United States, whereas only 6 percent went to Japanese firms.[74] The importance of scoring points with the United States is also proven the other way around. The absence of strong U.S. pressure was an important reason why Japan did not provide active support in the 1994 Mexican peso crisis, contrary to its action in the 1980s debt crisis.[75]

Japan was trying to use ODA as a substitution for defense contributions to the United States, as discussed earlier. GoJ provided strategic aid to countries bordering conflict or to Central American and Caribbean countries at U.S. request.[76] But there was still much criticism in the United States of Japan's ODA programs. Washington did not view Japanese ODA, as a share of GNP, as sufficient burden sharing. Calculating burden sharing as the combined total of aid and defense spending as a share of GNP, the United States contributed 6.83 percent in 1986 while Japan gave only 1.29 percent (see Table 2.2). In 1987 Congress wanted Japan to contribute 3 percent of GNP to the international community—1 percent on defense and 2 percent on ODA.[77] There was also much criticism of Japan's aid quality as measured by grant ratio and grant element. Japan's grant element of total ODA was 75.4 percent in 1987, lower than the DAC 1987–88 average of 90.4 percent, and its grant share was 46.6 percent in 1987, again lower than the DAC 1987–88 average of 78.4 percent.[78] In addition, Americans noticed the asymmetries in U.S. and Japanese aid approaches.[79] Armacost pointed out that "we seemed to wind up supporting many of the world's poorest countries," while Japanese aid "was concentrated in Asia; it focused on countries at the threshold of industrial success, relied mainly on loans rather than grants, and was heavily oriented to infrastructure projects in which Japanese suppliers of pipe, cement, and construction services were keenly interested."[80]

We should have a balanced view of Japanese development financing. On the one hand, it was to Japan's advantage to use foreign aid as substitution for international contributions. First, Japan's external spending was only a small part of its external earning. In 1981–91, Japan had a total of $530.1 billion in current account surpluses and $690.54 billion in merchandise trade surpluses but spent only $69.3 billion on ODA, merely one-tenth of its trade earnings.[81] Second, as Edward Lincoln observes, "foreign aid does (and will) lead to enhanced Japanese business opportunities in recipient countries."[82] Third, Japan's bilateral ODA remained tied with its economic and commercial interests.[83]

On the other hand, Japan was trying to be cooperative. For the recycling plans, Japanese went out of their way to prove their willingness to cooperate. Japanese policy makers, eager to score points with the United States, saw the debt crisis as a golden opportunity to demonstrate their international contributions. Top MOF officials who negotiated with Americans to implement the Brady Plan, often committed JExIm to lending programs without advance consultations with domestic partners in order to respond quickly to strong U.S. pressure.[84] Also, to overcome Japan's reputation for export promotion, Tokyo relied on nonproject loans and cofinancing with multilateral development banks to assure that loans were truly untied. To reduce criticism of its ODA, GoJ steadily increased the portion of loans open to procurement outside Japan, reaching 65.1 percent in 1988, compared to 18.0 percent for the United States and 39.3 percent for Germany.[85] Another way to appreciate Japan's efforts is that ODA grew faster than other items in the general account budget: ODA expenditures grew by 150 percent from fiscal 1980 to fiscal 1991, while defense grew by 100 percent, social welfare by 50 percent, and education and science by merely 25 percent.[86]

Nishigaki Akira, former president of OECF, and Shimomura Yasutami, a leading development specialist, also suggested that Japan's ODA program should be judged by its effectiveness. After all, whatever the financial conditions, development assistance should be ultimately judged by whether it has facilitated development in recipient countries. In this sense, Japan's ODA is cooperative for the recipient nations since Japanese money facilitates their development. But a high ratio of untying loans did not necessarily benefit American firms. By the late 1980s, only around 20 percent of the procurements for OECF loans went to developed nations, the United States included. In short, although cooperative for developing nations, Japanese ODA was less so for the United States.

Japan was hesitant to use sanctions. The number two economic superpower, Japan lagged far behind the number one United States in this regard. In their widely cited study, Gary Clyde Hufbauer et al. listed 107 cases of sanctions between January 1946 and January 1990. The United States was a "sender" individually or jointly 75 times (see

Table 2.4

Economic Sanctions: Japan Compared to Others, 1946–90
(number of cases)

Senders	Single	Joint	Total
I. Western countries			
United States	60	15	75
United Kingdom	1	5	6
Canada	3	1	4
France	1	1	2
West Germany	0	1	1
Japan	0	1	1
II. Communist countries			
Soviet Union	7	0	7
China	2	0	2
III. Developing nations			
Arab League	0	4	4
India	3	0	3
Indonesia	2	0	2
Total cases	84	23	107

Source: Calculated from Hufbauer et al., *Economic Sanctions Reconsidered,* pp. 16–27.
Other countries listed include Spain, South Vietnam, Nigeria, Australia, and South Africa. They are all listed once.

Table 2.4). In contrast, Japan was a sender only once, and a joint sender at that: Japan, West Germany, and the United States sanctioned Burma in 1988 over human rights violations.

Compared with development assistance, Japan was even less cooperative on economic sanctions. First, Japan was not that cooperative in supporting U.S.-led economic sanctions. As Table 2.5 shows, Japan cooperated with the United States less than did Europe, except when the targets were communist countries. After the Soviet invasion of Afghanistan in 1979, Japan joined the United States in imposing economic sanctions on the Soviet Union, with measures such as the boycott of the Moscow Olympics, postponement of economic cooperation negotiations, tightening of export credits, and restrictions on the export of machinery. In fact, Japan was more active than Europe at a significant cost: Its share of the Soviet trade with noncommunist countries dropped from second place to fifth. In a related case, after Vietnam invaded Cambodia in January 1979, Japan cut off aid to that country, siding with the West and China.

Table 2.5

Comparison of U.S., European, and Japanese Sanctions (1948–90)

Target	Period	United States			European Community			Japan		
		Export	Import	Financial	Export	Import	Financial	Export	Import	Financial
COMECON*	Since 1948	X			X			X		
North Korea	Since 1950	X	X	X						
Vietnam	Since 1957	X	X	X						
Cuba	Since 1960	X	X	X						
South Africa	Since 1962	X	X	X	X	X	X	X	X	X
Angola	Since 1974			X			X			
Cambodia	Since 1975	X	X	X	X		X			
Libya	Since 1978	X	X	X	X			X		
Iran	1979–81			X	X					
Pakistan	Since 1979			X						
Bolivia	1979–82			X						
USSR	1980–81	X								

Country	Period							
Iraq	Since 1980						X	X
Nicaragua	1981–90						X	X
Poland	1981–87	X					X	X
USSR	1981–82			X				X
Suriname	1982–88		X				X	
USSR	1983		X	X				X
Zimbabwe	1983–88				X		X	X
Grenada	1983						X	X
Iran	Since 1984				X		X	X
Panama	1987–90				X		X	
El Salvador	1987–88						X	
Haiti	1987–90			X	X		X	X
China	Since 1989	X	X	X	X	X	X	X
Iraq	Since 1990	X	X	X	X	X	X	X

Source: Hufbauer et al., *Economic Sanctions Reconsidered*, pp. 68–69. As they define in their book, export sanctions limit exports, import sanctions restrict imports, and financial sanctions impede finance, including the reduction of aid.

*Council for Mutual Economic Assistance.

Second, Japan often hesitated to join the United States in sanctions when its economic interests were at stake. As Schott has noted, Japan "usually restores the funds when relations normalize after a 'decent interval.'"[87] When Washington imposed sanctions on Iran after armed students seized U.S. embassy staff in Tehran in November 1979, Tokyo dragged its feet and agreed to join sanctions only after Europeans decided to do so. Iran was a major oil supplier to Japan. U.S. secretary of state Cyrus Vance complained to Okita Saburo, the Japanese foreign minister at the time, about Tokyo's "insensitivity" in buying large quantities of oil after Washington imposed an embargo on Tehran. Washington formally asked Tokyo to join the embargo in April of the next year. Okita then flew to Luxembourg for private discussions with the European foreign ministers to have a united policy. "At that time Japanese diplomacy was distressingly sandwiched between Iranian oil and United States friendship!" Okita explained.[88] Japan resumed aid to Iran in 1993. After the Iraqi invasion of Kuwait, Japan resisted pressure from the United States to act quickly to impose sanctions. It imported 170,000 barrels of crude oil a day from Iraq and 160,000 barrels a day from Kuwait, which Iraq had seized. The foreign ministry spokesman Watanabe Taizo called Iraq's invasion "extremely regrettable," but said "it takes time to decide what measures are appropriate to show our displeasure."[89]

Third, in some cases Japan actually softened the impact of U.S.-led sanctions. In June 1980, Japan and West Germany pressed the United States to allow rescheduling of Pakistan's $5.1 billion debt to a consortium of industrial nations despite U.S. sanctions on Pakistan over nuclear safeguards. In another case, in 1982 Washington tried to tighten COCOM controls in 1982 by adding new items such as dry docks and proposing a "no exception" policy on computers. The Soviets were using Japanese dry docks for building aircraft carriers. Along with Britain, France, and West Germany, Japan opposed expansion of the COCOM framework. After the June 1989 Tiananmen incident, Japan joined the United States and other Western nations in imposing sanctions on China. But Japan resumed aid to China a year later. Tokyo worked from inside to soften the Western position on China, a maneuver accepted by President George Bush, who could not do so himself in the face of congressional opposition.

Japan's hesitancy in supporting the United States in sanctions was caused not only by an interest in avoiding hard choices but also by its different notion of what works better to make countries change their behavior. In addition, Japanese did not really share some U.S. motives for imposing sanctions—namely, aiming to change a country's domestic political institutions or culture. Nishigaki and Shimomura argued that "persuasion is a superior approach" to coercive measures. "Wholehearted and sincere persuasion can help to get the developing country to understand what problems are a source of concern and where improvement is necessary. It can also help the country realize that a change in policy direction is in its own interest. Through this approach, we can hope to get the country in question to move in an improved direction by its own will, not merely to avoid penalties or reap rewards."[90] It is possible that this Japanese notion is misconstrued, but in the end it is what Japanese elites think that shapes Tokyo's approach to sanctions.

Aid Superpower in the 1990s

Japan emerged as the largest aid donor in the 1990s. Tokyo maintained a high level of ODA even after the bubble burst in 1991. Its yen-denominated ODA disbursements remained large, and dollar-denominated figures soared with yen appreciation. Given a decreasing Western interest in assisting developing nations in the post–cold war era, Japan's share of the total ODA disbursement among the DAC members increased from 16.8 percent in 1990 to 24.6 percent in 1995, when its share peaked. In 1991–97, Japan's net disbursements of ODA amounted to $79.9 billion, or 20.2 percent of the DAC total, compared to 16.9 percent contributed by the United States.[91]

Japan also tried to improve the quality of its ODA. According to a peer review published in March 1996, Japan's "volume performance has been accompanied for many years by a concerted effort to improve the quality of Japan's development cooperation."[92] One important indicator of cooperation the Japanese cited was the ratio of untied loans. The untied ratio of Japan's bilateral ODA was 98.9 percent in 1996—much higher than the 69.7 percent for DAC total. Regarding the grant element, which is generally considered a more important indicator of ODA quality, Japan also did well, reaching 67.0 percent in 1996—slightly higher than the 64.7 percent for total DAC. But Japan's grant share of 34.1 percent in 1996 was still considerably lower than 76.8 percent for DAC total.[93]

In a highly unusual move, Japan also attempted intellectual contributions in the area of development based on its own development experience and that of East Asian developing countries in the previous decades. As Anne L. Emig showed in her detailed account of Japan's challenge to the World Bank, Japanese gained confidence in the 1980s and decided to challenge the World Bank orthodoxy in the late 1980s when Japan's aid program in the Philippines came under World Bank criticism. GoJ articulated its viewpoints in the OECF Occasional Paper No. 1 in October 1991. In contrast to a market-driven World Bank approach to readjustment, Japanese offered an approach that encourages considerable government intervention in achieving economic development based on Asian experience. Respectful of the concerns of a major donor nation and facilitated by Japanese financing, the World Bank launched a major study of East Asian development experience, resulting in the 1993 World Bank report *The East Asian Miracle: Economic Growth and Public Policy*. The report gave little support for the Japanese approach, and the Japanese players involved did not attempt to replace the World Bank orthodoxy with the Japanese way. Nevertheless, in openly criticizing the World Bank Japan had certainly made a daring move, judging by its past behavior.[94]

Japan's success in the development area, its rising power, and its changing international security environment gave some Japanese confidence that Japan had figured out ways that fit current and future international relations better than a coercive U.S. approach. As a result, the talk in Japan was no longer burden sharing, but leadership sharing in nonmilitary areas.[95] Japanese still hoped to use economically based "international contributions" as substitution for reduction in trade surpluses and defense contributions.[96] As a primary example, Japan and the United States cooperated on global issues such as environment, population, AIDS, and narcotics in the "Common Agenda for U.S.–Japan Cooperation in Global Perspective" concluded in July 1993. But there was less U.S. push on the Japanese to increase ODA in the 1990s. As Donald C. Hellmann suggested, "an international division of labor in which America maintains order and the Japanese give aid (like the one the Bush administration agreed to)" was not acceptable and that "burden sharing must include military responsibilities roughly in proportion to economic power."[97]

In the early 1990s Japan also tried to shed its image of being driven mainly by commercial interests in favor of promoting "principled" use of economic power. Prime Minister Kaifu Toshiki announced that Japan would now consider a series of factors in making ODA decisions: military spending, development and production of weapons of mass production, trade in arms, efforts for promoting democratization and market economy, and human rights. These principles were incorporated in the

ODA Charter adopted by the cabinet in June 1992. The Charter is not legally binding and the Japanese government is free to interpret when to apply the principles listed in the Charter.

Of the principles listed in the Charter, Japan was most active on environmental protection, which involves incentives rather than sanctions. In addition, Japan became somewhat more assertive in arms control issues. In particular, Japan suspended its grant aid to China in August 1995 to protest China's nuclear testing, but it did not suspend yen loans, which were far more important to China than grant aid. In contrast, Japan has largely chosen not to use economic sanctions for human rights. In fact, the Ministry of Foreign Affairs includes both positive and negative linkage of foreign aid with human rights. *Japan's ODA 1997* includes only four cases of negative linkage: Sudan since October 1992, the Republic of the Congo since September 1991, Nigeria since March 1994, and Myanmar (Burma) since 1988. There is also a case of negative movement followed by positive movement: resuming aid to Haiti in October 1994 after President Jean-Bertrand Aristide returned to the country.[98]

Compared to the 1970s and 1980s, Japan cooperated even less with the United States in economic sanctions in the 1990s. Japan softened or lifted sanctions against a number of countries, such as Vietnam in 1992. In another case, Japan resumed aid to Iran in 1993 with a ¥38.6 billion ($347 million) loan for a hydroelectric power project. Japan did not want to change its position despite U.S. pressure on it to impose sanctions on Iran.[99] Washington's sanctions have not worked, in part because "the prospect of European and Japanese business ties has reduced Tehran's incentive to change its behavior."[100] Furthermore, Japan did not participate in new U.S. sanctions. Japan's limited cooperation stands out sharply because the United States has resorted more to economic sanctions in the 1990s. Based on a study by the Institute for International Economics, the United States currently imposes sanctions, in different forms, on twenty-six target countries, involving half of the world population.[101]

Conversely, Japan withheld bilateral aid from the Soviet Union and its successor state Russia in the late 1980s and the early 1990s, contrary to Western preferences. Tokyo's strategy was to "give humanitarian, technological, intellectual, and financial aid to Japan's northern neighbor in proportion to the degree of settlement reached on the northern territories issue."[102] Japan hoped to use massive aid, rumored to be around $25 billion, in exchange for the return of the disputed islands. Japan frustrated Germany's desire for a major aid package to Moscow in the London G-7 Summit in July 1991, resulting in criticism for its "selfishness." In response, Japan provided limited bilateral aid and did not stand in the way of aid packages by the multilateral institutions. Interestingly, Japan began its more serious aid program for Russia in the late 1990s based on its own strategic and economic interests in absence of Western pressure on Tokyo to do so.

A New Direction in the Late 1990s

Japan took a new direction in its use of economic power in the late 1990s. Japan's ODA disbursement fell by 34.9 percent in 1996 to $9.44 billion (excluding aid to Eastern Europe), the first time total aid fell below $10 billion since 1990.[103] The Japanese foreign ministry attributed this partly to a decline in the value of the yen. But Japan's contribution also declined by 24.6 percent in yen terms because of two additional factors: a downswing in Japan's contributions to multilateral institutions and an increase in repayments. In fact, with actual disbursements of $59.8 billion in the period 1993–97, Tokyo fell short of its fifth medium target of $70–75 billion.

More important, the Japanese government made an announcement in June 1997 that Japan would reduce the ODA budget for each fiscal year during a three-year period due to fiscal reform. Japan's ODA general account budget for fiscal 1998 (¥1047.3 billion) was cut by 10.4 percent, the first decrease since FY 1976. At ¥1389.1 billion, Japan's operational budget, which includes both general account budget and second budget drawing from the Fiscal Investment and Loan Program of the Trust Fund Bureau, saw a bigger cut of 17.1 percent over the previous year. Japan also ceased to set new medium-term quantitative targets in 1998. Given Japan's decade-long economic recession and shrinking domestic support for foreign aid, the era of rapid expansion of ODA has clearly come to an end.

However, Japan remains the world's largest donor, and Tokyo continues to use the ODA program to demonstrate its international contribution. Partly due to the Asian financial crisis, the Japanese ODA general account budget remained on the same level—a 0.2 percent increase for fiscal 1999 and a 0.2 percent decrease for fiscal 2000—and its operational budget actually fell by 11.2 percent for fiscal 1999 and 2.2 percent for fiscal 2000.[104] Japan's net disbursements of ODA rebounded to

$10.6 billion in 1998 and $15.3 billion in 1999.[105] As will be discussed in the next chapter, Tokyo has also disbursed billions of dollars in separate packages to help East Asia recover from the crisis. In a recent example, ahead of the G-8 summit held in Okinawa in July 2000, Tokyo announced a package of $15 billion, consisting of ODA and OOF (other official flows), over five years to help bridge "the digital divide" between developed and developing nations.

Japan has become more assertive in its ODA policy. The 1997–98 Asian financial crisis led to serious discussions among Japanese of the goals and methods of ODA. The Japanese Ministry of Foreign Affairs released a major periodic review of ODA, "Midterm Policy for ODA," in August 1998, which stated explicitly the need to use ODA to advance Japan's national interests, exhibiting rare boldness. To ensure its security and prosperity, Tokyo now wants to focus more on Asia and support domestic business by offering tied loans. In terms of priorities for aid projects, Japan wants to focus more on environment, public health, and education. In addition, Tokyo plans to improve transparency and efficiency in ODA administration.[106]

At the same time, Japan has also become somewhat more willing to use sanctions. After India's first three nuclear tests on May 11, 1998, Japan immediately suspended grants totaling $30 million and threatened to freeze part of its yen loans as well.[107] After India conducted two more tests, Japan froze new yen loans and recalled its ambassador to India. Tokyo also decided on a "cautious examination" of World Bank and ADB loans to India. As a Japanese foreign ministry official explained, Japan had taken "all conceivable measures at its disposal."[108] Although it did not cut off trade insurance, Japan emerged as the key supporter for the United States, compared with only a weak response from European nations. Japan and Canada joined the United States to push for a united front on economic sanctions on India at the G-8 summit in Birmingham, England, in May, an idea opposed by Russia, France, and Britain.[109] Japan's support was crucial as the largest bilateral donor to India and as a key ally to the United States in blocking loans to India in the international financial institutions.

After Pakistan announced its own nuclear tests on May 28 and 30, the Japanese government imposed sanctions similar to those leveled on India. Japan's proactive position on this issue cannot be explained by U.S. *gaiatsu* (foreign pressure). The Clinton administration did not pressure Tokyo to follow the U.S. lead. Moreover, if Japan wanted to avoid sanctions on India and Pakistan, it could have avoided them without strong U.S. criticism since the Europeans were not in line. Japan's unusually strong reaction to Indian and Pakistani nuclear tests was driven by its strategic concerns for nuclear proliferation and strong antinuclear sentiment at home. Funabashi Yoichi, the influential commentator of *Asahi shimbun,* observed that "Japan has been dealt the biggest blow from India's nuclear tests" and the country "bears special responsibilities to prevent nuclear proliferation." He argued that Japan should take actions "from this fundamental perspective" and not simply follow the United States and Europe.[110]

In another case, after North Korea's August 1998 test launch of a missile over Japan, Tokyo froze food and other humanitarian assistance to Pyongyang. The Japanese also demanded information concerning North Korea's alleged abduction of several Japanese nationals to be used as language teachers for spies in the early 1970s. In September 1999, under U.S. pressure, Pyongyang agreed not to test another ballistic missile and engaged in negotiations with Washington to improve relations. The Japanese government resumed food aid in March 2000.

Conclusion

Two features stand out in Japan's use of economic power in its relations with the United States. First, despite being the number two economic power in the world, Japan has largely chosen to support rather than confront the United States in noneconomic areas, even in the late 1980s, when Japan's economic power rose dramatically and the United States was widely perceived to be in a decline. Second, while making some concessions in defense and trade, Tokyo has consistently chosen less costly substitutes to meet U.S. demands—economic contributions for defense contributions, investments for consumption, and foreign aid for sanctions. Adding up these two features, we see a pattern of Japanese behavior: to demonstrate cooperation with the United States, but only selectively and at minimal cost.

It is easier to describe than to explain the pattern of Japanese behavior. Japan's relations with the United States provide inconclusive evidence to support any particular theoretical approach. Most cases in this chapter show a confluence of factors. I will provide partial explanations on three levels here. A more comprehensive explanation will be provided in the conclusion chapter when Japan's relations with the United States are compared to its relations with East Asia and the three international financial institutions.

On the first level, the rise and fall in Japan's power are obviously important: Japan adopted a more active approach to economic statecraft when its power was on the rise. "As our economic strength has increased, so has our responsibility to the world," Prime Minister Miyazawa Kiichi asserted.[111] "The United States has become exhausted," according to Ozawa Ichiro, then the LDP secretary-general and now the leader of the Liberal Party, a conservative opposition party. "It is time for Japan to assume responsibilities appropriate to its wealth."[112] Japan's rising power also explains U.S. pressure for greater contributions. Conversely, Japan's declining power explains in part its decreasing international contributions. But it is important to note that when its economic power was growing Japan chose to support rather than challenge the United States or go its own way, and Japan has been hesitant to use sanctions for noneconomic objectives. This leads to my second level explanation.

Japan's choice of cooperative rather than confrontational means for managing the United States can be partly explained by the source of its rising power, reinforced by its past experiences of dealing with that country. Japan has increased power under peculiar circumstances, resulting externally from its security alliance with the United States and an interdependent global economy, both of which are crucial features of the Pax Americana. For Japan to turn against the United States, two conditions would have to exist: First, the United States would have to cease to be a major contributing factor to Japan's prosperity and power. But Japan continues to rely on the United States for security and prosperity. Second, the United States would have to follow a global strategy that is fundamentally detrimental to Japanese interests. Washington has increased pressure on Tokyo over the years, which has caused resentment and even anger among Japanese. But Washington remains committed to the security alliance, which necessitates compromise with Tokyo. As a result, Japan's behavior can be explained by *gaiatsu* from the United States on the one hand and interdependence on the other hand.

It is difficult to separate the causal impact of U.S. hegemony from that of interdependence and international institutions on Japan's policy toward the United States. The two arguments reinforce each other and are strengthened by other factors, such as learning and norms. But power considerations seem to be logically more salient. First, Japan is more likely to cooperate with the United States in the absence of international institutions than in the absence of U.S. hegemony if the two can be separated. Second, it is not surprising that power considerations rather than institutional considerations dominate in a bilateral relationship. Empirically, the importance of the security alliance and of the U.S. market, technology, and global leadership is the focal point in Japanese thinking.

U.S. hegemony and interdependence, however, do not explain the extent to which Japan supports rather than confronts the United States. After all, few U.S. allies are as willing as Japan to avoid confrontation with the United States, despite their far weaker economic power.

One important reason why the Japanese apparently prefer cooperative to confrontational means to get what they want is that many Japanese are concerned about the consequence of confronting the United States. The Japanese have learned a lesson from their recent history.[113] Nishihara Masashi, a leading Japanese security expert, commented that "the bitter lesson Japan learned from World War II was that it should not disregard the immense strength of the United States and its allies; incurring their hostility was a fatal mistake."[114] Inoki Masamichi, a former president of the National Defense Academy, commented as follows:

> In the final analysis, we were crazy to declare war on the United States and Britain. Think about it. The United States produced 230 million tons of oil annually—Japan, 300,000 tons. America produced 50 to 60 million tons of steel, while Japan had finally managed to boost its output to 3 or 4 million tons. The men at the helm didn't even have the sense to consider the ramifications. Or rather, they thought that with luck the war wouldn't drag on. With luck! How utterly irresponsible! It was a reckless, foolish war.[115]

This line of argument sees Japan's defeat as a strategic blunder, while avoiding judging its moral responsibility. Nevertheless, such a bitter lesson reinforced the importance of maintaining the alliance with the United States.

On the other hand, Japan has learned to employ tools such as foot dragging, stonewalling, last-minute concessions, brinkmanship, market-opening packages, and deliberation groups. This learning is almost ritualized.[116] It is to Japan's advantage to negotiate with, rather than confront, the United States. This is in part because the United States does not have a good institutional memory of what has been negotiated with Japan. The American Chamber of Commerce in Japan reported early in 1997 that of forty-five trade agreements signed between the United States and Japan since 1980, only thirteen have been successfully implemented.[117] In addition, the Japanese government has also learned to exploit *gaiatsu* to make domestic vested interest groups accept difficult adjustments—more reason that *gaiatsu* is not necessarily negative for Tokyo.

Moreover, while Japanese have to some extent used their constitutional constraints and domestic antimilitarist sentiments to justify their weak support for the United States, they do respond to cultural factors when defining their security interests. Japanese strategic preferences for nonmilitary solutions, which are salient in the domestic context, constrain what the Japanese government is willing and able to do militarily abroad.[118]

On the third level, how do we explain the fact that although Japan cooperates with the United States it often comes up short, using less costly substitution? Interdependence has not generated sufficient incentives for Japan to make drastic changes in its earning behavior. And Washington's *gaiatsu* explains only part of Japanese behavior—there is not an exact correlation between U.S. pressure and Japanese cooperation. Japan's substitution of economic for defense contributions and investment for consumption amounts to a smart strategy to optimize its gains while forcing suboptimal outcomes on its stronger partner. This leads to two more questions: Why does Japan behave this way? How does Tokyo get away with its strategy? I will answer the second question first, shedding light on the first.

Japan has largely gotten away with its approach for two reasons. First, U.S. pressure is often vague. In such situations, Japan selects the institution and arena that maximize its gains and minimize its adjustment costs. Second, when the United States exerts explicit pressure on Japan, how much Japan yields depends on the bargaining situation. As Leonard J. Schoppa points out in his work on *gaiatsu* in trade negotiations, raw power has little to do with negotiation outcomes. In a two-level game, U.S. pressure works only when there is domestic support in Japan for the outcome at which the pressure is directed.[119] Although the United States is frustrated with Japan's limited cooperation, it is left without many options. On the one hand, the United States holds important cards, such as military protection of Japan, the world's largest market, global political leadership, and protectorship of sea lanes, all of which are crucial for Japan's interests. On the other hand, Washington cannot easily call Japan's bluff. As Susumu Yamakage points out, "the U.S. cannot close its own market if it wants its threat against Japan to remain effective. Japan can simply promise that it will open its market so long as the U.S. maintains an open market, and prolong that promise." But he also recognizes that "Japan must give up its own best-possible outcome if it wishes to stabilize its relationship with the U.S."[120] Japan has indeed consistently chosen second-best scenarios not only in trade negotiations but also in other areas. One may also argue that Washington also asked more than it could, knowing a second-best outcome was likely. But such public pressure was not sustainable, since it created a negative impression of the United States among the Japanese public.

This disadvantage for the United States in bargaining situations results from different national purposes. Bargaining outcomes are no doubt influenced by preferences of the players. As I.M. Destler pointed out, Japan's "overriding postwar need was to *build* prosperity" while for the United States, "the need was to *maintain* prosperity," and "that made all the difference."[121] Such a crucial difference explains Japan's bottom line in dealing with the United States: It is least willing to accept U.S. demands in the areas of trade and technology and less willing to cooperate in the defense arena than in the economic realm. In contrast, the United States is more willing to accommodate Japan given its conviction about maintaining its prosperity through a global free trade regime secured by its extensive security arrangements all over the world.

Such an asymmetry in the strategic thinking between Japan and the United States is certainly related to their relative positions in the world. The United States has been a hegemon, while Japan was a country catching up and, more recently, an economic superpower unused to its position. However, the difference in Japanese and U.S. strategic visions reflects the entrenched ideas and norms in the two nations: The elites in the two nations often have different understandings of what causes a nation to rise and fall and how a nation should behave. Steven K. Vogel observed that "the combination of a deep-seated free trade ideology with powerful pressure for protection has produced a distinct pattern in U.S. policy toward Japan during recent years." By contrast, "the postwar tradition of industrial protection and promotion remains firmly embedded in Japanese ideology and institutions despite Japan's increasing stake in the free trade regime." A combination of the United States and Japanese ideologies has aggravated frictions.[122]

Without understanding the nature of the modern Japanese state, it is difficult to understand Japanese foreign policy and Japanese–American relations. The Japanese state emerged in the Meiji Restoration under a survival-of-the-fittest international environment and developed a strong nationalist ethos to catch up with the West. While the military side of the state was destroyed during World War II, the catch-up mind-set remained in the economic side of the state. The strong nationalist ethos and the lesson learned from military defeat combined to push Japan into a neomercantilist path, which could thrive in an open international economic system only because of the cold war imperative.[123] Eric Heginbotham and Richard J. Samuels argued that Japanese foreign policy is still driven by what they call "mercantile realism," a synthetic concept that appreciates control of technology and wealth as central to national security.[124] Japan has surely become more exposed to the international system and has become more internationalist in its outlook. But its adamant refusal to open its domestic market and allow foreign ownership in its own country and its reluctance to share technologies reveal a deep-rooted neomercantilist ideology. A neomercantilist ideology does not exclude cooperation with the United States, since the United States is central for Japan's acquisition of wealth, technology, and security. It just means that Japan wants to shape the terms and content of its cooperation based on its own preferences.

Notes

1. Takashi Inoguchi, "Japan's Images and Options: Not a Challenger, But a Supporter," *Journal of Japanese Studies* 12, no. 1 (1986), p. 111. For similar arguments, see Yoichi Funabashi, "Introduction: Japan's International Agenda for the 1990s," in Yoichi Funabashi, ed., *Japan's International Agenda* (New York: New York University Press, 1994), pp. 1–27.

2. Morita Akio and Ishihara Shintaro, *"No" to ieru Nihon* [The Japan that can say "no"] (Tokyo: Kobunsha, 1989).

3. Clyde Prestowitz, *Trading Places: How We Allowed Japan to Take the Lead* (New York: Basic Books, 1988); Chalmers Johnson, "Trade, Revisionism, and the Future of Japanese-American Relations," in Kozo Yamamura, ed., *Japan's Economic Structure: Should It Change?* (Seattle: Society for Japanese Studies, 1990), pp. 105–36; Pat Choate, *Agents of Influence* (New York: Alfred A. Knopf, 1990); James Fallows, "Containing Japan," *Atlantic Monthly,* May 1989, pp. 40–54; Karel van Wolferen, *The Enigma of Japanese Power* (New York: Vintage, 1990); Lester C. Thurow, *Head to Head: The Coming Economic Battle Among Japan, Europe, and America* (New York: William Morrow, 1992); Jeffrey E. Garten, *A Cold Peace: America, Japan, Germany, and the Struggle for Supremacy* (New York: Basic Books, 1992).

4. George Friedman and Meredith LeBard, *The Coming War with Japan* (New York: St. Martin's Press, 1991).

5. Kenneth Dam et al., "Harnessing Japan: A U.S. Strategy for Managing Japan's Rise as a Global Power," *Washington Quarterly* 16, no. 2 (Spring 1993), p. 32.

6. For a critical article on the revisionists, see Brink Lindsey and Aaron Lukas, "Revisiting the 'Revisionists': The Rise and Fall of the Japanese Economic Model," Cato Institute, *Trade Policy Analysis,* no. 3 (July 31, 1998).

7. This is a classic example of a junior alliance partner caught in a dilemma between "abandonment" and "entrapment." See Glenn Snyder, "The Security Dilemma in Alliance Politics," *World Politics* 36, no. 4 (July 1984), pp. 461–95. For how this dilemma plays out in Japan's defense relations with the United States, see Michael J. Green, *Arming Japan: Defense Production, Alliance Politics, and the Postwar Search for Autonomy* (New York: Columbia University Press, 1995).

8. See Shigeru Yoshida, *The Yoshida Memoirs,* trans. Yoshida Kenichi (Cambridge: Riverside Press, 1962), pp. 8–9. For similar views by other conservative politicians, such as Shidehara Kijuro and Ugaki Kazushige, see Watanabe Akio, "Sengo nihon no shuppatsuten" [The departure point of postwar Japan], in Watanabe, ed., *Sengo nihon no taigai seisaku* [Postwar Japanese foreign policy] (Tokyo: Yuhikaku, 1985), pp. 10–11.

9. Shimoda Takeso, *Sengo nihon gaiko no shogen* [Testimony on postwar Japanese diplomacy] (Tokyo: Gyosei mondai kenkyusho, 1984), vol. 1, pp. 50–51.

10. Watanabe, "Sengo nihon no shuppatsuten," pp. 11–19.

11. John W. Dower, *Empire and Aftermath: Yoshida Shigeru and the Japanese Experience, 1878–1954* (Cambridge: Harvard East Asia Monographs, 1979), p. 36.

12. Hugh Patrick and Henry Rosovsky, "Japan's Economic Performance: An Overview," in Patrick and Rosovsky, eds., *Asia's New Giant* (Washington, DC: Brookings Institution, 1976), p. 45.

13. Robert M. Orr, Jr., "The Aid Factor in U.S.–Japan Relations," *Asian Survey* 28, no. 7 (July 1988), pp. 744–45.

14. Joseph P. Keddell, Jr., *The Politics of Defense in Japan: Managing Internal and External Pressures* (Armonk, NY: M.E. Sharpe, 1993), pp. 78–124.

15. Foreign Economic Policy Study Group of the Policy Research Council, "Taigai keizai seisaku kenkyu gurupu hokkokusho" [Report by the Foreign Economic Policy Study Group], *Sekai keizai hyoron* 24, no. 6 (June 1980), p. 54.

16. Susan Pharr, "Japan's Defensive Foreign Policy and the Politics of Burden Sharing," in Gerald Curtis, ed., *Japan's Foreign Policy After the Cold War: Coping with Change* (Armonk, NY: M.E. Sharpe, 1993), p. 243.

17. Masahiro Sakamoto, "Japan's Role in the International System," in John H. Makin and Donald C. Hellmann, eds., *Sharing World Leadership? A New Era for America and Japan* (Washington: American Enterprise Institute, 1989), p. 179.

18. Juichi Inada, "Japan's Aid Diplomacy: Economic, Political or Strategic? *Millennium: Journal of International Studies* 18, no. 3 (1989), pp. 399–414; Dennis T. Yasutomo, *The Manner of Giving: Strategic Aid and Japanese Foreign Policy* (Lexington, MA: Lexington Books, 1986).

19. Seizaburo Sato and Yuji Suzuki, "A New Stage of the United States–Japan Alliance," in Makin and Hellmann, eds., *Sharing World Leadership?* pp. 161–62.

20. Japan accounted for 14.61 percent of world total GNP, the U.S. for 26.07 percent, and the EC for 24.81 percent in 1987–89 on average. IMF, *World Economic Outlook,* May 1993, p. 117.

21. Kuriyama Takakazu, "Gekidono 90 nendai to nihongaiko no shintenkai" [The great upheaval of the nineties and the new directions in Japanese diplomacy], *Gaiko forum* (May 1990), p. 16.

22. See Steven Vogel, "The Power Behind 'Spin-Ons': The Military Implications of Japan's Commercial Technology," in Wayne Sandholtz et al., *The Highest Stakes: The Economic Foundations of the Next Security System* (New York: Oxford University Press, 1992), pp. 55–80.

23. Richard J. Samuels, *"Rich Nation Strong Army": National Security and Technological Transformation of Japan* (Ithaca: Cornell University Press, 1994), pp. 231–44.

24. Ibid., p. 319.

25. Michael H. Armacost, *Friends or Rivals? The Insider's Account of U.S.– Japan Relations* (New York: Columbia University Press, 1996), pp. 88–90.

26. Kitaoka Shinichi. "Wangan senso to nihon no gaiko" [The Gulf War and Japan's diplomacy], *Kokusai mondai* 377 (August 1991), pp. 9–10.

27. H. Norman Schwarzkopf, with Peter Petre, *It Doesn't Take a Hero* (New York: Bantam Books, 1992), p. 365.

28. Francis Fukuyama and Kongdan Oh, *The U.S.–Japan Security Relationship After the Cold War* (Santa Monica: Rand, 1993), pp. viii–ix.

29. Japan actually spends more on defense if we adopt NATO standards, which also include spending for defense R&D, coast guards, space programs, and pensions for veterans. The International Institute for Strategic Studies estimated in October 1996 that based on the NATO standards Japan's real defense expenditure accounted for 1.6 percent of GNP. "The Real Cost of Japanese Defense," *Economist,* October 12, 1996, p. 38. But this number was still much lower than that of the United States.

30. See Patrick M. Cronin and Michael J. Green, *Redefining the U.S.–Japan Alliance: Tokyo's National Defense Program*, McNair Paper 31 (Washington: Institute for National Strategic Studies, National Defense University, November 1994); David L. Asher, "A U.S.–Japan Alliance for the Next Century," *Orbis* 41, no. 3 (Summer 1997), pp. 354–58; Mike M. Mochizuki, "American and Japanese Strategic Debates: The Need for a New Synthesis," in Mochizuki, ed., *Toward a True Alliance: Restructuring U.S.–Japan Security Relations* (Washington: Brookings Institution, 1997), pp. 43–82; Yoichi Funabashi, *Alliance Adrift* (New York: Council on Foreign Relations Press, 1999).

31. Chester Dawson, "Blueprint for Controversy," *Far Eastern Economic Review,* July 13, 2000, pp. 19–20.

32. U.S. Department of State, "Background Notes: Japan," May 1997.

33. Joseph S. Nye, Jr., "The Case for Deep Engagement," *Foreign Affairs* 74, no. 4 (July/August 1995), p. 98.

34. Armacost, *Friends or Rivals?* p. 87.

35. I.M. Destler, "Has Conflict Passed Its Prime? Japanese and American Approaches to Trade and Economic Policy," *Maryland/Tsukuba Papers on U.S.–Japan Relations,* Center for International and Security Studies at Maryland, School of Public Affairs, University of Maryland at College Park and Graduate School of International Political Economy, University of Tsukuba, March 1997, p. 9.

36. Susumu Yamakage, "The Logic of U.S.–Japan Interdependence: Political Games of Market Access," *USJP Occasional Paper 89–09,* Program on U.S.–Japan Relations, Harvard University.

37. For more on the dispute, see I.M. Destler, Haruhiro Fukui, and Hideo Sato, *The Textile Wrangle: Conflict in Japanese–American Relations, 1969–1971* (Ithaca: Cornell University Press, 1979).

38. Japan's trade surplus in goods grew from $17.16 billion in 1977 to an annual average of $94.75 billion in 1986–88, and its current account surplus grew from $10.91 billion to an average of $84.15 billion in 1986–88. If we include services, Japan's trade surpluses were reduced somewhat, with an average of $72.01 billion in 1986–88. IMF, *International Financial Statistics Yearbook,* 1997, pp. 498–99.

39. Edward Lincoln, *Japan's Unequal Trade* (Washington: Brookings Institution, 1990); Paul Krugman, ed., *Trade with Japan: Has the Door Opened Wider?* (Chicago: University of Chicago Press, 1991).

40. IMF, *International Financial Statistics Yearbook,* 1997, pp. 116–21.

41. For Japanese trade negotiation style, see Amelia Porges, "U.S.–Japan Trade Negotiations: Paradigms Lost," in Krugman, ed., *Trade with Japan,* pp. 305–27. For a general study on Japan's international negotiating style, see Michael Blaker, *Japanese International Negotiating Style* (New York: Columbia University Press, 1977).

42. T.J. Pempel, "From Exporter to Investor: Japanese Foreign Economic Policy," in Curtis, ed., *Japan's Foreign Policy After the Cold War*; pp. 105–36.

43. Japan's share of outflow of global direct investment in this period was 19.3 percent, compared to 14.9 percent for the United States and 44.8 for the European Community countries. Japan External Trade Organization, *JETRO White Paper on Foreign Direct Investment 1994,* March 1994, p. 1.

44. Japan Ministry of Finance, *Financial Statistics of Japan,* various years.

45. Kiyohiko Fukushima, "Japan's Real Trade Policy," *Foreign Policy* 59 (Summer 1985), p. 23.

46. Dennis J. Encarnation, *Rivals Beyond Trade: America Versus Japan in Global Competition* (Ithaca: Cornell University Press, 1992). Also see Mark Mason, *American Multinationals and Japan* (Cambridge: Council on East Asian Studies, Harvard University, 1992).

47. Robert Gilpin, *The Political Economy of International Relations* (Princeton: Princeton University Press, 1987), pp. 328–36.

48. Amitabha Chowdhury, "Okita and Kurosawa Speak Up," *Asian Finance,* August 15, 1986, p. 38.

49. James Sterngold, "Tokyo Panel Asks Wider Japan Help to Poorer Nations," *New York Times,* June 4, 1990, A1.

50. Ibid.

51. Robert D. Putnam and Nicholas Bayne, *Hanging Together: Cooperation and Conflict in the Seven-Power Summits* (Cambridge: Harvard University Press, 1987), pp. 62–107.

52. Fallows, "The White Peril," p. 20.

53. Paul Kennedy, *The Rise and Fall of the Great Power* (New York: Random House, 1987).

54. U.S. State Department, "Background Note: Japan," May 1997.

55. James Sterngold, "Intractable Trade Issues with Japan," *New York Times,* December 4, 1991, p. D1.

56. See C. Fred Bergsten and Marcus Noland, *Reconcilable Differences? United States–Japan Economic Conflict* (Washington: Institute for International Economics,

1993); Laura D'Andrea Tyson, *Who's Bashing Whom? Trade Conflict in High-Technology Industries* (Washington: Institute for International Economics, 1992).

57. Of the rest of the agreements, 18 were marginally successful, 10 failed, and 4 had mixed results. The rating was based on surveys of the affected American firms about whether the trade agreement in question worked. Paul Blustein, "Business Group Downplays Japan Trade Pacts' Effects," *Washington Post,* January 14, 1997, pp. D1, D4.

58. Nye, "The Case for Deep Engagement."

59. C. Fred Bergsten, "Japan and the United States in the World Economy" (paper prepared for Conference on Wisconsin–U.S.–Japan Economic Development, Lake Geneva, Wisconsin, June 19, 1998).

60. Edwin O. Reischauer Center, *The United States and Japan in 2000: Seeking Focus* (Paul H. Nitze School of Advanced International Studies, Johns Hopkins University, 2000), p. 20.

61. Adam S. Posen, *Restoring Japan's Economic Growth* (Washington: Institute for International Economics, September 1998), pp. 41–54.

62. Associated Press, "Clinton Wants Japan Economic Reform," May 4, 1998.

63. Sonya Ross, "Clinton Presses Japan over Economy," Associated Press, May 3, 1999.

64. Bergsten, "Japan and the U.S. in the World Economy."

65. IMF, *International Financial Statistics,* June 2000, p. 430.

66. IMF, *Direction of Trade Statistics Yearbook,* 1999, p. 274.

67. *JEI Report,* no. 30B (August 4, 2000), pp. 6–7.

68. As an example, the Bank of Japan intervened heavily in June–July 1999 to drive down the yen value, a move interpreted by many Americans as a clear move for Japan to export its way out of recession. Paul Blustein, "Japan Contradicts Policy with Yen Moves," *Washington Post,* July 9, 1999, p. E1.

69. *International Financial Statistics Yearbook,* 1997, p. 499; *International Financial Statistics,* June 2000, p. 430.

70. JExIm merged with the Japan International Cooperation Agency (JICA) to create the Japan Bank for International Cooperation (JBIC) in October 1999.

71. Alan Rix, *Japan's Economic Aid: Policy-Making and Politics* (New York: St. Martin's Press, 1980), pp. 28–39.

72. Saburo Okita, *Japan's Challenging Years: Reflections on My Lifetime* (Sydney: George Allen and Unwin, 1983), p. 90.

73. OECD, *Development Cooperation 1993 Report,* p. 159, and 1994, p. A6.

74. Akio Hosono, "The United States and Japan in Development Assistance and International Cooperation," in Sato and Destler, eds., *Leadership Sharing in the New International System,* pp. 114–15. For similar arguments, see Saori N. Katada, "Two Aid Hegemons: Japanese-American Interaction and Aid Allocation to Latin America and the Caribbean," *World Development* 25, no. 6 (June 1997), pp. 931–45.

75. Saori N. Katada, "The Japanese Government in Two Mexican Financial Crises: An Emerging International Lender-of-Last-Resort," *Pacific Affairs* 71, no. 1 (Spring 1998), pp. 61–79.

76. Yasutomo, *Manner of Giving;* Robert M. Orr, Jr., *The Emergence of Japan's Foreign Aid Power* (New York: Columbia University Press, 1990), pp. 103–36.

77. Former World Bank President Robert McNamara also argued in Tokyo that Japan should contribute 1 percent of GNP to ODA by the end of the 1990s. Anthony

Rowley, "Redefining Aid," *Far Eastern Economic Review,* May 23, 1991, pp. 18–19.

78. *Development Cooperation 1989 Report,* p. 208. Grant ratio refers to the percentage of grants or free money in total ODA. Grant element measures softness of a loan, in the form of the present value of an interest rate below the market rate over the life of a loan. Grant element increases with the length of the maturity and gap between the commercial interest rates and ODA rates.

79. Robert M. Orr, Jr., "Collaboration or Conflict? Foreign Aid and U.S.–Japan Relations," *Pacific Affairs* 62, no. 4 (Winter 1989/90), pp. 476–89.

80. Armacost, *Friends or Rivals?* p. 23.

81. Data are from *Development Cooperation,* various years and *International Financial Statistics Yearbook,* 1997, pp. 157–58. If we include services, Japan's trade surpluses in this period amounted to $437.17 billion.

82. Lincoln, "Japan in the 1990s: A New Kind of World Power," *Brookings Review* (Spring 1992), p. 17.

83. See Margee Ensign, *Doing Good or Doing Well? Japan's Foreign Aid Program* (New York: Columbia University Press, 1992).

84. Anne L. Emig, "Activating the Export–Import Bank of Japan as a Development Lending Agency."

85. *Development Cooperation 1990 Report,* p. 220.

86. Akira Nishigaki and Yasutami Shimomura, *Japan's Aid: Historical Roots, Contemporary Issues and Future Agenda* (Tokyo: The Overseas Economic Cooperation Fund, January 1996), pp. 14–16.

87. Jeffrey J. Schott, "Statement Before the Committee on International Relations of U.S. House of Representatives," June 3, 1998.

88. Okita, *Japan's Challenging Years,* pp. 100–101.

89. Colin Nickerson, "After Hesitating, Japan Agrees to Sanctions against Iraq," *Boston Globe,* August 4, 1990, p. 2.

90. Nishigaki and Shimomura, *Japan's Aid,* p. 28.

91. Calculated from OECD, *Development Cooperation,* various years.

92. *Development Cooperation 1996 Report,* p. 148.

93. *Development Cooperation 1998 Report,* pp. A49–50.

94. Emig, "Japan's Challenge to the World Bank: An Attempt at Intellectual Leadership" *The Japanese Economy* 27, no. 1 (January–February 1999), pp. 46–96). For a collection of influential Japanese essays that attempted to articulate Japanese development philosophy, see Kenichi and Izumi Ohno, eds., *Japanese Views on Economic Development: Diverse Paths to the Market* (London: Routledge, 1998).

95. See Hideo Sato, "Global Leadership Sharing: A Framework of Analysis," in Sato and Destler, eds., *Leadership Sharing in the New International System,* pp. 1–29.

96. Japanese Ministry of Foreign Affairs still sees ODA as a pillar in Japan's international contribution. *Wagakuni no seifu kaihatsu enjo,* 1996, pp. 15–16.

97. Donald C. Hellmann, "The United States and Asia in an Age of International Upheaval," *Current History* 91 (December 1992), p. 403.

98. *Japan's ODA,* 1997, pp. 67–72.

99. Interview with a senior OECF official, May 10, 1995, Washington, DC.

100. Patrick Clawson, "Iran," in Richard N. Haass, ed., *Economic Sanctions and American Diplomacy* (New York: Council on Foreign Relations Press, 1998), p. 94.

101. Gary Hufbauer, "The Snake Oil of Diplomacy: When Tensions Rise, the U.S. Peddles Sanctions," *Washington Post,* July 12, 1998, p. C1. He and Jeffrey Schott and Kimberly Ann Elliott have written the third edition of *Economic Sanctions Reconsidered* (Washington: Institute for International Economics, forthcoming).

102. Motohide Saito, "Japan's 'Northward' Foreign Policy," in Curtis, ed., *Japan's Foreign Policy After the Cold War,* p. 285.

103. MFA, *Japan's ODA,* 1997, pp. 9–10.

104. ODA budget data are from http://www.mofa.go.jp/policy/oda/budget/2000.

105. Data are from http://www.oecd.org/dac.

106. See Marc Castellano, "Japan's Foreign Aid Program in the New Millennium: Rethinking 'Development,'" *JEI Report,* no. 6A (February 11, 2000).

107. "Tokyo to Freeze Aid Grants to New Delhi," *Asahi shimbun,* May 13, 1998.

108. "Japan Suspends Loans to India, Recalls Ambassador," *Asahi shimbun,* May 15, 1998.

109. Martin Crutsinger, "Clinton Pushes for India Rebuke," Associated Press, May 15, 1998. In the end, the G-8 summit only condemned the tests and failed to make a concerted effort at sanctioning India.

110. Yoichi Funabashi, "India Thumbs Its Nose at Established World Order," *Asahi Shimbun,* May 18, 1998.

111. Quoted in T.R. Reid, "Japan OK's Deployment of Its Troops," *Boston Globe,* June 9, 1992, p. 2.

112. Quoted in Colin Nickerson, "US, Japan Drift Dangerously Apart," *Boston Globe,* November 25, 1991, p. 8.

113. For a detailed discussion of the Japanese experience of defeat, see John W. Dower, *Embracing Defeat: Japan in the Wake of World War II* (New York: W.W. Norton, 1999).

114. Masashi Nishihara, "Japan's Receptivity to Conditional Engagement," in James Shinn, ed., *Weaving the Net: Conditional Engagement with China* (New York: Council on Foreign Relations Press, 1996), p. 180.

115. Ronald Dore and Inoki Masamichi, "Reviewing the Structure of Japan-U.S. Relations," *Japan Echo* 19, special issue (1992), p. 40.

116. John Creighton Campbell, "Japan and the United States: Games that Work," in Curtis, ed., *Japan's Foreign Policy After the Cold War,* pp. 43–61.

117. David S. Broder, "Trade: The Monitors Are Missing," *Washington Post,* December 10, 1997, p. A25. In fact, as Clyde Prestowitz noted, "Chamber officers could find no one in the U.S. government who had even a list of all the deals—much less any idea of whether their terms actually were being observed." Clyde Prestowitz, "Keeping on Top of Trade," *Washington Post,* December 9, 1997, p. A23.

118. For discussion on the culture of security, see Peter J. Katzenstein, *Cultural Norms and National Security: Police and Military in Postwar Japan* (Ithaca: Cornell University Press, 1996); Thomas U. Berger, *Cultures of Antimilitarism: National Security in Germany and Japan* (Baltimore: Johns Hopkins University Press, 1998).

119. Leonard J. Schoppa, *Bargaining with Japan: What American Pressure Can and Cannot Do* (New York: Columbia University Press, 1997).

120. Yamakage, "Logic of U.S.–Japan Interdependence," pp. 16–18.

121. Destler, "Has Conflict Passed Its Prime?" p. 5. The italics are by Destler.

122. Steven K. Vogel, "The 'Inverse' Relationship: The United States and Japan at the End of the Century," in Robert J. Lieber, ed., *Eagle Adrift: American Foreign Policy at the End of the Century* (New York: Longman, 1997), pp. 194–97.

123. In fact, Michael Schaller argues that Japan's government-guided, export-driven approach was nurtured by early U.S. policy to combat communism. Schaller, *Altered States: The United States and Japan Since the Occupation* (New York: Oxford University Press, 1997).

124. Eric Heginbotham and Richard J. Samuels, "Mercantile Realism and Japanese Foreign Policy," *International Security* 22, no. 4 (Spring 1998), pp. 171–203.

3

Unique Leader in East Asia

Japan's economic relations with its Asian neighbors are largely complementary, unlike its clear competition with the West. But Japan seeks advantages through economic cooperation with the region, aiming to enhance its competitiveness versus the West and to maintain a structural lead over other Asian nations. Japan's pursuit of self-interests is not unique among nations. What is unique is that Japan eschews virtually all but economic tools of diplomacy, and even there it prefers cooperative to punitive measures. "Normal" powers in the region, such as the United States and China, combine military, diplomatic, and economic statecraft—both cooperative and punitive—to advance broad national interests.

How cooperative has Japan been in using economic power in East Asia? To answer this question, we need to consider what Japan intends to accomplish in the region and how the countries in the region evaluate Tokyo's efforts. For most Asian nations, a perfectly cooperative Japan should spend as little on defense as possible, transfer official and private financial resources, open its market to Asian goods, serve as the lender of last resort, and avoid sanctions on its neighbors. However, Japan picks and chooses where and how much it cooperates. It is a unique and selective leader. It plays an indirect military role and seldom uses sanctions against other nations. Even in the economic realm Japan has not taken the lead on all issues. In his classic work on the Great Depression, Charles Kindleberger provided a list of leadership responsibilities.[1]

1. Maintaining a relatively open market for distress goods.
2. Providing countercyclical, or at least stable, long-term lending.
3. Policing a relatively stable system of exchange rates.
4. Ensuring the coordination of macroeconomic policies.
5. Acting as a lender of last resort by discounting or otherwise providing liquidity in financial crisis.

Japan has led in providing official and private lending and investments, although its influence also comes from its example as the first modernized non-Western nation, its model of development, and its impact on the incentive structures for the East Asian nations. In contrast, Japan has participated but not led in coordination on macroeconomic policies and policing of a stable system of exchange rates. Noticeably, Japan has played a limited role in opening its market for distress goods.

Japan has been successful in its Asia strategy *for its own purposes*. Japan has thrived and consolidated its hold on the region despite strong historical resentment among its Asian neighbors. Most important, if one recalls the competing visions and designs for East Asia in the 1950s and 1960s, Asia's realities are closer to Japan's visions than those of other major powers, including the United States, China, and Russia. East Asia looks like a formation of flying geese, with Japan at the center. It is not Soviet style communist nor Chinese style communist nor U.S. style capitalist, although the Asian financial crisis may change this. To be sure, what emerged in Asia is due to both the interaction among countries large and small and underlying historical forces. But Japan's "economical" approach to the region helped it come out on top. In contrast, the United States, China, and Russia paid heavy human, financial, psychological, and moral costs for their hegemonic endeavors in the region—the Korean War and the Vietnam War being primary examples. "This congruence between Japan's vision and the one widely accepted in Asia is not accidental," as Susan Pharr and Ming Wan argued. "Rather, such congruence has been achieved, in no small measure, as a result of the success of Japan's Asia strategy."[2]

Tokyo's ability to exercise regional leadership has been called into question by three crises shaking up the region in the late 1990s. In March

1996, China staged a missile exercise off the island of Taiwan as a harsh response to Taiwan President Lee Teng-hui's visit to the United States in the previous year and as intimidation to prevent Taiwan's move toward independence. In response, two U.S. carrier battle groups steamed to the region, the largest show of U.S. naval force in the region since the end of the Vietnam War. This event dashed any wishful thinking that the region had been transformed in a way that privileged Japan's economics-based, nonconfrontational approach. The United States reasserted itself in the region based on traditional means of power. In contrast, Japan has served as a junior partner and reluctantly allowed its security alliance with the United States to be more regionalized. Then in September 1999 East Timor erupted in chaos after a referendum that had overwhelmingly supported independence from Indonesia. Japan did little to stop the bloodshed. In contrast, the United States pressured the Indonesian government to accept international peacekeeping forces and Australia took the lead in sending troops into East Timor.

In the economic realm, Japan's leadership was tested when a severe financial crisis started in Thailand in the summer of 1997 and blazed throughout the region. Initially, Japan actively responded to Thailand's collapse and made a commitment of considerable financial resources, in contrast to a weak American position. But when the crisis deepened and the Americans vetoed Japan's proposal to create a regional monetary arrangement, Japan retreated and let the International Monetary Fund (IMF) and the United States take the center stage. Tokyo was widely criticized as failing to rise to the occasion in an area where it enjoys comparative advantage. Japan was seen as unable to reform its economy and open its market to distress goods from the region. In response, Tokyo committed billions of dollars to help the region recover and quietly promoted regional trade and financial cooperation—efforts that came to be appreciated by its Asian neighbors. Despite its continued economic recession, Japan emerged from the Asian financial crisis as a stronger economic leader.

Japan's selective leadership in Asia is explained by its bargaining position, its historical legacy, its norms, and its ideas. Like other nations, Japan has sought strong bargaining positions in Asia, which allow it to achieve its immediate and long-term objectives. But seeking and utilizing bargaining situations are a learned process influenced by one's instrumental norms and ideas. Japan has learned from, adapted itself to, and shaped the patterns of its interaction with other nations. Japan has learned to be cautious, nonconfrontational, and interested mainly in economic issues. Japan's emphasis on both cooperation and competition is best captured in the distinct Japanese theory of "flying geese." Japan is the head goose, followed by other Asian nations according to their stage of development. The head goose assists its followers, consistent with market forces. In the end, every goose benefits from such an arrangement, but the head goose enjoys a structural competitive edge.

This chapter includes four sections. The dynamic in Japan's relations with East Asia is different from its relations with the United States. While the United States has mostly treated its security relationship with Japan as a high priority since 1952, Asian nations primarily want a cooperative Japan in the economic realm. The first section evaluates Japan's economic cooperation with the region. The second section examines how and why Japan has seldom used economic sanctions against its Asian neighbors. The third section assesses Japan's indirect strategic role in the region. The fourth section concludes this chapter.

Economic Cooperation

What Japan means by economic cooperation is essentially transfer of official and private economic resources to developing countries to facilitate development (Figure 3.1). Japan's definition of economic cooperation is broad. It includes not just official flows, which are what people normally have in mind when talking about assistance to developing nations, but also private capital flows. Japan's official development assistance (ODA) often serves as seed money for private flows. But this definition of economic cooperation is also much narrower than Kindleberger's definition of economic leadership. It focuses on transfer of financial resources, and omits, most noticeably, an open market for distress goods and lender of last resort during financial crises as tools of economic statecraft.

How the Japanese define economic cooperation explains how they evaluate their performance in this area. They argue, correctly, that both official and private flows of resources promote growth. "The large contribution of private Japanese corporate activity, especially overseas direct investment, to economic development in Asia is widely recognized," pointed out Nishigaki and Shimomura.[3] Japanese government publications on ODA all highlight Japan's substantial contributions to Asian economic growth.[4]

Figure 3.1

Definition of Japan's Economic Cooperation

- Official Development Assistance (ODA)
  - Bilateral ODA
    - * Grant Aid
    - * Technical Cooperation
    - * ODA Loans, etc.
  - Multilateral ODA
    - * Contributions, etc., to United Nations Agencies, etc.
    - * Contributions, etc., to International Financial Institutions, etc.
- Other Official Flows (OOF)
  - * Official Export Credits
  - * Direct Investment and Others
  - * Finances to Multilateral Institutions
- Private Flows (PF)
  - * Private Export Credits
  - * Direct Investment and Others
  - * Finances to Multilateral Institutions
- Grants by Private Voluntary Agencies

Source: OECF, *The Overseas Economic Cooperation Fund Annual Report,* 1997, p. 31. The definition of the Ministry of International Trade and Industry (MITI) is virtually identical. See MITI, *Keizai kyoryoku no genjo to mondaiten* [Current conditions and issues of economic cooperation], 1994, p. 1.

The Americans are skeptical. In the late 1980s and early 1990s, some journalists suggested that Japan was recreating its wartime design for a "Greater East Asia Coprosperity Sphere," but using economic rather than military means this time.[5] Scholars and analysts were also concerned. Walter Hatch and Kozo Yamamura saw Asia in "Japan's embrace," arguing that the Japanese government and the business community cooperated in creating a potentially exclusive production alliance in the region as an extension of the Japanese domestic base.[6] Such alarming remarks reflected American concerns for their own position in the region. East Asia "was subsumed into the global rivalry between the Americans and the Japanese," suggested Dennis J. Encarnation.[7] U.S. views shifted with the Asian financial crisis. Unable to reform its economy and resolve its banking crisis, Japan is now seen as uncooperative in helping to revive the troubled economies in the region. The new American criticism combines both self-interests in preventing a surge of Asian exports to the United States and broader concerns for social, economic, and political stability in the region.

By contrast, Asians have largely seen Japan as cooperative. In fact, some Asians sought Japanese economic leadership. Malaysian prime minister Mahathir Mohamad's "Look East" policy, announced in 1981, called for emulating the Japanese development model. Singapore's prime minister Lee Kuan Yew also indicated strong interest in learning from Japan in the 1980s. As the largest donor to East Asian nations, Japan has facilitated realization of the development objectives of its East Asian neighbors. Foreign aid factors heavily in the strategic and development thinking of China and the Association of Southeast Asian Nations (ASEAN). Japan's "request-based" aid is largely consistent with the priorities of the recipient nations, although Japanese companies and consultants are often involved in designing projects to present to Tokyo for assistance. The gap in assessment of Japan's economic cooperation with Asia between Americans and Asians reflects different needs and goals. Asian nations seek to better their economies rather than compete with Japan at this stage, while the United States competes with Japan head-on.

Economic Diplomacy Through the Early 1970s

Articulated first by Prime Minister Yoshida Shigeru, "economic diplomacy" was defined in the first White Paper of Diplomacy in 1957 as "peaceful expansion of our economic power" in foreign markets.[8] Under this policy, Asia was important as a source of supply for resources and a market for exports. Japan started official assistance in technical cooperation with Asian nations by joining the Colombo Plan in 1954.[9] Tokyo then used war reparations to establish diplomatic relations with Southeast Asian nations in the 1950s. Japan signed reparation agreements with Burma (effective April 1955), the Philippines (July 1956), Indonesia (April 1958), and South Vietnam (January 1960), paying a total of ¥356,552 million ($990.4 million). Japan also compensated the following nations: Thailand in 1955 (revised 1962), Laos in 1958, Cambodia in 1959, Burma in 1963, South Korea in 1965, Singapore in 1968 and 1970, Malaysia in 1967, and Micronesia in 1969, making a total of $485 million in grants and $196.3 million in loans.[10] With reparations, Japanese firms provided goods and services to those Asian nations, which stimulated Japan's economy after the Korean War boom and allowed Japanese to reenter regional markets.[11] In fact, prominent leaders of business groups such as the Federation of Economic Organizations

(Keidanren) and the Chamber of Commerce and Industry often represented the government in negotiations.[12] Japan's reparations largely ended in the mid 1960s.

In the 1960s Japan used "economic cooperation" to promote exports, secure a supply of resources, and improve relations with the nations important for its economy. Believing that "tied loans have the effect of spurring the export of Japanese goods," Japanese aid officials themselves have acknowledged, the Government of Japan (GoJ) "actively extended yen loans to these [Asian] countries throughout the 1960s to comply with the export promotion policy."[13] Japan's ODA to Southeast Asia increased moderately from $130.6 million in 1963 to $211.3 million in 1969. Virtually all its aid went to Asia in this period—98.7 percent in 1963 and 100 percent in 1969.[14] At the second Asian Development Bank (ADB) annual meeting in April 1969, Japan announced its plan for a twofold increase in aid to Asia within five years. Starting in 1972 Japan's aid to ASEAN surpassed that from the United States. Japan's ODA program facilitated Japanese companies penetrating the Southeast Asia markets. But rapid Japanese economic advance in the region caused serious local resentment, fully displayed during the visit by Prime Minister Tanaka Kakuei to Thailand and Indonesia in January 1974.

The United States encouraged Japan to reenter the region to serve its own economic and strategic interests. To reduce the U.S. financial burden and prevent a communist takeover in Japan, Washington believed that it was essential for Japan to import cheap materials from Southeast Asia and export cheap goods to the region. In fact, the Eisenhower government became involved in Indochina conflicts largely to protect Japan, based on the belief that if Southeast Asia fell to communism Japan would be forced to accommodate communism to survive economically. Dulles urged Yoshida to use reparations to facilitate Japan's economic interests in the region.[15] Washington continued to encourage Japanese economic cooperation with Southeast Asia in the 1960s as a contribution to its escalating war efforts in Vietnam and a counterweight to communist influence in the region.

The flip side of Washington's cold war strategy of integrating Japan with Southeast Asia and the Western world was its determination to keep the country from the communist orbit. In particular, the United States forced Japan to keep away from mainland China—its largest trading partner before the war—although the United States did tolerate Japan's moderate trade with China to meet Japan's perceived economic needs. Under the principle of *seikei bunri,* or separation of politics from economics, Japan maintained moderate trade with China through "unofficial channels."[16]

Japan's trade relations with China revealed its different opinion of China and other Asian communist countries from that of the United States as well as its national priority to promote economic growth. Ogata Sadako commented that "not many Japanese regard Communist China as a 'cold war' enemy, nor do they accept the 'China-communism-enemy' equation that is so widely held in the United States."[17] Japanese politicians of different convictions virtually all advocated trade with communist countries for commercial reasons and to drive a wedge between the Soviet Union and Asian communist countries.[18] In the case of Vietnam, while supporting U.S. policy in Vietnam, the Japanese government avoided direct involvement in the war and maintained a moderate trade relationship with North Vietnam even at the height of the war.[19] As for North Korea, after normalizing relations with South Korea in June 1965, Japan left room for improving relations with the North by refusing to recognize the South Korean government as governing all Korea. Tokyo also maintained informal contacts with North Korea and became North Korea's largest nonsocialist trading partner.

However, there was little evidence that Japan, against its best economic interests, engaged Asian communist countries to transform them and that Asian communist countries could be transformed through economic interaction with noncommunist countries. In fact, Beijing's own trade interests in the 1950s were driven by a strategic objective to divide Japan and the United States as well as by economic necessity. China's failure in the late 1950s to alter Japanese politics in its favor revealed the strength of the U.S.–Japan alliance and its own economic weakness. As China plunged into the Great Famine of 1959–61, Japanese trade came to be motivated more by pragmatic economic interests than by mere political consideration. As the economic gap between the two nations widened in subsequent years, Japan would gradually enhance its bargaining position vis-à-vis China.

Courting Asia in the 1970s and 1980s

Japan adapted its economic approach in Southeast Asia in the 1970s and used ODA as a main instrument to repair ties with the region. Three factors explain this shift. First, the first oil crisis in 1973–74 highlighted the importance of Southeast Asia for securing energy supplies and shipping lanes. Second, the anti-Japanese demonstrations in Southeast Asia during Tanaka's visit in January 1974 necessitated cooperative moves to alleviate economic grievances. Third, ASEAN wanted Japan to play a more active economic role in the region at the end of the Vietnam War. ASEAN wanted preferential access and removal of nontariff barriers to the Japanese market, an export stabilization arrangement with Japan, and $1 billion in aid for five industrial projects. Prime Minister Fukuda Takeo visited Southeast Asia in August 1977 and spelled out the "Fukuda Doctrine," including three principles: a pledge not to become a military power, a "heart-to-heart" conversation with the countries in the region, and promotion of a stable relationship between ASEAN and Indochina. Japan provided the $1 billion loan for the industrial projects as requested, but did not respond to ASEAN pleas to open its domestic market for ASEAN goods. Washington praised the Fukuda Doctrine and agreed that a greater Japanese role would compensate for decreased American involvement in the region in this period.[20] Consistent with its new approach, Japan's ODA to ASEAN doubled in ten years, from $380 million in 1975 to $800 million in 1985 (Table 3.1).

Japan expanded economic cooperation with virtually the whole region. Tokyo normalized diplomatic relations with Beijing in 1972 and launched its ODA program in China in 1979 in support of Deng Xiaoping's economic reform.[21] Japan provided the first of the four yen loan packages to China, totaling ¥350 billion ($1.5 billion in 1979 dollars) for 1980–84. Japan offered aid and expanded trade with Vietnam after that country's unification in 1975 but had to suspend assistance after the Vietnamese invasion of Cambodia. After France resumed humanitarian aid to Vietnam in December 1981, Japan offered similar assistance in January 1982 despite objections from ASEAN.[22] In October 1984 Foreign Minister Abe Shintaro promised $170–250 million a year in aid to Indochina if Vietnam withdrew from Cambodia.[23] Besides generous bilateral ODA, the Export-Import Bank of Japan (JExIm) offered substantial credits (which count as other official flows [OOF] in Organization for Economic Cooperation and Development [OECD] terminology) to other East Asian nations, totaling $11.05 billion in FY 1980–85, or 37.9 percent of total bank commitments.[24] In addition, Japan's massive contributions to the World Bank and the ADB helped the countries in the region as well. Japan's financing of the two banks will be discussed in detail in the next chapter. Japan's increasing official

Table 3.1

Regional Distribution of Bilateral Japanese ODA (net disbursement basis, $ million, % of total)

	1975		1980		1985		1990	
Asia	638	75.0	1,383	70.5	1,732	67.7	4,117	59.3
Northeast Asia	76	8.9	82	4.2	392	15.3	835	12.0
Southeast Asia	426	50.1	861	43.9	962	37.6	2,379	34.3
(ASEAN)	380	44.7	703	35.8	800	31.3	2,299	33.1
Southwest Asia	133	15.6	435	22.2	375	14.7	898	12.9
Central Asia								
Others	3	3.9	5	0.3	3	0.1	4	0.1
Middle East	90	10.6	204	10.4	201	7.9	705	10.2
Africa	59	6.9	223	11.4	252	9.9	792	11.4
Latin America	47	5.6	118	6.0	225	8.8	561	8.1
Oceania	5	0.6	12	0.6	24	0.9	114	1.6
Europe	0	0.0	-2	—	1	0.0	158	2.3
Eastern Europe							153	2.2
Unallocatable	11	1.3	23	1.2	122	4.8	494	7.1
Total Bilateral ODA	850	100.0	1,961	100.0	2,557	100.0	6,940	100.0

Asia	5,745	54.4	4,145	49.6	3,076	46.5	5,372	62.4
Northeast Asia	1,606	15.2	869	10.4	529	8.0	1,211	14.1
Southeast Asia	2,592	24.6	1,858	22.2	1,416	21.4	2,438	28.3
(ASEAN)	2,229	21.1	1,694	20.3	1,345	20.5	2,356	27.4
Southwest Asia	1,435	13.6	1,320	15.8	964	14.6	1,463	17.0
Central Asia	67	0.6	80	0.9	145	2.2	228	2.7
Others	44	0.4	18	0.2	21	0.3	33	0.4
Middle East	721	6.8	561	6.7	513	7.8	392	4.6
Africa	1,333	12.6	1,067	12.8	803	12.1	950	11.0
Latin America	1,142	10.8	986	11.8	715	10.8	553	6.4
Oceania	160	1.5	198	2.4	159	2.4	147	1.7
Europe	153	1.5	200	2.4	134	2.0	144	1.7
Eastern Europe	138	1.3	130	1.6	54	0.8	47	0.6
Unallocatable	1,303	12.3	1,200	14.4	1,213	18.4	1,048	12.2
Total Bilateral ODA	10,557	100.0	8,356	100.0	6,613	100.0	8,606	100.0

Source: Ministry of Foreign Affairs (MFA), *Japan's ODA*, various years and http://www.mofa.go.jp/policy/oda/summary/1999.

Notes: 1. Unallocatable refers to aid programs that are impossible to be designated to any particular country, including items such as research projects and student training programs.

2. Five countries in Central Asia and three countries in the Caucasus became eligible for ODA in 1993 and 1994, respectively.

flows facilitated its direct investment in East Asia since the early 1970s, a development allowed by the Japanese government's gradual relaxing of restrictions on capital exports. Japan's Foreign Direct Investment (FDI) in East Asia reached $1.85 billion in FY 1983.[25]

Japan used economic cooperation to smooth relations with Asian nations. Japan's ODA to China was in part a substitute for war reparations, which Beijing renounced in 1972. In the early 1980s, Prime Minister Nakasone Yasuhiro used an official visit and Japanese aid to revive bilateral relations with Korea, which had grown strained as a result of Japan's trade surplus and charges by the Chun Doo-Huan government that Japan failed to appreciate Korea's role as a bulwark against communism. Whereas Japanese prime ministers traditionally made their first trip abroad to Washington, Nakasone traveled first to Seoul, signaling the high priority he gave to improving relations with Korea. He also negotiated a $4 billion aid package over seven years, including $1.85 billion in ODA loans, $350 million in yen bank loans, and $1.8 billion in JExIm loans.[26]

In addition, Japanese believed that their economic exchange with Asian nations, especially the communist ones, would have a long-term positive impact on these nations. As former foreign minister Okita Saburo argued about China, "China is now at the stage of introducing the price mechanism into a socialist planned economy and by trial and error she is groping for the system best suited to her particular conditions. Thus I feel that we should look at China from a long-term point of view and cooperate with her as much as possible on that basis."[27] But a note of caution is needed here. Japan's economic interests and its transformative logic point in the same direction in this case. And Japan's economic interests were principal ones. The Japanese government and business community were upset when the Chinese government canceled some projects in 1980, including a major steelworks in Shanghai. Japanese were not concerned enough about transforming China to take a loss.

"Embracing" Asia After the Late 1980s

Heart-to-heart conversation with Southeast Asia turned into a full embrace in the late 1980s. The term "embrace," originally used by Hatch and Yamamura, essentially means a Japan-centered multitier production alliance in Asia.[28] I use the term broadly here to indicate both Japan's intention and effort to integrate economically with other Asian countries, and Asian nations' acceptance of this behavior. It should be noted that embrace is a more appropriate characterization of Japan's relations with ASEAN nations than its relations with the rest of the region, China in particular. China has growing economic strength. It receives most foreign direct investment from overseas Chinese and imports technologies from the United States and Europe, as well as Japan.

Japan's growing economic ties with East Asia were impressive. As previously, ODA led the way, increasing from $1.35 billion (52.9 percent of the total) in 1985 to an annual average of $3.5 billion (36.6 percent) in 1995–96 (Table 3.1). Japan was by far the largest bilateral donor for virtually all East Asian nations (Table 3.2). Take China for example. Japan provided the second yen loan (1985–89), totaling ¥470 billion ($2.3 billion in 1984 dollars), the third yen loan (1990–95), totaling ¥810 billion ($6.3 billion in 1988 dollars), and the first three years of the fourth yen loan, which started in 1996, totaling ¥580 billion (about $6.7 billion).

JExIm continued to be a major source of financing for East Asia. Between FY 1986 and FY 1990, the bank committed $16.7 billion in credits to East Asian nations, or 40.2 percent of total lending. This was impressive given that JExIm also played a key role in assisting the heavily indebted nations in Latin America. The bank provided $34.1 billion in credits to East Asia between FY1991 and FY1996, or 39.6 percent of the total.[29] This included trade and investment credits as well as so-called untied loans to support development, all offered on near-commercial terms.[30]

Japan's ODA served as seed money for Japanese private capital. Most yen loans funded infrastructure projects, which significantly improved key areas such as electric power, transportation, telecommunications, agriculture, and water supply (Table 3.3), and thus also improved the investment environment for Japanese firms. In addition, the Japanese government adopted policy measures to encourage investments.[31] While Japan invested a total of $19.2 billion in East Asia in the thrity-five years from FY 1951–85, its total investment soared to $27.7 billion in the five years from FY 1986–90. Japan's FDI in Asia was heavily concentrated in the manufacturing sector. Besides FDI, Japanese banks became a major source of private loans to the region, supplying $118.9 billion to South Korea, China, Indonesia, Thailand, Taiwan, Malaysia, and the Philippines as of the end of June 1997—fully one-third of global bank lending to these countries (Table 3.4).

Japan's trade followed its investment in Asia.[32] Trade with East Asia

Table 3.2

List of Key East Asian Countries to Which Japan Is Top Donor (net disbursement basis, $ million, % of total)

	1985		1990		1991		1992		1993	
China	388	67.6	723	51.0	585	46.3	1051	50.6	1351	60.2
Indonesia	161	32.1	868	57.2	1066	60.9	1357	68.8	1149	60.1
Malaysia*	126	62.0	373	81.3	200	73.2	157	80.6		
Thailand	264	68.5	419	57.2	406	63.5	414	59.5	350	62.2
Myanmar	154	60.8	61	73.8	85	79.8	72	87.1	69	88.7
Philippines	240	54.9	647	58.8	459	53.2	1031	67.0	758	56.8
Vietnam**							281	59.4		

	1994		1995		1996		1997	
China	1479	61.8	1380	54.5	862	51.6	577	47.0
Indonesia	886	56.9	892	68.5	966	90.9	497	62.9
Malaysia*			65	60.7				
Thailand	383	70.4	667	80.7	664	82.7	468	77.9
Myanmar	134	93.7	114	90.5	35	77.7	15	62.7
Philippines	592	62.8	416	55.6	415	55.4	319	56.2
Vietnam**			170	31.0	121	25.8	233	39.7

Source: MFA, *Japan's ODA* and *Wagakuni no seifu kaihatsu enjo* [Japan's ODA], various years, and http://www.mofa.go.jp/policy/oda/summary/1999.

* Malaysia did not seek additional ODA in 1993–94 due to the rising debt burden caused by the yen appreciation.

** Due to its participation in sanctions against Vietnam, Japan did not become Vietnam's largest donor until 1992. Japan offered $11.5 million in 1993, behind Sweden, Italy, France, Germany, and Australia, and $79.5 million in 1994, behind France and Italy.

Table 3.3

Contributions of Japanese ODA Loans to Major Asian Recipient Countries

Country	Electric Power	Transportation	Telecommunications	Agriculture, Fisheries, Water Supply
Indonesia	Construction of 14% of total installed capacity (excluding small-scale facilities) of 14,372 MW.	Construction and rehabilitation of 12% (799 km) of total railways. Construction of 15% (56 km) of total toll roads.	Construction of 50% (2,500 km) of microwave route. Construction of 73% of total junction network in Jakarta.	Construction of irrigation facilities covering 9% (3,700,000 hectares) of total irrigated area. Construction of 60% (770,000 tons/day) of total treatment facilities for water supply in Jakarta.
China	Construction of 3% of total installed capacity of 210,000 MW. Provided loans for 8% of new capacity (75,000 MW) built under the eighth five-year development plan (1991–1995).	Electrification of 38% (3,842 km) of total electrified railway of 9,941 km (includes work in progress). Construction of 13% (56 berths) of total number of 359 10,000-class harbor berths.	Construction of 2% (1.286 million circuits) of total digital circuits of 57.01 million. Currently laying 4,700 km of long-distance transmission optical fiber cable between Beijing and Harbin, accounting for 5% of total installed capacity (10,000 km).	Provision of loans for the construction of 6 chemical fertilizer plants with a net production capacity of 1.43 million tons, accounting for 25% of the 5.70 million tons of capacity added during the eighth five-year plan (1991–1995).

(continued)

Table 3.3 (continued)

Country	Electric Power	Transportation	Telecommunications	Agriculture, Fisheries, Water Supply
Philippines	Construction of 8% of total installed capacity of 753 MW. Construction of 4% (274 km) of the permanent transmission line network.	Repair and improvement of 13% (3,500 km) of national roads. Development of international airports in Manila and Cebu. Construction/upgrading of light rail transit to relieve traffic congestion in Metro Manila.	Construction of 15% (87,000) of national telephone circuits.	Construction of wells and water supply facilities for 21% (13 million people) of total population. Construction of 7 pumping stations for flood control out of 10 stations in Metro Manila. Construction of irrigation facilities covering approximately 2% (29,000 hectares) of total irrigated areas.
Thailand	Construction of 15% (2,381 MW) of total installed capacity. Electrification of 23% (14,446 villages) of electrified villages in rural areas.	Construction of 10 of the major 14 bridges in Bangkok. Construction of 32% (65 km) of expressway in Bangkok. Construction of Bangkok International Airport.	Procurement of all the public coin telephones for direct wireless communication with regional and remote areas.	Construction of small-scale irrigation facilities covering 30% (1.5 million households) of total agricultural households.
Malaysia	Construction of 24% (2,774 MW) of total installed capacity.	Construction of 19% (182 km) of expressway.		

Source: Adapted from *OECF Annual Report*, 1997, p. 240.

Table 3.4

Outstanding International Bank Lending to Key Asian Nations (as of end of June 1997, $billion)

Nation	United States	Japan	Europe	World Total
S. Korea	10.0	23.7	36.3	103.4
China	2.9	18.7	28.1	57.9
Indonesia	4.6	23.2	22.5	58.7
Thailand	4.0	37.7	19.8	69.4
Taiwan	2.5	3.0	14.4	25.2
Malaysia	2.4	10.5	12.7	28.8
Philippines	2.8	2.1	6.8	14.1
Total	29.2	118.9	140.6	357.5
% of total	8.2	33.3	39.3	100.0

Source: The Economist, April 4, 1998, p. 42. The original source from Bank for International Settlements.

almost quadrupled, from $78.4 billion (25.5 percent of its global trade) in 1985 to $302.9 billion (39.8 percent) in 1996. Exports to East Asia surpassed those to the United States in 1991 and reached $176.3 billion in 1996, only slightly smaller than combined exports to the industrial countries of North America and Europe ($184.6 billion). Significantly, Japan's trade surpluses with East Asia increased from $7.8 billion (16.6 percent of its global surplus) in 1985 to $49.7 billion (80.6 percent) in 1996.[33]

Japanese firms moved into Asia to advance their interests. They showed little inclination to transfer advanced technologies and managerial skills to potential Asian competitors in host countries and often raised the technological sophistication only enough to export to third countries. In fact, instead of passing whole sectors to second-tier and third-tier countries, Japan maintained high-end products in different sectors at home.[34] Japanese firms that formed alliances with local firms may "lock in" their junior partners to a permanent dependency because of Japanese control of technologies and organizational skills.[35] In general, John Ravenhill concluded that Japanese multinationals did not bring as many positive benefits as American counterparts in Asia: Japanese expatriates dominated in management and technology positions.[36] In addition, Japan had no preferential trading arrangements with other Asian nations, thus making East Asia different from other regional trading blocs. Although Japan became an increasingly important market for Asian goods in the 1980s, most Asian exports still went to North America. Conversely, as Japan's FDI in Asia grew, its exports of capital goods and components to the region also increased sharply.

If Japan pursued its own best interest, why did other Asians consider its behavior cooperative? This cannot be explained by Japanese deception or Asian naïveté. Japan's reputation for pursuing economic and commercial interests was well established by now. There was concern among Japan's East Asian neighbors about dependence on Japan's technologies.[37] And Asians tended to be suspicious rather than trusting of Japan due to their memory of past aggression. The key was what Asians thought they needed from Japan to meet their main policy objectives of the time. Asians welcomed Japanese involvement in their economic development. Starting in the 1980s, governments throughout the region promoted foreign investments, largely equating introduction of foreign capital with faster economic growth. In fact, Asian nations complained when Japan's direct investment was small in their countries. Chinese, for example, were highly critical of the modest volume of Japanese FDI in China in the late 1980s.[38] The Chinese government approached Japanese firms to solicit investments, with some successes. Hitachi, the first Japanese electronics maker to invest in China, is a case in point.[39]

In short, Japan's economic relations with Asia were basically cooperative because they suited the mutual needs of the parties directly involved. Japan, as a mature economy, wanted a closer relationship with Asia for competitive economic reasons, while other Asian developing nations wanted Japan's input of capital, goods, technology, and expertise for economic development. More important, Japan's official and private transfer of capital and technology did assist economic development in other Asian countries, funding substantial infrastructure development and contributing to growth in manufacturing. As Table 3.3 shows, Japan contributed a considerable share of infrastructure projects in electric power, transportation, telecommunication, and water supplies in Indonesia, the Philippines, Thailand, Malaysia, and China. Despite much concern about Japan locking East Asian nations into a permanent formation of flying geese, Mitchell Bernard and John Ravenhill point out that the analogy fails to capture the complex realities in the region, which exhibit "shifting hierarchical networks of production linked both backward to Japanese innovation and forward to American markets for the export of finished goods."[40]

Tested in the Late 1990s

The Asian financial crisis tested Japan's ability to exercise economic leadership in the region. Japan went through three stages: starting with promise, retreating from a worsening crisis and deferring to the United States, and regrouping for a bigger role.

Japan started with promise. When the Thai baht collapsed in the summer of 1997, Tokyo responded. It was in Japan's interest to help Thailand. Half of Thailand's $90 billion foreign debt was owed to the Japanese government and private banks. In addition, a Thai default on foreign debt would trigger a full-fledged economic crisis, hurting the Japanese companies operating in Thailand and forcing more bad loans on Japanese banks. In a $17 billion rescue package orchestrated by the IMF in August, Japan led bilateral donors with $4 billion, matching the IMF's commitment. The United States, Germany, Britain, France, and Canada provided assistance only through the IMF, the World Bank ($1.5 billion), and the ADB ($1.2 billion). To contemporary observers, it looked as though there were indeed a division of labor in the international monetary system, with the United States taking responsibility for the Americas, the European Union for Eastern Europe and Africa, and Japan for East Asia. After all, the United States offered $20 billion as part of a $50 billion package for Mexico in the Peso Crisis of 1994. In addition, Washington's passive reaction to the Thai crisis was in sharp contrast to its intervention during the Taiwan Strait Crisis of March 1996, suggesting an America that wanted to act as a security guarantor but not a lender of last resort in the region.

Japan's active role, compared to a weak U.S. response, prompted the media to see the country as willing and able to "come to the rescue" of the region.[41] In fact, some Asians called for closer regional cooperation, with "anti-American and pro-Japanese undertones."[42] At the annual meeting of the IMF–World Bank in Hong Kong in September, Japan proposed an Asian Monetary Fund (AMF), which would include $100 billion in contributions from Asian nations, but not the United States. However, U.S. Treasury Secretary Robert Rubin and Deputy Treasury Secretary Lawrence Summers were concerned that the AMF would weaken the IMF conditionality and threaten U.S. economic leadership. The treasury officials lobbied hard and killed the Japanese plan.[43] Besides American opposition, Beijing also opposed the Japanese plan because of fear that Japan would take a leadership role in the region at China's expense.

Japan retreated after this humiliating defeat and the United States took the center stage in assisting Indonesia and South Korea. But Japan provided more money than any other bilateral donor. Tokyo contributed one-third of total bilateral commitments in the three IMF-sponsored rescue packages: $4 billion of the $17 billion package for Thailand in August, $5 billion of the $43 billion package for Indonesia in November, and $10 billion of the $60 billion package for South Korea in December. The IMF, World Bank, and ADB committed $59.7 billion.[44] Financial contribution is a selling point for Japan. By its own calculation Japan contributed $43 billion to the Asia crisis by mid 1998, compared to $11 billion from the United States, $5.4 billion from Europe, and $1.2 billion from China (Table 3.5). Prime Minister Obuchi Keizo stressed Japan's $43 billion contribution in his speech at the UN General Assembly on September 21, 1998.

However, Asia needed much more than financial contributions from Japan. With an economy accounting for almost two-thirds of the total gross domestic product (GDP) of East Asia, Japan's economic revival was central to the revival of the whole region. But Prime Minister Hashimoto Ryutaro stated explicitly on November 25, 1997, that Japan did not want to be a locomotive for Asia. The Asia Pacific Economic Cooperation (APEC) forum in November 1998 failed to achieve tariff reduction in nine industries by 2020 because of Japan's refusal to lower tariffs in fishing and forestry industries. Before the meeting GoJ reportedly considered a $200 million aid package over five years to improve the fishing and lumber industries in Asian countries. Americans and Australians saw Tokyo's move as yet another example of "checkbook diplomacy" to win Asian support, a charge Japanese angrily rejected.[45]

To make things worse, Tokyo failed to produce reform measures strong enough to convince foreign countries and the international market that it fully grasped the magnitude of its economic difficulties. The resulting weak yen impeded the ability of the regional economies to compete in exports. Not surprisingly, Americans were most vocal. "Rather than absorbing more imports," Edward J. Lincoln warned, "Japan will shift its burden through more exports to the United States. . . . Tokyo is quite willing to let the United Sates underwrite the Asian recovery."[46] His frustration with the Japanese paralysis was widely shared in the U.S. policy community. After praising China's "great statesmanship and strength in making a strong contribution to the stability" of Asia "by maintaining the value of its currency," President Bill Clinton stated at the joint press conference in Beijing on June 27, 1998, that the key for Asia's revival "is for the plans to reform the financial institutions in

Table 3.5

Japan's Financial Contributions to the Asian Crisis Compared to Other Major Powers (by mid 1998)

Japan	United States	Europe	China**
Total: $42 billion	Total: $11 Billion	Total: $5.4 billion	Total: $1.2 billion
1. Financial aid with IMF: $19 billion $4 billion for Thailand, $5 billion for Indonesia, $10 billion for South Korea	1. Financial aid: $8 billion $3 billion for Indonesia and $5 billion for South Korea	1. Financial aid: $5 billion $5 billion for South Korea (from EU)	1. Financial aid: $1 billion
2. Trade insurance: $15 billion $1 billion for Thailand, $1 billion for Indonesia, and $13 billion for the three countries in fiscal 1997	2. Trade insurance: $2.75 billion $1 billion for Thailand, $1 billion for Indonesia, and $750 million for South Korea	2. Credits: $300 million for Thailand and Indonesia from Germany?	2. Trade insurance: $200 million
3. JExim (two-step loans,* investment financing, and others): $7.5 billion $2.5 billion in the February 1998 emergency package and $5 billion in the current package	3. Others (power plant financing: the Overseas Private Investment Corp.): $400 million	3. Economic and technical cooperation: $50 million	
4. Others (human resources training and others): $1 billion			

Source: Internal background materials prepared by Japan International Cooperation Agency (JICA) and Economic Cooperation Bureau of MFA for the Japanese delegation attending the Tidewater meeting of aid donors in Washington, DC, June 1998.

* Two-step loans are loans given to the developing governments, which lend to local companies.
** China offered $1 billion for the IMF package for Thailand. China also offered $400 million to the Indonesian package. In addition, Beijing offered $200 million of export credit to Jakarta during Chinese Foreign Minister Tang Jiaxuan's visit there in April 1998.

Japan and take other steps that will get growth going and get investments going in Japan to be made."

Equally damaging to Japan's leadership in the region in the long run was growing criticism from Asian nations. During an interview right before Clinton's visit to China in June 1998, Chinese President Jiang Zemin stated that "the weakening of the yen and other currencies will inevitably have an impact on China's exports."[47] Tung Chee-hwa, Hong Kong's chief executive, told Clinton in July that "a stable yen exchange rate and a healthy Japanese economy is essential, not only for the financial stability of Asia but for the world as a whole."[48] "The weakness of the yen and Tokyo's slowness in putting its economy in order, particularly its foot dragging," Malaysia's then Deputy Prime Minister Anwar Ibrahim warned, "is threatening the fragile banking system and making the regional situation gloomy indeed."[49] In a joint communiqué issued on July 25, 1998, ASEAN foreign ministers urged Japan to "expedite the implementation of its economic measures in support of the economic recovery of ASEAN countries."[50] However, we should also remember that Asians were also highly critical of the high-handed IMF approach to the Asian crisis.

In response, Tokyo took new initiatives and regained lost ground.[51] Finance Minister Miyazawa Kiichi launched a new $30 billion loan package for Asia in October 1998. According to the "New Miyazawan Plan," which was separate from Japan's ODA program, GoJ committed to use JExIm to guarantee loans and purchase government bonds by Thailand, Malaysia, Singapore, Indonesia, the Philippines, and South Korea. Different from the IMF, GoJ imposed few conditions on the recipient countries. In December 1998, Tokyo announced a separate special loan facility totaling ¥600 billion ($5.5 billion) to assist Asia. When the Miyazawa Plan was exhausted by mid 1999, Tokyo announced a ¥2 trillion ($16.7 billion) bond guarantee program. Even though Asia was recovering, the Japanese Ministry of Foreign Affairs released a report in September 1999 recommending human resource development. At the ASEAN summit in Manila in November 1999, Prime Minister Obuchi Keizo announced a new aid plan of $500 million for regional human resource development and personnel exchange between Japan and Asia. By the end of 1999, the Japanese government used the figure of $80 billion as Japan's financial contributions to the Asian financial crisis in various programs. Right before the Group of Eight (G-8) summit held in Okinawa in July 2000, Tokyo announced a $15 billion aid package to bridge "the digital divide" in the world. Vaguely consisting of both ODA and OOF, the money will be used mainly for Asian nations.

To some extent, Japan's activism since late 1998 has followed its traditional script for economic cooperation—namely, provision of financial resources—but has failed to open its markets or revive its own economy through economic restructuring, which would enable absorption of more distress goods from Asia. Despite repeated requests from regional leaders, Japan has done little to serve as an engine of growth in the trade area. In yen terms, Japan imported only 2.7 percent more from Asia in 1999 than in 1998. In addition, Japanese banks continued to retreat from Asia, reducing their outstanding loans to the region from $123.8 billion in mid 1997 to $74.8 billion at the end of June 1999, thus reducing available credits crucial for economic recovery.[52]

However, Japan's approach is also unusual for two reasons. First, Japan has become more explicit in linking its cooperation with its own interests. As discussed in the previous chapter, the Japanese Ministry of Foreign Affairs made such a connection in its review of ODA in August 1998, in blunt language unheard of previously. The Miyazawa Plan reflects Tokyo's desire to play a more prominent leadership role in Asia and to encourage wider use of the yen in the region. The $5.5 billion special loan facility for Asia stipulated that contracts would go to Japanese companies. More broadly, in the aftermath of the Asian financial crisis, Tokyo wants more ODA to go to Asia, which is more important for its security and prosperity. As Japan became a global power, Asia's share of Japan's bilateral ODA disbursements shrank from 75.0 percent in 1975 to 59.3 percent in 1990 and a low of 46.5 percent in 1997. By sharp contrast, Asia received 62.4 percent of Japan's bilateral ODA in 1998 (Table 3.1).

Second, Japan has used its financial assistance to further regional cooperation and enhance its leadership. Until the Asian financial crisis, Japan had preferred multilateralism on the global level to regional integration and had shown little inclination to exclude the United States from any serious regional grouping. As a primary example, Tokyo did not support Mahathir's attempt to create an exclusive East Asian group even though Japan was expected to play a leadership role in the group. However, Japan had a change of mind due to the Asian financial crisis, the failure of the World Trade Organization (WTO) and APEC to promote further trade liberalization, the advance of regional integration in Europe and North America, and increasing popularity of the idea of regional blocs.

Despite its failure to establish an Asian Monetary Fund in 1997, Japan has continued to seek a regional financial arrangement for East Asia. At the deputy ministerial–level talks at the ASEAN summit in November 1999, ASEAN financial officials recommended that Japan, China, and South Korea take the lead in creating a regional fund. ASEAN also wanted to turn the Miyazawa Plan into a permanent support facility—an idea that Tokyo endorsed. ASEAN nations, China, Japan, and South Korea created a currency swap scheme in Chiangmai, Thailand, in May 2000. The Chiangmai initiative was very similar to the Japanese plan, except that ASEAN took the lead, which made the plan acceptable to China. Japan is also renewing its effort to internationalize the yen, which will enhance its influence and reduce dependence on the U.S. dollar.

Even more significant, Japan is now seeking bilateral and regional free trade agreements. In a dramatic change of policy, the Ministry of International Trade and Industry (MITI) in its 1999 trade white paper emphasized the benefits of regional free trade agreements. The 2000 MITI trade white paper released in May again urged Japan to negotiate bilateral and regional free trade agreements. The report concluded that East Asian economic regionalism would benefit Japan. Japan is now discussing free trade arrangements with South Korea and Singapore. In February 1999, the South Korean government proposed to include China. There are also serious discussions to link an eventual Northeast Asian free trade area with the ASEAN Free Trade Area (AFTA), which is being implemented.

What do Japan's closer economic ties with East Asia mean for the United States? On the one hand, it is in U.S. economic and strategic interest to see East Asia recover. Thus Japan's financial assistance to the region benefits the United States as well. On the other hand, East Asian economic integration may benefit Japan more than the United States. After all, Japan and other East Asian nations are pursuing greater regional cooperation partly because they are resentful toward the IMF's perceived heavy-handedness during the Asian financial crisis. The United States has resisted East Asian monetary cooperation precisely because such cooperation will weaken the influence of the IMF, which it dominates. While East Asian regionalism may well become a building block for global free trade, it may lead to discrimination against outsiders—similar to that seen in European integration—and lead to creation of a tripartite global economy.[53] Japan's leaning toward East Asia, therefore, has important global ramifications in the long run.

Economic Sanctions

In sharp contrast to economic cooperation, Japan has seldom initiated action to impose economic sanctions on its Asian neighbors. Sanctions come in three forms: restricting exports, restricting imports, or restricting finance to inflict costs on target nations.[54] Since Japan has been unwilling to impose trade sanctions, its main instrument in sanctions is reduction of foreign aid. The 1992 ODA Charter articulated the principles to guide Japanese foreign aid—namely, prevention of aid for military use, environmental protection, democratization, transition to market economy, and human rights. In its 1997 *ODA Annual Report,* MFA emphasizes "positive linkage" to implement these principles, as well as "negative linkage." Positive linkage refers to carrots and negative linkage to sticks, judging by the concrete cases discussed in the report. Nowhere is the word sanction used in the report. Moreover, before applying negative linkage, GoJ is to cautiously examine (1) whether the target nation will react adversely, (2) how the population at large will be affected, and (3) whether the target country has started moving in the right direction.[55] These qualifying conditions virtually exclude all East Asian nations from Japan's use of negative linkage unless under strong U.S. pressure. It is implicit punishment if Japan does not offer carrots given to other countries, especially rivals. But Japan has sought to ensure balance in the distribution of aid among regional countries in order to avoid the impression of favoritism.[56]

A Reluctant U.S. Follower Through the 1960s

Japan did not initiate any sanctions in this period (see Table 3.6), but under the structural weakness of postwar Occupation followed by efforts to restore its standing in the West, Japan followed the U.S. lead and participated in sanctions against communist countries, especially China and North Korea. Japan became a member of the Coordinating Committee on Multilateral Export Controls (COCOM), the U.S.-led regime that restricted exports to communist countries.

China trade was a contentious issue in Japan's relations with the United States in this period. Japan wanted access to the China market to export goods and import materials. But after the Korean War broke out in June 1950 Washington forced Japan to adopt even stricter sanctions on China and North Korea than Western European members of COCOM, resulting in severe restrictions on Sino–Japanese trade.[57] Japan lobbied for some relaxation in the restrictions in the late 1950s because Great Brit-

Table 3.6

Sanctions in East Asia Since 1945

Case Numbers	Principal Sender	Target Country	Active Years	Goals of Sender
49–1	U.S. and CHINCOM	China	1949–70	1. Retaliation for communist takeover and assistance to North Korea; 2. Deny strategic and other materials.
50–1	U.S. and UN	North Korea	1950–	Withdraw attack on South Korea.
54–1	U.S. and South Vietnam	North Vietnam	1954–	1. Impede military effectiveness of North Vietnam; 2. Retribution for aggression in South Vietnam.
56–1	U.S.	Laos	1956–62	1. Destabilize government; 2. Prevent communist takeover.
57–1	Indonesia	Netherlands	1957–62	Control of West Irian.
60–1	Soviet Union	China	1960–70	1. Retaliation for China's break with Soviet policy; 2. Impair Chinese economic and military potential.
63–1	Indonesia	Malaysia	1963–66	Promote "Crush Malaysia" campaign.
63–2	U.S.	Indonesia	1963–66	1. Cease "Crush Malaysia" campaign; 2. Destabilize Sukarno government.
63–3	U.S.	South Vietnam	1963	1. Ease repression; 2. Remove Nhu; 3. Destabilize Diem.

Case	Sender(s)	Target	Period	Objectives
73–1	U.S.	South Korea	1973–77	Improve human rights.
75–1	U.S. and Canada	South Korea	1975–76	Forgo nuclear reprocessing.
75–2	U.S.	Kampuchea	1975–79	1. Improve human rights; 2. Deter Vietnamese expansionism.
76–1	U.S.	Taiwan	1976–77	Forgo nuclear reprocessing.
77–1	Canada	Japan and EC	1977–78	Strengthen nuclear safeguards.
78–1	China	Albania	1978–83	Retaliation for anti-Chinese rhetoric.
78–2	China	Vietnam	1978–88	Withdraw troops from Kampuchea.
88–1	Japan, Germany, and U.S.	Burma	1988–	1. Improve human rights; 2. Restore democracy.
89–1	U.S. and West	China	1989–	Retaliation for Tiananmen Square.
90–1		Thailand		
95–1	Japan	China	1995–97	Protest over nuclear testing.

Source: Data for the period of 1945–89 are from Hufbauer, Schott, and Elliott, *Economic Sanctions Reconsidered*, vol. 1, pp. 17–27. Information for Japan's role in 1945–89 is summarized from the case studies in Hufbauer, Schott and Elliott, *Economic Sanctions Reconsidered*, vol. 1 and vol. 2. Data for the 1990s are provided by the author.

ain had challenged the U.S. export-control initiative and President Dwight Eisenhower was privately sympathetic to British and Japanese arguments. Washington came to realize by the late 1950s that to maintain trade control on China the United States needed to accommodate allies like Japan.[58] Ironically, Japan's victory did not bring any immediate benefits. Beijing suspended trade with Japan in May 1958 because of Prime Minister Kishi Nobusuke's refusal to connect politics with economics in relations with China and his strong support for the United States and Taiwan.

Greater Independence in the 1970s and 1980s

Based on growing economic power, the Japanese started talking about using economic statecraft to ensure Japan's comprehensive security. But they mainly resorted to cooperative means to encourage stability and moderation in other Asian nations, which would enhance their own security. Although still sensitive to U.S. concerns, Tokyo also showed greater independence from Washington by not actively participating in U.S.-led sanctions in the region. There were three cases in the two decades in which Japan used punitive economic measures against Asian nations.

In the first case, Japan joined the United States in pressuring the South Korean military government for a better treatment of dissident leader and later president Kim Dae Jung. When South Korean secret agents kidnapped Kim from a Tokyo hotel in August 1973, Japan reduced economic aid to South Korea. Both the United States and Japan put pressure on the Korean government to spare Kim's life after a death sentence was handed down in September 1980. Prime Minister Suzuki Zenko warned that further economic aid to South Korea would be suspended if Kim's death sentence were carried out. Kim's sentence was changed to life imprisonment in January 1981.[59] But the most important external pressure came from the United States.

In the second case, in a symbolic departure from Washington, Tokyo decided to provide ODA to Hanoi in October 1975, soon after Vietnam's unification. Japan provided ¥27.5 billion ($112 million based on current exchange rates) in grants and loans to Vietnam between October 1975 and July 1978. In December 1978 Tokyo committed another ¥14 billion ($66.5 million) for 1979. The Vietnamese army invaded Cambodia a week later. Japan was initially hesitant to freeze aid because of its prior commitment, Hanoi's continuous request for Japanese aid, and concern over diminishing influence if ties were reduced. Tokyo suspended aid only in January 1980. The Soviet Union had invaded Afghanistan in December 1979. With growing reaction in China and ASEAN against Soviet influence in the region, Japan had to respond. GoJ adopted a pro-ASEAN stance regarding its policy toward Vietnam, though official communication continued. Japan resumed humanitarian aid and cultural cooperation in 1983, but it remained sensitive to U.S. antagonism to Vietnam,[60] as well as Chinese and ASEAN opposition to Hanoi and its own broader concern for regional stability.

In the third case, COCOM regulations remained an issue between Japan and China. During negotiations for the first bilateral official trade agreement after the two nations normalized diplomatic relations in September 1972, Beijing pressured Tokyo to remove the COCOM restrictions, but without any success.[61] Bilateral trade grew rapidly and the overall relationship improved steadily, but the Japanese continued to use COCOM as justification for not sharing technologies and information—a cause of continuous resentment on the Chinese side. The situation improved somewhat in 1986 when Washington relaxed its export licensing procedures and COCOM restrictions were also loosened. Japan and China could now engage in joint ventures involving equipment and technology previously forbidden. But COCOM remained an issue.[62] In a highly publicized case, in 1987 after MITI punished the Toshiba Machinery Company for selling advanced equipment to the Soviet Union by suspending the company's trade with communist countries for a year, Toshiba had to cancel $900 million worth of contracts with China.[63]

A Principled Approach Since the Late 1980s?

Japan became more active in sanctions in Asia in the late 1980s. In 1988 Japan, along with the United States and Europe, imposed sanctions on Burma after the military junta seized power. In the following year, Japan froze yen loans to China after the Chinese army repressed demonstrators in Beijing in June. But Tokyo resumed the loans a year later. Both cases involved human rights and democracy.[64]

Japan has been trying to articulate principles to guide its foreign aid program since the late 1980s. Prime Minister Kaifu Toshiki announced in 1991 that Japan would consider arms spending, democratization, market reform, and human rights in its ODA policy. These objectives were incorporated in the ODA Charter as a cabinet decision in June 1992. Henceforth, aid decisions would support environmental protection, prevention of aid for military use, limits on military spending and arms production, democratization, transition to market economy, and human rights.

Japan's adoption of the charter does not mean that it is now sanction-happy. In fact, the Japanese have avoided using the term "sanction." To implement the charter, Japanese emphasize "positive linkage" as well as "negative linkage." In addition, the charter includes escape clauses, such as overall bilateral relations, humanitarian concerns, and country-specific considerations. In many cases Japan has not applied the charter. A comprehensive foreign ministry list in 1997 includes only four examples of positive linkage, four of negative linkage, and two "where negative movement has occurred, followed by positive movement."[65] East Asia has not been the primary target for Japan's negative linkage. Of the six punitive cases, three involve African countries (suspension of aid to Congo since September 1991, Sudan since October 1992, and Nigeria since March 1994), and one involves Haiti during 1991–94.[66] The only East Asian cases are Myanmar (Burma) and China.

The Japanese government reviewed its aid policy toward Myanmar after the release of Aung San Suu Kyi from house arrest in July 1995 and decided to resume humanitarian assistance to the country on a case-by-case basis. But in the absence of significant progress Tokyo did not provide any grant aid or yen loans for new projects. In a change of policy, Japan provided a $19.5 million loan to Myanmar in February 1998 for repair on a runway at the Yangoon international airport. Suu Kyi criticized Japan's decision, saying it "belittles human rights in this year that commemorates the golden anniversary of the Universal Declaration of Human Rights of the United Nations."[67] Prime Minister Obuchi promised Myanmar leaders during the ASEAN meeting in November 1999 that Japan would consider resuming limited ODA if the Myanmar military government made progress in reform. A bilateral workshop was held in Rangoon in June 2000 to discuss Japanese support for Myanmar's economic reform. Japan's resumption of aid would upset the West, which continues to take a hard line on Myanmar. But Tokyo will not resume aid until the workshop issues a progress report a year later.[68]

Japan suspended grant aid to China in August 1995 in protest of Beijing's May nuclear test. This was a significant case not because of the amount of money involved but because Japan sanctioned its most important Asian neighbor on its own initiative and alone. Tokyo's decision stemmed from the strong antinuclear emotion of the Japanese public and the timing of China's tests—right after the extension of the Non-Proliferation Treaty, Prime Minister Murayama Tomiichi's visit to Beijing, and Japan's earlier warning to China over the testing issue.[69] Although annoyed by Tokyo's decision, the Chinese government understood that Japan had to make a symbolic gesture due to domestic politics and would compensate China in other ways.[70] Japan resumed grant aid in March 1997 after China announced its decision to stop nuclear tests, but its grant aid freezing was a minor factor in the decision. China stopped nuclear tests mainly to avoid international isolation.

Japan's reluctance to use sanctions is demonstrated by its decision not to suspend loan aid to China even while freezing grant aid. Japan would have gotten China's attention if it had cut its loans,[71] but it is unlikely even this would have induced China to cancel its nuclear tests. A drastic decision like freezing loans would have compromised Japan's strategic interests in maintaining a good neighborly relationship with China. As a China specialist in the Japanese Foreign Ministry recognized, "MOFA's position is that it is important to promote the bilateral relationship with China. ODA is an integral part of that. Japan cannot drastically cut ODA without sacrificing the overall relationship."[72] But the Japanese policy elites encountered increasing public and media criticism of China—a common theme in numerous interviews.

Japan's negative use of economic power has been insignificant compared to the extent of its economic cooperation with other Asian countries. Compared with disbursement levels the year before the freeze, China lost $129.5 million in 1995–96—merely 5.8 percent of total Japanese aid to China in this period. Similarly, Myanmar lost around $160 million a year after the 1988 freeze. China and Myanmar's losses in 1995–96 accounted for 7.2 percent of Japan's disbursements to East Asia.[73] In fact, Tokyo tends to use positive linkage to implement the ODA charter. As a notable example, GoJ has been active in assisting China's environmental protection, committing $1.8 billion of loans, grant aid, and technical assistance during 1988–95.[74] Environmental protection has become a focus in Japanese aid to China. During Jiang Zemin's visit to Japan in November 1998, GoJ agreed to offer ¥390 billion (about $3.2 billion) of ODA loans to China in 1999–2000, 43 percent of which is related to the environment.

It is also important to note what Japan has not done. Japan differed from the United States regarding Vietnam. Japan was eager to forge economic ties with Vietnam but was sensitive to the U.S. embargo on Vietnam that had been in effect since the end of the war. After Hanoi introduced economic reform in the mid 1980s and withdrew from Cambodia in 1989, Japan gradually expanded its aid program in Vietnam. Tokyo resumed humanitarian aid in 1990 and offered a commodity loan (¥45.5 billion, or $359.3 million) in 1992 and project loans (¥52.3 billion, or $470.4 million) in 1993.[75] Japan also lobbied the United States to stop blocking loans to Vietnam from multilateral institutions. Japan joined France and other donors at the 1993 IMF/World Bank meeting in pressing to refinance Vietnam's arrears of $140 million and Cambodia's $51 million to allow resumption of multilateral aid to these two countries. A donor meeting in Paris in November 1993 pledged $1.8 billion in aid to Vietnam for 1994.[76] Japan stepped up its economic cooperation with Vietnam soon after the United States lifted its trade embargo in February 1994 and normalized diplomatic relations with Vietnam in July 1995. In recent years, Japan refused to sanction Cambodia after Second Prime Minister Hun Sen waged a bloody coup against First Prime Minister Prince Norodom Ranariddh on July 5, 1997. Japan also avoided pressuring Indonesia over East Timor.

Japan's passivity in sanctions stands out against U.S. activism in this area in the region. The U.S. government now imposes some forms of economic sanctions on five countries in East Asia: Burma since 1988 (now a ban on new U.S. investments), Cambodia since 1992 (aid reduction), China since 1989 (limited export restrictions), Indonesia since 1991 (military aid restrictions and a ban on arms sales), and North Korea since 1950 (comprehensive trade and financial sanctions). In addition, the United States imposed trade restrictions on Vietnam from 1954 on. The United States and Vietnam signed a trade agreement only in July 2000, with resistance to improved trade relations coming mainly from Hanoi in recent years.

Why has Japan not used sanctions against other Asian nations more often? The simple answer is that Japanese have not found it in their interest to do so. Japanese generally believe that it is more effective to provide incentives than punishment to modify behavior.[77] More important, since Japan's foreign policy toward Asia has been heavily economics-based, it naturally prefers not to adopt measures that would hurt its economic and commercial interest. The fact that Japan has participated in any sanction has much to do with its interest in appearing to be on the right side of the West and history.

Japan has recently shown signs of being more willing to use economic sanctions to advance its interests. Tokyo suspended food aid in protest of North Korea's testing of a ballistic missile over Japan on August 31, 1998. In addition, Japan threatened not to sign the final agreement for the Korean Peninsula Energy Development Organization (KEDO) to build two nuclear reactors in North Korea in return for the North's ending of its nuclear program. Japan had agreed to contribute $1 billion for KEDO. Urged by the United States and South Korea, Japan finally signed a contract to contribute $1 billion to KEDO on May 5, 1999. Two months later Tokyo threatened to freeze aid if North Korea proceeded to test another ballistic missile.[78] Under U.S. pressure, North Korea agreed in September 1999 to suspend its missile program in return for economic assistance. Tokyo lifted the embargo on food aid in December 1999 and resumed food aid through the UN World Food program in March 2000.

Japan is also acting more assertively toward China. Due to growing sentiment among Japanese that Tokyo should take into consideration Beijing's military spending and dual-use infrastructure projects when formulating aid policy, the Japanese government has decided to offer aid to China on a single-year basis, unlike its previous multiyear method.[79] This shift represented a subtle form of punishment for another major power in the region. Due to alleged Chinese naval espionage incursions into Japan's 200-mile exclusion zone near the disputed islands (Diaoyutai/Senkaku), the LDP postponed decisions to support a $161 million loan to a railway and airport expansion project. Beijing strongly objected to the linkage of the loan and its naval activities.[80]

Political and Security Role

Japan's political and security roles in East Asia have gradually expanded. Still, its political moves remain tentative and its security role limited, restrained by domestic politics, a security alliance with the United States, and resistance of its Asian neighbors. Japan has been more successful in playing a *political* role in Southeast Asia than in Northeast Asia and more successful in playing a *security* role in Northeast Asia than in Southeast Asia due to different power balances, historical memory, and domestic politics.

A U.S. Follower Through the 1960s

Japan's political and security roles in East Asia in this period were minimal. Japan followed the U.S. lead, but it often had different views from

Washington on political and military affairs and tried hard to avoid entanglement in U.S. adventures in the region.

In the 1950s Japan contributed to its alliance with the United States by providing military bases and hosting U.S. combat troops—a crucial link in the U.S. cold war strategy in Asia. While Japanese valued their security relations with Americans, they did not accept some basic U.S. views toward Asia and were not obliged to assist U.S. military operations outside Japan. Yoshida did not see China as a permanent threat, based on his understanding of Chinese history and nationalism. He and his followers preferred to lure China away from the Soviet Union through economic engagement. But the United States forced Japan to side with the Taiwan government, which restricted Japan's ability to maneuver in Asia and created tense domestic division.

How Japan's security ties with the United States were viewed in the region depended on which side of the cold war one was on. The noncommunist countries preferred Japan's security alliance with the United States to a communist or a rearmed Japan. Communist countries saw the U.S.–Japan alliance as a threat, but Moscow and Beijing aimed at America as the true threat.

The revised U.S.–Japan Security Treaty of 1960 removed a clause that allowed U.S. military forces to be deployed in times of domestic crisis in Japan, but Japan remained reluctant to support the United States outside Japan. To contain communism in Asia, Americans believed that it was essential to keep Japan, with its industrial potential, hardworking people, and military virtues, from falling into communist orbit. To accomplish that Japan needed Southeast Asia as a supplier of resources and as an export market. While the United States focused on the war in Vietnam, Japan emerged as the largest economic power in Southeast Asia during the war, benefiting from war procurements and increased exports to other Asian nations producing materials for the U.S. military forces.

The Korean Peninsula had been strategically important for Japan since the Meiji Restoration. For Americans, Japanese, and South Koreans, defense of South Korea was directly linked with defense of Japan in both an operational and a psychological sense. But the Japanese government did not acknowledge the importance of South Korea to its own security until 1969, when Sato did so in a joint statement with Nixon in exchange for the return of Okinawa.[81] His statement and subsequent clarifications convinced South Koreans that Japan recognized their importance for its own security and would support dispatching U.S. troops from Japan to the peninsula if necessary—though GoJ did not want any direct involvement in military actions or logistic support. Seoul also used this security linkage in later years to extract greater economic aid from Tokyo.[82]

Great Independence in the 1970s and 1980s

Several events prompted Japan to seek greater independence in its foreign policy in the 1970s. On July 15, 1971, Richard Nixon shocked the Japanese by announcing his plan to visit China. He shocked them again a month later by stopping free convertibility of the U.S. dollar with gold and imposing a 10 percent import surcharge. Japan was shocked yet again in 1973 when the Organization of Petroleum Exporting Countries (OPEC) embargoed oil, setting off the first of two oil crises that decade.

Japan's own economic success in the previous decades also meant that the country could no longer hide behind the United States. Japan was now recognized as one of the five power centers in the world, along with the United States, the Soviet Union, China, and Europe. This meant greater U.S. pressure for burden sharing and heightened suspicion by Asian nations. Japan also wanted renewed U.S. commitment to its defense. The fall of Saigon in 1975 ironically made defense a legitimate topic in Japan and eased tension in Japanese–U.S. defense relations.[83] Japan was concerned about a U.S. withdrawal from South Korea. Japan increased its defense expenditure but did not take on more defense responsibilities until the end of the 1970s. In the face of a growing Soviet military presence in Asia, Japan agreed to monitor Soviet submarines, to block the Sea of Okhotsk on its northern front, and to monitor and defend sea lanes within 1,000 nautical miles to the south. As stated bluntly by former senior foreign ministry official Okazaki Hisahiko, "Japan is contributing to Asia's security by holding off the Soviet Union in Northeast Asia, but our military power can't be used for anything else."[84]

Given the grave security situation at the end of the 1970s, South Koreans did not object to Japan's increasing security role despite concern about a revival of a Japanese military threat. China, too, accepted Japan's greater security role in Northeast Asia because of mounting Soviet pressure on its borders. In the summer of 1972 Beijing decided to support the U.S.– Japan Security Treaty and Japan's Self-Defense Force, much to the amazement of leftists in Japan. After 1978 China encouraged Japan to be more active militarily to alleviate the Soviet pressure on Chinese borders. China's encouragement of a closer U.S.–Japanese security tie did not last long, however. By 1982 Beijing started criticizing Japan's militarism.

Japan made its most significant political initiative in Southeast Asia, a region more receptive to Japanese involvement. In August 1977 Prime Minister Fukuda Takeo announced the first official Japanese foreign policy doctrine since the war, to guide Japan's relations with the region. As discussed earlier, the Fukuda Doctrine included three principles: (1) Japan will not become a military power, (2) Japan will establish relations with ASEAN based on a "heart-to-heart" understanding, and (3) Japan will be an equal partner of ASEAN and facilitate mutual understanding between ASEAN and Indochina. The doctrine indicated Japan's greater interest in playing a political role in the region, but it is worth noting that Japan had to renounce a greater military role in the region to take it on. The Fukuda Doctrine did not succeed in bridging ASEAN and Indochina. After Vietnam invaded Cambodia, Japan froze aid to Vietnam in 1980. China secured the front line state against Vietnam and the United States renewed its defense role in the region. In contrast, Japan became "a sometimes reluctant supporter of ASEAN."[85]

Fukuda's successors, Suzuki Zenko and Nakasone Yasuhiro, visited ASEAN countries in 1981 and 1983, respectively, to further relations with this important regional group. Both prime ministers emphasized Japan's political role in the region. In fact, Nakasone linked Japan's economic security with ASEAN's.[86] While Japan became more active politically in the region compared to its own past record, its political influence, not to mention its security influence, remained limited. Over the Cambodia issue, Japan's role was largely limited to a would-be financial provider, while the United States, China, the Soviet Union, and Vietnam engaged in the more conventional power game, which relied on diplomacy and military statecraft as well as economic statecraft and propaganda. Japan's greater economic cooperation did not neatly translate into greater political influence. When Japan lost a vote for a seat in the UN Security Council in 1978 to Bangladesh, Japanese were shocked to find that several ASEAN members that received Japanese aid did not support its bid.[87]

Japan also used economic aid for strategic purposes, often at the request of the United States and key Asian nations. When the United States was negotiating base rights with the Philippines, it urged Japan to participate in a multilateral assistance program.[88] In another case, Japan increased aid to Thailand, which took in massive numbers of refugees from Cambodia. Tokyo also engaged in active aid programs in the South Pacific to counter growing Soviet influence. In addition, Japan's launch of financial aid to China in 1979 had unmistakable strategic signifi-cance. At the same time, Japan did not want to emphasize the strategic dimension of its aid programs. Seoul requested $10 billion in project loans in the summer of 1981, shocking Tokyo with both the size of the request and the use of Korean security needs as justification. In the end, Tokyo provided $4 billion in December 1982, including restrictions to guard against military uses.[89]

Japan Reorients in the 1990s

Since the end of the cold war, Japan has been reassessing its foreign policy toward Asia, with two developments in parallel. First, Japan has made some bold political and security moves in Southeast Asia on its own initiative, but with little success. Second, Japan has been drawn into a tighter security arrangement with the United States, with great security implications for Northeast Asia.[90]

The bold initiatives began in July 1991 when Foreign Minister Nakayama Taro made a surprising proposal to treat the post-ministerial conference as a forum for regular Japan–ASEAN security discussions. His proposal received a cool reaction from his ASEAN hosts, which in turn surprised Japan. ASEAN was not as worried about security issues at this time as Japan was. They also did not want to exclude China and the Soviet Union from a security dialogue, when the perceived threat from these two nations was decreasing.[91] In June 1992 Japan hosted an international conference on reconstruction of Cambodia and offered 20–25 percent of the $800 million in aid to that country. In October 1992 Japan sent 200 military engineers to join UN peacekeepers in Cambodia under its new UN Peacekeeping Operations Cooperation Act. In January 1997 Prime Minister Hashimoto proposed a regular summit forum between Japan and ASEAN to discuss security as well as trade and investment. ASEAN leaders were again cool to the idea because such an arrangement would have angered China.[92] Indeed, China's Xinhua News Agency criticized Hashimoto's move.[93]

ASEAN has been more receptive to a greater Japanese political and security role than Northeast Asia. But its support is also conditional. Thai security specialist Kusuma Snitwongse pointed out that "ASEAN has accepted the positive nature of Japan's political and military roles; its military actions have been acceptable when carried out within a multilateral framework, such as the United Nations. Japan's independent military role, however, is cause for concern, and maintenance of the U.S.–Japanese alliance is seen as a guarantee against independent posturing."[94] Similarly, Prasert Chittiwatanapong recognizes that ASEAN wants a greater Japanese political and security role without corresponding expansion in its military capabilities. ASEAN remains cautious toward Japan because of its lack of remorse for its past aggression.[95] ASEAN is also interested in engaging China despite its concerns about the intentions and growing power of its northern neighbor.[96]

In Northeast Asia, Japan has been drawn into a greater security role as a U.S. partner. Of the three hot spots in Asia (the Korean peninsula, the Taiwan Strait, and the Spratly islands), two are in Northeast Asia and the other involves China and ASEAN nations. The U.S.–Japan Security Treaty was reaffirmed in April 1996, extending cooperation between the two nations to the region. The two signed new defense guidelines in September 1997. After passing implementing laws for the guidelines in May 1999, Japan will now do more to assist the United States in responding to crises in regions surrounding Japan. This will involve logistic support, fueling, minesweeping, naval blockade, and use of civilian airports, ports, and hospitals.

Both the U.S. and Japanese governments have refused to clarify whether the "areas surrounding Japan" include the Taiwan Strait. GoJ has said the concept is contingent upon circumstances and does not refer to a specific geographic area. Like Washington, Tokyo has also refused to rule out Taiwan being covered by the new guidelines, although some senior officials and LDP politicians have departed from the party line. Nevertheless, the new guidelines cover Northeast Asia for any practical purpose.[97]

The Chinese government has seized every opportunity to convey to Americans and Japanese its strong opposition to Japan's enlarging security role in the region and the expansion of the U.S.–Japan Security Treaty. China's second defense white paper, released in July 1998, asserted that "the enlargement of military blocs and the strengthening of military alliances have added factors of instability to international security" and that "directly or indirectly incorporating the Taiwan strait into the security and cooperation sphere of any country or any military alliance is an infringement upon and interference in China's sovereignty." China obviously targets the U.S.–Japan Security Treaty and the new guidelines.[98] During his visit to Beijing in early July 1999, Prime Minister Obuchi did not succeed in convincing his Chinese hosts that a closer Japan–U.S. military cooperation does not aim at China.

However, other Asian nations differ with China in their assessment of the new guidelines. The Philippines, Australia, Taiwan, Indonesia, and Vietnam all support the guidelines as contributing to regional security, and some of these countries want to see a tighter U.S.–Japan security relationship as a check on a rising China. Even South Korea cautiously supports the guidelines as important for its security. Thailand is a rare exception, which has expressed reservations about Japan's expanding defense role.[99]

On top of the new guidelines for U.S.–Japan defense cooperation, the Theater Missile Defense (TMD), which the United States has been urging Japan to develop jointly, is causing disputes between Japan and China. The TMD system is designed to protect Japanese and U.S. military forces in Japan from ballistic missile attacks, presumably from North Korea and China. The Clinton administration proposed the joint project in 1993 and the two countries formed a working group to study the issue. But the Japanese government dragged its feet because of its concern about offending China and the high cost and uncertain technologies of the TMD system. Chinese feel that such a system would deny its nuclear deterrent and thus make China vulnerable. Beijing has recently increased criticism of the U.S.-led system for the region, with strongly worded articles in the People's Liberation Army newspaper and warnings by senior government officials. The Chinese government is particularly opposed to any suggestion that Taiwan be included in the plan. However, after North Korea launched a rocket over Japan on August 31, 1998, Tokyo now has a stronger justification for participating in the TMD program. In fact, Tokyo is also strengthening its own defense capability.

On the Korean Peninsula, Japan continues to finance the Korean Peninsula Energy Development Organization (KEDO), created in 1994 to provide two nuclear reactors to North Korea at a cost of $5 billion in exchange for a freeze on that country's nuclear weapons program. With $1 billion committed, Japan is a major contributor, next only to South Korea (one-half to two-thirds of the total cost). Tokyo suspended its financial contributions to KEDO the day after the North Korean launch, reacting more negatively than Seoul and Washington. Japan has since resumed participation in KEDO, although it has threatened to freeze aid if North Korea launches another ballistic missile.

In contrast to its role as a financier, Japan has not been included in the most sensitive multilateral security dialogue in the region—the four-way dialogue between the two Koreas, China, and the United States. Despite its high stake in a peaceful Korean Peninsula, Japan has not been invited to play a direct role because of regional sensitivities toward any involvement by a former colonial master that brutalized Korea.

Japan's limited leadership and influence in the political and security areas stand out against other key players in the region. The United States continues to act as policeman in the region and it asserted itself during the 1996 Taiwan Strait crisis. China, while causing tensions in the South China Sea and the Taiwan Strait, has also been the key to resolving security issues such as the Korean Peninsula and Cambodia, in consultation with the United States. For entrepreneurial leadership, ASEAN nations deserve more credit than Japan, the United States, and China for creating and expanding the only viable multilateral institution in the region. It is Australia that provided the initial momentum for APEC by convening the first ministerial-level conference in 1989.[100] Malaysian prime minister Mahathir boldly championed the "all-Asian" East Asia Economic Group (EAEG) in December 1990.[101] ASEAN created the ASEAN Regional Forum (ARF) in July 1994, which now includes ASEAN members, China, the European Union, India, Japan, South Korea, Russia, the United States, and some other countries. True, Japan played a role in suggesting such a forum,[102] but the shift in the U.S. position on multilateralism in security dialogues in the region was more important in making ARF a possibility.[103]

Tokyo has become more assertive since late 1998. As a primary example, Japan has adopted a more proactive approach toward the Korean Peninsula. Prime Minister Obuchi first strengthened policy coordination with the United States and South Korea. He then proposed a six-way dialogue, including Japan and Russia, to supplement the four-party talks (the United States, China, and the two Koreas) in an important policy speech at the ASEAN-plus-three (China, Japan, and South Korea) summit held in Hanoi in December 1998. Tanaka Akihiko, a noted Japanese international relations specialist, praises Obuchi's move as "unprecedented in the entire period since the end of World War II" because "in the past the Japanese government has been extremely cautious about proposing ideas concerning the international order in Northeast

Asia."[104] Moreover, the Japanese government is enhancing its war fighting ability and mulling over revision of laws to better prepare for any military threat to the country. Norota Hosei, the chief of the Defense Agency, openly called for revisions of the defense-related laws in March 1999.[105] A few days earlier, Japanese destroyers chased and fired at two suspected North Korean spy ships that had intruded into Japanese waters—the first time the Japanese military force had been employed in actions. To enhance its influence in the region and the world, GoJ sought to represent Asian voices in the G-8 summit to be held in Okinawa in July 2000. Former prime minister Obuchi visited Southeast Asia to listen to their concerns. Foreign Minister Kono Yohei, who played an important role preparing for the G-8 summit, also made a trip to Southeast Asia to listen to the opinions of regional leaders. However, Beijing indicated that the G-8 summit had nothing to do with China. Premier Zhu Rongji would visit Japan in October 2000 as planned rather than ahead of the G-8 summit in Okinawa as the Japanese side had hoped.

Conclusion

Economic cooperation is the dominant theme in Japan's relations with East Asia. Until very recently, Japan has not asserted itself by using economic sanctions against other Asian countries or converting its massive economic and technological capabilities into military might or taking up greater security and political roles in the region. Japan is not altruistic in its dealings with Asia. Even during the peak of Japan's economic cooperation with Asia in the late 1980s and early 1990s, Japanese companies, driven by economic interests rather than concerns for Asian brotherhood, intended to remain in a commanding position in the region—with control of production processes and key technologies—and to seek competitive advantages over their Western competitors. This does not, however, negate Japan's cooperation. Tokyo has been cooperative in that it seeks to facilitate realization of the development objectives of its Asian neighbors and tries to avoid appearing threatening to their security interests.

Japan picks and chooses where it cooperates—a pattern of behavior that maximizes gains and minimizes adjustment costs for Japan but weakens the perceived sincerity of its action and limits its leadership role in the region. As a unique leader, Japan promoted regional economic development and set the tone for regional international relations

in the 1980s. Despite an initial setback during the 1997–98 Asian financial crisis, Japan has emerged as a stronger economic leader based on its
massive financial assistance and efforts to promote regional economic
integration. Furthermore, Japan has become more assertive in security,
political, and economic policy.

To explain Japan's approach toward Asia, we need to examine Japan's
power, the constraints it confronts, and its own preferences. First, Japan's
economic power rose rapidly in the late 1980s and has relatively declined since the early 1990s. Rising or declining, Japan's economic dominance in the region is overwhelming. If we use GDP as a crude yardstick
for a nation's economic power, Japan is more than twice as large as the
rest of the East Asian nations combined (Figure 3.2). Its relative power
explains its willingness and capacity to impact developments in the region as well as expectations by other countries of its contributions and
anticipation of its inevitable political and security role. It is true that
Japan has experienced a decade of economic stagnation and recession.
However, the country remains the world's second largest economy and
much more powerful economically than the rest of the region combined.
Thus Japan maintains a significant structural power in Asia.

However, structural realism, as understood by international relations
specialists in the United States, does not explain Japan's foreign policy
behavior toward Asia well. Japan has not acted assertively as a regional
hegemon based on its economic and technological capabilities. This may
be explained to some extent by the constraining factors on Japan. The
United States is by far the most important constraining factor. Figure
3.2 shows that Japan's total share of East Asia GDP shrinks to one-third
if we include the United States. And the Japanese know that few Asian
nations will support Japan in any major quarrel with the United States.
But as discussed in Chapter 2, this does not explain why Japan has not
always acted in East Asia in the way that would best advance U.S. interests—namely, specifying its security role in the region in support of the
U.S. military forces and opening its market to divert Asian goods from
the U.S. market.

To a less extent, Japan is also being checked by China. In fact, China's
rapid economic growth for the past two decades has convinced some
analysts that China rather than Japan will be the dominant force in the
region in the future. Despite its huge foreign aid to China, Japan does
not enjoy as much bargaining leverage over China as it appears. From
the Chinese perspective, Japan needs China's support and influence in

Figure 3.2

Shares of Regional GDP Among the United States, Japan, China, and the Rest of East Asia
(percentages are shares among the four)

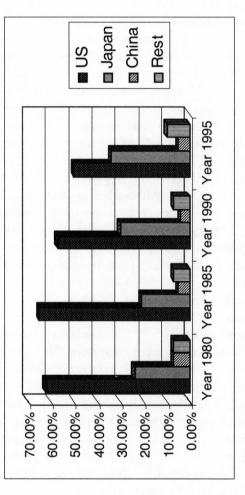

Source: Calculated from IMF, *International Financial Statistics Yearbook,* various years. Data for GDP of Hong Kong and Taiwan are from Far Eastern Economic Review, *Asia Yearbook,* various years.

Note: "Rest of East Asia" in this table includes Hong Kong, Indonesia, South Korea, Malaysia, the Philippines, Singapore, Taiwan, and Thailand.

GDP figures for Taiwan and Hong Kong in 1995 were actually from 1994.

Exchange rate is period average rate.

order to become a political major power. And Chinese see Japan's aid to China as mutually beneficial. Despite growing concerns in Japan about China's rise,[106] Tokyo has so far adopted only moderate precautionary measures.

Japan's reluctance to balance against China is related to a third constraining factor—namely, the historical legacy of its past aggression in the region. As Funabashi observes, Japan is burdened by "its past misdeeds and its ad hoc attempts to resolve them."[107] In the most recent case, history overshadowed Jiang's visit to Tokyo in November 1998. Beijing was hoping that Tokyo would make a written apology similar to the one it had made to South Korean president Kim Dae Jung, who had visited Japan a month earlier. GoJ expressed "deep remorse and a heartfelt apology" to Seoul in a joint written communiqué signed by Kim and Obuchi. In contrast, Obuchi only made an oral apology to Jiang. While disagreeing with Chinese over history, Taiwan, and U.S.–Japan defense guidelines, Tokyo agreed to offer ¥390 billion (about $3.2 billion) of ODA loans to China. Although economic cooperation may smooth bilateral relations, it does not resolve the root problem of historical grievances. History explains why Japan is more accepted in the economic arena than in other arenas. History also explains why Japan has been more hesitant to sanction East Asian nations than countries outside the region.

History also explains Japan's easier relations with Southeast Asia than with Northeast Asia. To Chinese and Koreans, Japan's past aggression is an issue that is very much alive.[108] Chinese leaders have never failed to call upon the Japanese to draw correct historical lessons. In contrast, Southeast Asians have not shown the same degree of animosity toward Japanese. As Table 3.7 (Question One) shows, almost half of those polled in China and South Korea believe that Japan should compensate the victims of the war to improve relations with their country. In contrast, less than 20 percent of those polled in Indonesia, Malaysia, Thailand, and Vietnam feel that way. The poll (Question Two) also shows that Southeast Asia is more enthusiastic about and satisfied with Japanese economic cooperation than Northeast Asia.[109]

While history explains why Japan does not want to expand militarily, it does not explain why Japan is not more cooperative in opening its market to other Asian nations, transferring technology and skill, or exercising leadership in the time of economic crisis—all of which are very much desired by the rest of East Asia. Also, it is puzzling why Japan does not make a full apology in order to exercise a stronger leadership.[110] Furthermore, the Japanese have often used Asian opposition as an excuse for not taking actions they do not want to take in the first place.[111]

To understand Japan, we should also consider its own strategic preferences, which are shaped by its identity as well as its ideas about the world, Asia, and norms of proper state behavior. As discussed in the previous chapter, Heginbotham and Samuels argue that Japan's foreign policy has been consistent with "mercantile realism." What makes Japan's thinking about East Asia different from its relations with the United States is its vision of transforming Asia. Japan does not balance China, for example, because it believes engagement is the most effective way of dealing with Beijing.[112] The logic is extended to other communist Asian countries to draw them into the global economy. Watanabe Toshio suggested that "the disintegration of the cold war structure in Asia is being propelled by two forces. One is the drive in the Communist countries to revitalize their economies through links with their noncommunist neighbors, and the other is the impulse in these neighbors to open new frontiers for their own economic expansion by responding to the communist countries' needs."[113] While hedging against an uncertain future with its greater defense cooperation with the United States since the mid 1990s, Japan remains driven by mercantilist calculations rather than a structural realist stratagem.

Japan's approach to East Asia is reinforced by learning from its dealing with the region. Japan has learned the hard way that uncooperative measures arouse strong resistance from Asian nations. Japan was shocked by Southeast Asia's anti-Japan demonstrations in the 1970s. Japan certainly knows the high diplomatic costs that will be involved if it is insensitive to Chinese and Korean concerns. By avoiding confrontation and seeking cooperation with East Asia, Japan has partially succeeded in reducing the hostility and suspicion of its Asian neighbors. As Table 3.7 (Question Three) shows, despite all the problems between Japan and other East Asian countries, it is striking that less than 10 percent of those polled in China and South Korea and less than 3 percent in four Southeast Asian nations believe that Japan's relations with their countries will become somewhat worse or much worse in the twenty-first century than now.

Ideas do change, and things learned can be unlearned. Japan is undergoing a profound reevaluation of its most basic assumptions about na-

Table 3.7

How Asians View Japan

Question One: What do you think Japan should do to improve relations with your country? Pick as many answers as you like from the following options.

	China	Korea	India	Indonesia	Malaysia	Thailand	Vietnam
Promote Japanese investments	49.5	11.8	62.8	28.8	45.6	42.9	71.6
Control Japanese investments	2.5	5.4	6.4	18.7	11.1	10.5	1.5
Increase imports from your country	54.8	32.2	48.5	39.6	51.6	57.0	46.2
Expand economic and technical cooperation	57.3	44.4	45.4	56.3	46.9	43.9	69.2
Pay attention to global environment and resources	22.7	11.7	13.6	22.1	17.5	30.3	20.6
Compensate the victims of the war	49.9	48.4	4.5	17.0	18.8	6.4	18.9
Reduce military power	22.9	11.8	3.8	1.4	9.3	2.1	3.6
Play an active role in international politics	19.8	19.4	11.2	5.2	15.7	7.5	3.8
Accept laborers from your country	28.1	6.5	34.2	28.6	32.4	44.9	33.2
Respect your country's culture and history	65.7	66.3	13.9	20.8	28.5	21.7	30.9
Advocate Asia's position vis-à-vis the U.S. and Europe	14.6	6.6	6.2	4.5	7.8	4.2	2.4
Others	0.8	1.2	0.6	0.2	1.6	0.7	0.8
I have no answer	1.8	4.1	9.9	5.2	3.8	0.3	4.1

Question Two: Do you think Japan's economic and technical cooperation with your country has been helpful in your country's development? (For Japanese, the question is whether Japan's economic and technical cooperation has been helpful for its partner countries' development.)

	Japan	China	Korea	India	Indonesia	Malaysia	Thailand	Vietnam
Very helpful	25.8	15.5	17.9	42.8	31.2	33.2	35.7	35.5
Somewhat helpful	53.9	71.8	59.3	46.1	59.9	53.1	50.9	53.2
Not very helpful	13.8	8.3	16.5	4.3	1.3	8.6	11.0	5.3
Not helpful at all	1.8	0.9	2.1	1.9	1.1	0.7	2.3	1.4
I can't answer	4.7	3.5	4.2	4.9	6.5	4.4	0.1	4.6

Question Three: Do you think your country's relations will become better or worse in the twenty-first century than now or remain unchanged?

	China	Korea	India	Indonesia	Malaysia	Thailand	Vietnam
Much better	5.0	5.8	54.5	39.3	31.6	30.1	65.5
Somewhat better	46.2	51.1	33.3	44.4	47.4	46.5	22.6
No change	38.3	31.9	4.7	10.3	14.4	20.4	7.5
Somewhat worse	4.6	8.2	1.0	1.2	0.8	2.7	0.6
Much worse	0.4	0.9	0.8	—	0.1	0.3	0.4
I can't answer	5.6	2.1	5.6	4.9	5.7	—	3.4

Source: Yomiuri Daily, September 19, 1996, p. 10. The surveys were conducted, with samples of about 1,000 each, in the countries so named in May–July 1996. Margins of errors not provided.

Note: Questions were translated and numbered by the author.

tional defense. The catalyst is North Korea's August 1998 missile testing, which for many Japanese posed the most direct and immediate threat to Japan over the past fifty years.[114] In an emotional overreaction to the threat of missile attacks, of which many countries have been fully aware for decades, some Japanese are questioning their previous naïveté about security issues and becoming doubtful about the effect of Japan's checkbook diplomacy. As reflected in government policy, GoJ issued its longest ever annual defense report on July 27, 1999, which makes clear Japan's right to use military force to prevent foreign attacks—a clear shift in defense policy. Using the North Korean threat as justification, the report essentially asks for more arms and enhanced military preparedness. The report also lists some potential problems with China.[115] Japan may well emerge a more assertive and normal country from its shock. However, while hedging against a potentially indifferent United States for Japanese security needs, mainstream Japanese thinkers still regard the U.S.–Japan Security Alliance as the best choice for its national defense. Moreover, while Japan may respond assertively against North Korea, it will continue to seek better relations with most other Asian neighbors through economic cooperation.

Notes

1. Charles Kindleberger, *The World in Depression, 1929–1939,* p. 289.
2. Susan J. Pharr and Ming Wan, "Japan's Leadership," pp. 135–36.
3. Nishigaki and Shimomura, "Japan's Aid," p. 30.
4. There is surely dissent in Japan. Japanese critics among academics, journalists, and politicians have questioned the motives, approaches, and effects of Japan's ODA programs. See Yasutomo, *New Multilateralism in Japan's Foreign Policy,* pp. 16–26. But their views do not significantly affect Japanese decision-making.
5. For just one citation, see David E. Sanger, "Power of the Yen Winning Asia: New 'Co-prosperity' Is Displacing U.S.," *New York Times,* December 5, 1991, D1.
6. Walter Hatch and Kozo Yamamura, *Asia in Japan's Embrace: Building a Regional Production Alliance* (New York: Cambridge University Press, 1996).
7. Dennis J. Encarnation, *Rivals Beyond Trade,* p. 152.
8. Sueo Sudo, *The Fukuda Doctrine and ASEAN: New Dimensions in Japanese Foreign Policy* (Singapore: Institute of Southeast Asian Studies, 1992), pp. 2–3.
9. Japan paid $10.6 million for receiving trainees from Asia and sending Japanese experts to Asian countries. *Japan's ODA 1994,* pp. 12–13.
10. *Keizai kyoryoku no genjo to mondaiten,* 1987, pp. 4–6. Japan's official reparations were completed in July 1976 and its compensations were completed in April 1977.
11. Yamakage Susumu, "Ajia taiheiyo to nihon" [Asian Pacific region and Ja-

pan], in Watanabe Akio, ed., *Sengo nihon no taigai seisaku* [Postwar Japanese foreign policy] (Tokyo: Yuhikaku, 1985), pp. 136–43.

12. Sudo, *Fukuda Doctrine and ASEAN,* pp. 44–48.

13. *Japan's ODA 1994,* p. 13.

14. Alan Rix, *Japan's Economic Aid,* pp. 32–34.

15. Michael Schaller, *Altered States,* pp. 96–112.

16. The bilateral trade volume experienced ups and downs due to political factors, varying from $151 million (2.6 percent of Japan's total) in 1956 to $23.5 million (0.3 percent) in 1960. The bilateral trade steadily grew in the 1960s, from $47.5 million (0.5 percent) in 1961 to $901 million (2.06 percent) in 1971, right before Nixon's visit to China. Trade data between 1950 and 1963 are from Hiroshi Yashiki, *Nichu boeki annai* [Information of Japan–China trade] (Tokyo: Nihon keizai shimbunsha, 1964), p. 159. He used custom statistics compiled by MOF. Trade data after 1964 are from the Japanese Ministry of Finance, *Financial Statistics of Japan,* various years.

17. Ogata Sadako, "Japanese Attitudes toward China," *Asian Survey* 5, no. 8 (August 1965), p. 389.

18. Schaller, *Altered States,* pp. 77–95.

19. Thomas R. Havens, *Fire Across the Sea: The Vietnam War and Japan, 1965–1975* (Princeton: Princeton University Press, 1987).

20. Sudo, *Fukuda Doctrine and ASEAN,* pp. 91, 102–109, 244; Marjorie L. Suriyamongkol, *Politics of ASEAN Economic Cooperation: The Case of ASEAN Industrial Projects* (Singapore: Oxford University Press, 1988), pp. 164–215.

21. For Sino–Japanese economic relations in this period, see Chae-Jin Lee, *China and Japan: New Economic Diplomacy* (Stanford: Hoover Institution Press, 1984).

22. Juichi Inada, "Stick or Carrot? Japanese Aid Policy and Vietnam," in Bruce M. Koppel and Robert M. Orr, Jr., eds., *Japan's Foreign Aid: Power and Policy in a New Era* (Boulder: Westview, 1993), pp. 117–19.

23. Havens, *Fire Across the Sea,* pp. 245–58. Indochina was also a good test case of the limit of Japan's cooperation with Asia. With millions of refugees from Indochina, Japan only accepted a few thousand as permanent residents. Instead, Tokyo offered hundreds of millions of dollars in funding for the international relief efforts.

24. Calculated from JExIm, *Annual Report,* various years.

25. MOF, *Financial Statistics of Japan,* 1984, p. 73.

26. Brian Bridges, *Japan and Korea in the 1990s: From Antagonism to Adjustment* (Aldershot, UK: Edward Elgar, 1993), pp. 14–16, 101–102. Japanese aid was not the only factor in improved relations. Equally important were Nakasone's apologies and greater respect for the Korean culture and history.

27. Okita Saburo, *Japan's Challenging Years,* p. 95.

28. Hatch and Yamamura, *Asia in Japan's Embrace.*

29. JExIm, *Annual Report,* various years.

30. For a discussion of JExIm, see Emig, "Activating the Export-Import Bank of Japan as a Development Lending Agency."

31. Shojiro Tokunaga, "Japan's FDI-Promoting Systems and Intra-Asia Networks: New Investment and Trade Systems Created by the Borderless Economy," in Tokunaga, ed., *Japan's Foreign Investment and Asian Economic Interdependence: Production, Trade, and Financial Systems* (Tokyo: University of Tokyo Press, 1992), pp. 20–25.

32. The JExIm 1996 survey of Japanese multinational corporations shows that the biggest reason for Japanese FDI in East Asia was to maintain and expand export markets. "EXIM Japan FY 1996 Survey: The Outlook of Japanese Foreign Direct Investment," *Kaigai toshi kenkyusho ho* 24, no. 1 (January 1997), pp. 27–29. The JExIm 1997 survey showed similar results. "EXIM Japan FY 1997 Survey: The Outlook of Japanese Foreign Direct Investment," *Kaigai toshi kenkyusho ho* 24, no. 1 (January 1998), p. 30.

33. IMF, *Direction of Trade Statistics Yearbook,* various years. East Asia here includes Brunei, Cambodia, China, Hong Kong, Indonesia, Laos, Macao, Malaysia, Myanmar, North Korea, the Philippines, Singapore, South Korea, Taiwan, Thailand, and Vietnam.

34. Mitchell Bernard and John Ravenhill, "The Pursuit of Competitiveness in East Asia: Regionalization of Production and Its Consequences," in David P. Rapkin and William P. Avery, eds., *National Competitiveness in a Global Economy* (Boulder: Lynne Rienner, 1995), pp. 103–31.

35. Tokunaga, "New Investment and Trade Systems," p. 43; Hatch and Yamamura, *Asia in Japan's Embrace,* p. 194.

36. John Ravenhill, "Japanese and U.S. Subsidiaries in East Asia: Host-Economy Effects," in Dennis J. Encarnation, ed., *Japanese Multinationals in Asia: Regional Operations in Comparative Perspective* (New York: Oxford University Press, 1999), pp. 261–84.

37. These concerns, always present in Northeast Asia, have also been growing in Southeast Asia since the late 1980s. Bernard and Ravenhill, "Pursuit of Competitiveness in East Asia," pp. 117–19, and Haruhiro Fukui, "East Asian Perspectives on U.S.–Japan Leadership Sharing" (paper presented at the 37th ISA conference, San Diego, April 16–20, 1996), pp. 11–14. As for the Chinese, a senior official of the Chinese State Science and Technology Commission expressed a widely shared view in China that "Japanese do give money, but are *xiaoqi* [stingy]" because they "are very cautious when discussing projects and are always concerned that they might leak technology and expertise to China." Discussion with the official, June 2, 1995.

38. A Chinese scholar characterized Japan's FDI in China in the 1980s as "four smalls": (1) FDI in China was only 0.5 percent of Japan's total FDI in 1986; (2) Japan's cumulative FDI in China was only 8 percent of the total foreign direct investment in China; (3) only 15 percent of Japan's FDI in China in 1981–86 was in the manufacturing sector; and (4) there was only a small amount of investment for each project. Wang Xinsheng, "Ji Zhonghua quanguo Riben jingjixuehui diwujie nianhui" [The fifth annual conference of All China Association of Japanese Economy], *Riben wenti* 26, no. 4 (1989), p. 63.

39. Eric Harwit, "Japanese Investment in China: Strategies in the Electronics and Automobile Sectors," *Asian Survey* 36, no. 10 (October 1996), p. 987.

40. Mitchell Bernard and John Ravenhill, "Beyond Product Cycles and Flying Geese: Regionalization, Hierarchy, and the Industrialization of East Asia," *World Politics* 47, no. 2 (January 1995), pp. 171–209. Also see Dennis J. Encarnation, ed., *Japanese Multinationals in Asia: Regional Operations in Comparative Perspective* (New York: Oxford University Press, 1999).

41. "Japan to the Rescue," *Economist,* October 11, 1997, pp. 89–90.

42. Henny Sender, S. Jayasankaran, and John McBeth, "Not a Happy Bunch," *Far Eastern Economic Review,* October 2, 1997, p. 69.

43. David Wessel and Bob Davis, "How Global Crisis Grew despite Efforts of a Crack U.S. Team," *Wall Street Journal,* September 24, 1998, A1; Nicholas D. Kristof, "Japan Sees Itself as a Scapegoat of Washington in the Asia Crisis," *New York Times,* September 21, 1998, p. A1.

44. The size of the packages all increased after initial announcements due to new commitments from bilateral donors. My number is based on the total commitments available shortly after announcements of each of the three packages. The media often used $100 billion as the total for the three IMF packages. Japan's share of the total bilateral packages would then be 50 percent.

45. Eric Altbach, "APEC Squabbles over Trade, Politics Overshadow U.S.–Japan Aid Plan," Japan Economic Institute, *JEI Report,* no. 44B (November 20, 1998), p. 8.

46. Edward J. Lincoln, "Japan's Financial Mess," *Foreign Affairs* 77, no. 3 (May/June 1998), p. 65.

47. "Upbeat Jiang on Asia's Woes," *Washington Post,* June 21, 1998, p. C1.

48. John F. Harris, "Clinton Vows Help to Asia," *Washington Post,* July 3, 1998, p. A1.

49. Sandra Sugawara, "Treasury Official May Go to Tokyo," *Washington Post,* June 17, 1998, p. A23.

50. Tom Raum, "Japan's Next Leader Pledges to Lift Country Out of Recession," *Washington Post,* July 27, 1998, p. A24.

51. Marc Castellano, "Rapid Recovery in Southeast Asia Strengthens Japan-ASEAN Economic Relations," *JEI Report,* no. 24A (June 23, 2000).

52. Marc Castellano, "Japan's Recovery Crucial to East Asian Rebound," *JEI Report,* no. 11B (March 17, 2000), p. 7.

53. Fred Bergsten, "Towards a Tripartite World," *Economist,* July 15, 2000, pp. 23–26.

54. Hufbauer et al., *Economic Sanctions Reconsidered,* pp. 36–38.

55. *Japan's ODA,* 1997, pp. 64–72.

56. A case in point: When Japan provided the first yen loan to China in 1979, it assured ASEAN by including the balance of ODA to China with the ODA to ASEAN as a principle guiding aid to China.

57. Tanaka Akihiko, *Nitchu kankei, 1945–1990* [Japan–China relations, 1945–1990] (Tokyo: Tokyo daigaku shuppankai, 1991), pp. 44–49; Wu Xuewen, Lin Liande, and Xu Zhixian, *Zhongri guanxi* [Sino–Japanese relations, 1945–1994] (Beijing: Shishi chubanshe, 1995), pp. 56–61.

58. Schaller, *Altered States,* pp. 77–95.

59. Bridges, *Japan and Korea in the 1990s,* pp. 12–14.

60. The U.S. Senate passed the Kasten Resolution in September 1987, criticizing Japan's trade with Vietnam. Japan had become Vietnam's second-largest trading partner. Shortly afterward, Honda abandoned its plans for a motorcycle assembly plant in Vietnam. Wolf Mendl, *Japan's Asia Policy: Regional Security and Global Interests* (London: Routledge, 1995), p. 118.

61. Wu, *Zhongri guanxi,* pp. 205–206.

62. Allen S. Whiting, *China Eyes Japan* (Berkeley: University of California Press, 1989), pp. 116–17.

63. Qingxin Ken Wang, "Recent Japanese Economic Diplomacy in China: Political Alignment in a Changing World Order," *Asian Survey* 33, no. 6 (June 1993), p. 640.

64. For Japan's approach toward human rights in Asia in contrast to the U.S. approach, see Ming Wan, *Human Rights in Chinese Foreign Relations: Defining and Defending National Interests* (Philadelphia: University of Pennsylvania Press, 2001), chapter 5; and "Human Rights and U.S.–Japan Relations in Asia: Divergent Allies," *East Asia: An International Quarterly* 16, no. 3/4 (Autumn/Winter 1998), pp. 137–68.

65. *Japan's ODA,* 1997, pp. 67–72.

66. Japan also "punished" some other African nations: suspension of aid to Gambia in September 1994 and reduction of aid to Kenya and Malawi. *Japan's ODA 1996,* p. 41.

67. "Suu Kyi Faults Japan Aid to Myanmar," Associated Press, April 8, 1998.

68. Marc Castellano, "Japan Looks Toward Resumption of Aid to Myanmar— Eventually," *JEI Report,* no. 25B (June 30, 2000), p. 8.

69. Interviews with Japanese diplomats at the Japanese embassy, Washington, DC, May 22, 1995 and in Cambridge, MA, June 2, 1995.

70. Discussion with a senior official of the Chinese Science and Technology Commission on June 2, 1995. He commented that "China has already expressed its view. Japanese are shrewd. They made a symbolic gesture, but will compensate China in other ways. . . . China also understands the current situation in Japan. The coalition government is unstable, with different factions. [Japan] needs to express its views."

71. As recognized by a senior Japan specialist in the China Institute of International Studies, which is attached to the Chinese foreign ministry, Japan does have leverage, as it gives more bilateral aid to China than anybody else. Interview, Beijing, May 20, 1996.

72. Interview, Cambridge, MA, March 16, 1995.

73. Calculated from *Japan's ODA,* various years. Japanese grant aid to China was reduced from ¥7,847 million ($76.8 million) in FY 1994 to ¥481 million ($5.1 million) in FY 1995 and ¥2,067 million ($19.0 million) in FY 1996.

74. See Susan J. Pharr and Ming Wan, "Yen for the Earth: Japan's Pro-Active China Environment Policy," in Michael B. McElroy, Chris P. Nielsen, and Peter Lydon, eds., *Energizing China: Reconciling Environmental Protection and Economic Growth* (Cambridge: Harvard University Committee on the Environment, Harvard University Press, 1998), pp. 601–38.

75. *Japan's ODA,* 1994, pp. 313–14.

76. Ronald Bruce St. John, "Japan's Moment in Indochina: Washington Initiative . . . Tokyo Success," *Asian Survey* 35, no. 7 (July 1995), pp. 678–79.

77. As stated by a Japanese Foreign Ministry official who was involved in the negotiations of the second yen loan to China, "Japan should help China to develop economically and socially. It is not a good idea to put pressure on China." Interview, Cambridge, MA, April 9, 1996.

78. "Japan May Freeze Aid to North Korea," Associated Press, July 13, 1999.

79. *Sankei shimbun,* February 2, 1999, p. 1.

80. John Pomfret, "Rocky Road for China–Japan Talks," *Washington Post,* August 29, 2000, p. A14.

81. The sentence is as follows: "The Prime Minister deeply appreciated the peacekeeping efforts of the United States in the area and stated that the security of the Republic of Korea was essential to Japan's own security."

82. Ho Hahn Bae, "Policy Toward Japan," in Youngnok Koo and Sung-joo Han, eds., *The Foreign Policy of the Republic of Korea* (New York: Columbia University Press, 1985), pp. 178–79.

83. Havens, *Fire Across the Sea,* pp. 242–43.

84. Okazaki Hisahiko and Sato Seizaburo, "Redefining the Role of Japanese Military Power," *Japan Echo* 18, no. 1 (1991), p. 25.

85. Charles E. Morrison, "Japan and the ASEAN Countries: The Evolution of Japan's Regional Role," in Takashi Inoguchi and Daniel I. Okimoto, eds., *The Political Economy of Japan: The Changing International Context,* vol. 2 (Stanford: Stanford University Press, 1988), p. 423.

86. Sueo Sudo, "Japan-ASEAN Relations: New Dimensions in Japanese Foreign Policy," *Asian Survey* 28, no. 5 (May 1988), pp. 509–25.

87. Robert M. Orr, Jr., "The Rising Sun: Japan's Foreign Aid to ASEAN, the Pacific Basin and the Republic of Korea," *Journal of International Affairs* 41, no. 1 (Summer/Fall 1987), p. 60.

88. Inada Juichi, "Ajia josei no hendo to nihon no ODA" [The changes in Asia and Japan's ODA], *Kokusai Mondai* 360 (March 1990), pp. 48–50.

89. Orr, "The Rising Sun," pp. 56–57.

90. See Mike M. Mochizuki, *Japan Reorients: The Quest for Wealth and Security in East Asia* (Washington: Brookings Institution, 1998); Cronin and Green, *Redefining the U.S.–Japan Alliance*; Yoshihide Soeya, "Japan: Normative Constraints Versus Structural Imperatives," in Muthiah Alagappa, ed., *Asian Security Practice* (Stanford: Stanford University Press, 1998), pp. 198–233.

91. Prasert Chittiwatanapong, "Japan's Roles in the Posthegemonic World: Perspectives from Southeast Asia," in Tsuneo Akaha and Frank Langdon, eds., *Japan in the Posthegemonic World* (Boulder: Lynne Rienner, 1993), pp. 205–18.

92. "Japan and Asia: Not so Fast," *Economist,* January 18, 1997, p. 37.

93. *World Journal,* January 20, 1997, p. A10.

94. Kusuma Snitwongse, "Securing ASEAN's Future: An Overview of Security in Southeast Asia," *Harvard International Review* 14, no. 2 (Spring 1994), p. 9.

95. Chittiwatanapong, "Japan's Roles in the Posthegemonic World," pp. 201–31.

96. See Jusuf Wanandi, "ASEAN's China Strategy: Towards Deeper Engagement," *Survival* 38, no. 3 (Autumn 1996), pp. 117–28; Derek da Cunha, "Southeast Asian Perceptions of China's Future Security Role in Its 'Backyard,'" in Jonathan D. Pollack and Richard H. Yang, eds., *In China's Shadow: Regional Perspectives on Chinese Foreign Policy and Military Development* (Rand, conference proceedings, 1998), pp. 115–26; Allen S. Whiting, "ASEAN Eyes China: The Security Dimension," *Asian Survey* 37, no. 4 (April 1997), pp. 299–322.

97. This is a widely shared view among Chinese officials and scholars: "Americans are smart. They do not specify whether the guideline covers Taiwan," an influential Chinese international relations specialist mused. "Japanese are less careful. They do not have to spell things out." Discussion with a scholar, May 21, 1998. Now that the Diet has passed laws authorizing the guidelines, Chinese scholars and officials are more certain that Japan will support the U.S. militarily in crises involving Taiwan and North Korea. Interviews in Beijing and Shanghai, May and June 1999.

98. For China's criticism of the U.S.–Japan alliance, see Banning Garrett and Bonnie Glaser, "Chinese Apprehensions about Revitalization of the U.S.–Japan Alliance," *Asian Survey* 37, no. 4 (April 1997), pp. 383–402.

99. Edwin O. Reischauer Center for East Asian Studies, School of Advanced International Studies, Johns Hopkins University, *The United States and Japan in 1998: Adapting to a New Era,* p. 68.

100. One may argue that Australia was really doing what Japan wanted. It is true that APEC suited Japanese needs. But it also suited most other countries' needs. Even with strong converging interests, someone still has to take the initiative.

101. While not necessarily accepting his idea, some Japanese officials admired Mahathir's courage. A foreign ministry official praised Mahathir as the leader of a small country who dares to stand up to the United States. "These things should have been said by Japanese," he said. Interview, March 24, 1994.

102. Japan contributed to the creation of ARF, starting with Nakayama's suggestion in 1991. Charles E. Morrison, "Southeast Asia and U.S.–Japan Relations," in Gerald L. Curtis, ed., *The United States, Japan, and Asia: Challenges for U.S. Policy* (New York: W.W. Norton, 1994), pp. 148–49.

103. Ralph A. Cossa, "Asian Multilateralism: Dialogue on Two-Track," *Joint Force Quarterly* 7 (Spring 1995), pp. 32–36.

104. Tanaka, "Obuchi Diplomacy," p. 8.

105. "Japan Defense Chief Wants Change," Associated Press, March 28, 1999.

106. This sentiment was reflected in an influential study on China drafted by Kojima Tomoyuki, Abe Junichi, Takahara Akio, and Takai Kiyoshi, and cosigned by sixty-seven academic and business leaders. Policy Council of the Japan Forum on International Relations, *The Policy Recommendations on the Future of China in the Context of Asian Security,* January 1995. See also Satoshi Morimoto, "Chinese Military Power in Asia: A Japanese Perspective," in Jonathan D. Pollack and Richard H. Yang, eds., *In China's Shadow: Regional Perspectives on Chinese Foreign Policy and Military Development* (Rand, conference proceedings, 1998), pp. 37–49; Michael J. Green and Benjamin L. Self, "Japan's Changing China Policy: From Commercial Liberalism to Reluctant Realism," *Survival* 38, no. 2 (Summer 1996), pp. 35–58. For opposing Japanese views, see Amako Satoshi, ed., *Chugoku wa kyoika* [Is China a threat?] (Tokyo: Keiso shobo, 1997).

107. Yoichi Funabashi, "Tokyo's Depression Diplomacy," *Foreign Affairs* 77, no. 6 (November/December 1998), p. 29.

108. For an excellent study on the negative Chinese image of Japan, see Whiting, *China Eyes Japan.* It should be noted that, unlike that of China, South Korea's relationship with Japan has been facilitated by the policies of the United States, a common ally for the two countries. See Victor D. Cha, *Alignment Despite Antagonism: The United States–Korea–Japan Security Triangle* (Stanford: Stanford University Press, 1999).

109. For elite views, see Fukui, "East Asian Perspectives on U.S.–Japan Leadership Sharing." He points out that defying the logic of relative gains, Seoul prefers a more militarily and economically powerful United States to Japan, mainly because of Korea's different historical experiences with these two nations.

110. Former U.S. Ambassador Walter F. Mondale (from August 1993 to December 1996) commented that Japan would have a stronger leadership role to play in the world if it made a full apology for its atrocities in the war. "They need as a nation to speak more clearly. . . . There are elements in Japan who do not want to confront what went on in World War II." Barry Schweid, "Ex-Ambassador Seeks Japan Apology," Associated Press, April 9, 1997.

111. For example, Sato Seizaburo, a leading Japanese international relations specialist, argues that "the Japanese who play up the possible Asian objections are only using them as an excuse to avoid getting involved in any kind of dirty, dangerous, and difficult work overseas." Okazaki and Sato, "Redefining the Role of Japanese Military Power," p. 25.

112. Immediately after the Tiananmen Incident, Tanino Sakutaro, the director general of Asian Affairs of the foreign ministry at the time, commented that "we should remember that a more stable, affluent China will benefit not just itself but all of Asia and in fact the world. We need to avoid reacting emotionally and applying only Western values to each new set of political and social phenomena as it unfolds in China. Instead we should direct our efforts to bringing China into the framework of Asian peace, development, and prosperity." Quoted in Armacost, *Friends or Rivals*, p. 139.

113. Watanabe Toshio, "Drawing Communist Asia into the Free-World Economy," *Japan Echo* 18, no. 2 (1991), p. 59. We also need to have a sectoral view in this issue. Gaimusho is more concerned about Japan's political interests, whereas MITI wants to promote Japan's business interests. The resulting policy is a compromise of these divergent interests. Zhao Quansheng, "Japan's Aid Diplomacy with China," in Bruce M. Koppel and Robert M. Orr, Jr., eds., *Japan's Foreign Aid: Power and Policy in a New Era* (Boulder: Westview Press, 1993), pp. 163–87.

114. Morimoto Satoshi, "Confronting the North Korean Threat," *Japan Echo* 26, no. 1 (February 1999), p. 25.

115. The 2000 JDA White Paper, released on July 28, again highlighted China's defense developments as a concern for Japan.

4

Financier of International Institutions

This chapter discusses Japan's relations with the World Bank, the International Monetary Fund (IMF), and the Asian Development Bank (ADB). As a latecomer, Japan has faced institutional disadvantages in the two global institutions—the World Bank and the IMF. In contrast, the ADB is a rare case in which, for the first time since the World War II, Japan became a coleader with the United States and assumed top managerial positions in an international organization. Since there are not many occasions when Japan enjoys a dominant position, this case provides an interesting glimpse of what might be expected of Japan's behavior as a dominant power.

Japan's policy toward these three international financial organizations reflects its two-track foreign policy toward the United States and Asia. Japan tries to represent Asian interests in the global institutions and sees the ADB as serving Asia better than the World Bank. At the same time, Japan gives priority to its relations with the United States when it considers policies toward both global and regional institutions. However, Japan's multilateralism is not fully explained by its bilateral and regional foreign policy. Compared to its bilateral and regional policies, Japan's policy toward international organizations has been more cooperative, a fact reflected in its generous financial support. In fact, its

Portions of this chapter, which were originally written for this book, appeared as "Japan and the Asian Development Bank," in *Pacific Affairs*, Vol. 68, No. 4, Winter 1995/96, pp. 509–528, where they were first published. I wish to thank *Pacific Affairs* for permission to use them here.

cooperation stands out against America's increasing unwillingness to finance these institutions. Japan does not compete with the institutions per se but with other member states for benefits, positions, power ranking, and agenda setting.

Power affects Japan's calculations. Japan takes into consideration its bilateral and regional relations, which involve power concerns. It also has to consider the power factor within the institutions. But institutionalist arguments provide a better explanation for Japan's cooperation with the institutions. By definition, multilateral cases are better subject matter than bilateral cases for institutionalist arguments. First, the institutions constrain what member states can and cannot do and offer unique incentives for states. Second, how strongly Japan is connected with these institutions is correlated with how cooperative it is: Japan is more cooperative in the ADB than in the World Bank and the IMF. Moreover, Japan's policies toward the three financial institutions are shaped by norms and ideas based on its learning through its interaction with the institutions over the years. Tokyo is cooperative with the institutions partly because it has adopted a broader definition of national interests due to the constant interaction of Japanese officials with the institutions.

This chapter includes three sections. The first section examines Japan's relations with the IMF and the World Bank. The second section describes and explains Japan's support for the ADB. Section 3 concludes the chapter.

Japan's Relations with the IMF and the World Bank

Passivity and Low Profile Through the 1970s

Japan joined the IMF and the International Bank for Reconstruction and Development (World Bank) on August 13, 1952, as the fifty-second member, with both symbolic and substantive goals.[1] In a symbolic sense, Japan saw its membership in the IMF and the World Bank as "the first concrete step in returning to the international economy and society." In a substantive sense, Japan hoped to benefit from the IMF in terms of enhanced external credibility, participation in discussions of international monetary issues, and ability to purchase foreign currency in case of temporary international current account imbalance. From the Bank, Japan expected to receive investment capital and technical assistance.

In addition, Japan hoped to raise its external credibility in borrowing foreign capital based on its World Bank membership.[2]

Japan adopted a passive approach and preferred economic benefits to policy influence. The country received a standby credit line of $125 million from the Fund in 1957 and a credit line of $350 million in 1961 when it suffered another major balance of payments deficit.[3] In addition, Japan was the second largest World Bank borrower as of June 30, 1967, with a large share of its postwar infrastructure built with World Bank loans.[4]

Besides economic benefits, Government of Japan (GoJ) received an initial Fund quota of $250 million, as the ninth largest holder—substantially lower than its request of $330 million—to be equal to West Germany.[5] Since World Bank voting shares were linked with Fund quotas, Japan also occupied the ninth position in the Bank. Japan did not openly lobby for a larger quota in the late 1950s, but its ranking in the Fund and the Bank moved up to seventh by the mid 1960s, reflecting its growing economic significance (Tables 4.1 and 4.2).

Japan came of age in the mid 1960s, achieving free convertibility of the yen, joining the Organization of Economic Cooperation and Development (OECD) and hosting the IMF and the World Bank annual meeting in Tokyo in 1964. Japan became more interested in raising its status. In the 1964 Fund and Bank meeting, Finance Minister Tanaka Kakuei called for "selective adjustment of quotas in order to duly reflect actual economic conditions as they exist in the countries concerned."[6]

Japan's rising economic and financial power explained its heightened interest in a bigger quota and its partial success in achieving this objective. Japan became a net lender of private capital in 1965, and its reserves reached $3.7 billion in 1968. Japan emerged as a large surplus country in 1970–71. By February 1970, Japan had become the fifth largest voter in the Fund and the Bank. GoJ made its first loan to the Bank ($100 million) in February 1970 and issued its first public bond of $30.6 million for the Bank in 1971. Its influence increased, as it could appoint its own executive directors to the IMF and the World Bank starting from 1971.

Despite its advance in the two institutions, Japan did not demand a larger voting share and maintained its low profile. Japan was not an important player in the Fund reform, which created Special Drawing Rights (SDRs) and amended the Article of Agreements in 1968. Europeans proposed all the basic reforms, although there were some "associ-

Table 4.1

IMF Quota Increase for Major Countries (percentage of total)

	United States		Japan		Germany		Britain		France	
Initial quota October 1945	36.80	1	—	—	—	—	17.40	2	7.02	4
After Japan joined April 1953	31.48	1	2.86	9	3.78	6	14.88	2	6.00	4
Special quota increase April 1960	28.89	1	3.50	8	5.52	3	13.66	2	5.52	3
4th quota increase March 1965	24.52	1	3.44	7	5.70	3	11.59	2	4.68	4
5th quota increase February 1970	23.18	1	4.25	5	5.53	3	9.69	2	5.19	4
6th quota increase March 1976	21.55	1	4.28	5	5.56	3	7.50	2	4.92	4
7th quota increase February 1978	21.51	1	4.25	5	5.52	3	7.49	2	4.91	4

(continued)

Table 4.1 (*continued*)

	United States		Japan		Germany		Britain		France	
8th quota increase March 1983	19.90	1	4.69	5	6.00	3	6.88	2	4.98	4
9th quota increase June 1990	19.62	1	6.10	2	6.10	2	5.48	4	5.48	4
11th quota increase February 1998	17.521	1	6.279	2	6.135	3	5.065	4	5.065	4

Source: Calculated from *IMF Summary Proceedings* and *IMF Annual Report*, various years. Data for the 11th quota are from the IMF Press Release, no. 97/63, December 23, 1997. The Board of Governors approved the increase on February 6, 1998 (IMF Press Release, no. 98/2).

Notes: Initial quota, 1953 and 1960 quotas are capital subscriptions, and the rest are authorized quotas to which a member may or may not decide to subscribe.

The second quinquennial review of the quotas in January 1955 did not lead to any increase. Special general review dated in 1960 was authorized in February 1959.

The authorized total quota was $7.5 billion for the initial review, $21 billion for the fourth general review, $28.9 billion for the fifth review, 39 billion Special Drawing Rights (SDR) for the sixth review, 58.6 billion SDR for the seventh review, 90 billion SDR for the eighth review, 135.2 billion SDR for the ninth review, and 212 billion SDR ($288 billion) for the eleventh review. Japan's quota for the ninth quota increase was 8,241.5 million SDR for the ninth review and 13,312.8 SDR for the eleventh review.

Table 4.2

IBRD Capital Increase for Major Countries (percentage of total)

	United States		Japan		Germany		Britain		France	
Original December 1945	43.36	1	—	—	—	—	17.75	2	6.15	4
Japan joined May 1952	35.14	1	2.77	9	3.65	6	14.39	2	5.81	4
GCI & SCI September 1959	31.36	1	3.27	8	5.15	3	12.76	2	5.15	3
SCI after 4th quota increase April 1965	28.21	1	3.43	7	5.69	3	11.55	2	4.67	4
SCI after 5th quota increase July 1970	25.94	1	4.02	5	5.37	3	10.22	2	5.03	4
SCI after 6th quota increase February 1977	23.80	1	4.15	5	5.39	3	7.96	2	4.80	4

(continued)

Table 4.2 (continued)

	United States		Japan		Germany		Britain		France	
SCI–Japan, OPEC & France April 1979	23.16	1	5.22	5	5.25	3	7.55	2	5.23	4
GCI & China SCI January 1980	21.78	1	4.94	5	4.96	3	7.31	2	4.95	4
SCI after 8th quota increase August 1984	20.91	1	5.19	2	5.17	3	4.95	4	4.95	4
SCI–Japan & Others April 1987	18.91	1	6.69	2	5.17	3	4.95	4	4.95	4
GCI* April 1988	19.23	1	6.81	2	5.25	3	5.04	4	5.04	4

Source: For the figures except General Capital Increase (GCI) of April 1988, see Ogata, "Shifting Power Relations in Multilateral Development Banks," Appendix 3. The authorized capital stock for the IBRD was $10 billion initially, increased to $21 billion at the 1959 GCI, to $27 billion in December 1970, by around $44 billion in April 1980, and by $74.8 billion to a total of $171.4 billion at the GCI of 1988.

* This is an approximation based on the existing subscribed shares of the five nations as of June 30, 1988, and the increased shares authorized by the GCI on April 27, 1988. See *World Bank Annual Report*, 1988, pp. 168–71 and *World Bank Group Summary Proceedings*, 1988, pp. 225–32.

ate or consequential amendments that are the result of proposals by other members during the negotiations." Under European pressure, the Fund adopted measures to require 85 percent of the votes for quota adjustments, which gave the European Economic Community a collective veto power.[7]

Japan's bargaining position, institutional weakness, and core interests explained its behavior. First, Japan's financial contributions were not yet large enough for it to demand larger voting shares. As Table 4.3 shows, Japan's ratio of voting share by share of contributions was 0.87 in 1971—higher than other major Western nations. In particular, Japan only had a share of 4.44 percent of the initial replenishment for the International Development Agency (IDA), the soft loan window of the World Bank group. As Table 4.4 shows, Japan increased its share to about 5.5 percent for IDA-1 and IDA-2 (1965–71), but still ranked sixth among members. In addition, Europe had become the largest market for long-term external borrowings since 1966. In 1968, the World Bank borrowed more from Germany than from the United States. In contrast, Japan made its first loan to the Bank only in February 1970.[8]

Second, Japan was institutionally disadvantaged as a latecomer. The creation of the two institutions reflected the interests and capabilities of the United States. As the key designer of the Bretton Woods institutions, Washington helped define the mission of the Bank and the Fund as well as their rules and operating procedures. The two institutions were based in Washington, used English as their working language, and had a disproportionate share of Americans among senior staff.

Third, Japan was more interested in economic gains than policy influence. Table 4.5 shows that Japan's share of cumulative procurements by 1971 exceeded its share of contributions, with a ratio of 1.29. Only West Germany (1.36) did better than Japan among the five largest donors in the Bank.

The Bretton Woods system collapsed in the 1970s. But Japan made greater financial contributions to the Fund and the Bank. In particular, Japan's share of IDA contributions increased sharply to 11.00 percent for IDA-4 (1975–77) and 10.30 percent for IDA-5 (1978–80) (Table 4.4). Japan also contributed to Fund facilities. Its greater contribution reflected its rising economic and financial power. Japan became one of the three major economic powers in the world by the 1970s, along with Germany and the United States. And the nation accumulated considerable surplus capital by the late 1970s.

Table 4.3

Voting Powers Versus Contributions in the IBRD of Key Members

Members	By Mid 1966			By Mid 1971			By Mid 1981		
	Voting Share (A)	Contrib. Share (B)	A/B	Voting Share (A)	Contrib. Share (B)	A/B	Voting Share (A)	Contrib. Share (B)	A/B
United States	25.50	31.65	0.81	23.81	32.34	0.74	20.84	32.71	0.64
Japan	3.19	3.80	0.84	3.92	4.51	0.87	5.04	5.34	0.94
Germany	5.22	6.33	0.82	5.19	7.02	0.74	5.06	7.61	0.66
Britain	10.50	12.18	0.86	9.81	11.91	0.82	7.44	11.13	0.67
France	4.30	5.49	0.78	4.02	5.87	0.68	5.05	6.25	0.81
Total ($million)	4,004.6			5,402.1			10,235.5		

	By Mid 1991			By Mid 1999		
	Voting share (A)	Contrib. share (B)	A/B	Voting share (A)	Contrib. share (B)	A/B
Members						
United States	17.32	25.39	0.68	16.53	23.62	0.70
Japan	7.89	18.85	0.42	7.93	20.13	0.39
Germany	6.09	11.07	0.55	4.53	10.73	0.42
Britain	5.84	7.85	0.74	4.34	7.06	0.61
France	5.84	6.49	0.90	4.34	6.65	0.65
Total ($million)	78,253.4			107,656.7		

Source: Calculated from *World Bank Annual Report*, 1967–99.
Note: Contributions here include paid-in portions of subscriptions and donations to the IDA and other special funds.

Table 4.4

IDA Replenishments for Major Countries (percentage of total)

	United States		Japan		Germany		Britain		France	
Initial 1961–64	42.34	1	4.44	6	7.00	3	17.33	2	7.00	3
IDA-1 1965–68	41.89	1	5.54	6	9.75	3	12.97	2	8.31	4
IDA-2 1969–71	40.00	1	5.54	6	9.75	3	12.96	2	8.10	4
IDA-3 1972–74	39.33	1	5.90	6	9.59	3	12.74	2	6.15	4
IDA-4 1975–77	33.32	1	11.00	4	11.43	2	11.10	3	5.63	6
IDA-5 1978–80	31.22	1	10.30	4	10.91	2	10.60	3	5.38	6
IDA-6 1981–83	27.00	1	14.65	2	12.50	3	10.10	4	5.38	5
IDA-7 1986–87	25.00	1	18.70	2	11.50	3	6.70	4	6.60	5

IDA-8 1988–90	23.19	1	20.98	2	11.07	3	6.34	5	6.77	4
IDA-9 1991–93	21.61	1	20.75	2	11.49	3	6.70	5	7.60	4
IDA-10 1994–96	22.19	1	21.28	2	11.70	3	6.54	5	7.77	4
IDA-11 1997–99	20.86	1	18.70	2	11.00	3	6.15	5	7.02	4
IDA-12 2000–02	20.86	1	18.70	2	11.00	3	7.30	4	7.30	4

Source: Ogata, "Shifting Power Relations in Multilateral Development Banks," Appendix 1. The figures for IDA-9 are calculated from *World Bank Annual Report 1990*, p. 40; IDA-10 from *World Bank Annual Report 1993*, p. 58; IDA-11 from *World Bank Annual Report 1996*, p. 18; IDA-12 from *World Bank Annual Report 1999*, p. 20.

Table 4.5

Procurements Versus Contributions in the World Bank of Key Members

| | By Mid 1971 | | | By Mid 1980 | | | By Mid 1986 | | |
| | Procure. % | Contrib. % | A/B | Procure. % | Contrib. % | A/B | Procure. % | Contrib. % | A/B |
	(A)	(B)		(A)	(B)		(A)	(B)	
Members									
United States	24.0	32.3	0.73	17.3	31.3	0.55	13.0	28.8	0.45
Japan	5.8	4.5	1.29	11.8	9.2	1.28	10.3	16.1	0.64
Germany	9.5	7.0	1.36	10.9	10.8	1.01	7.9	10.7	0.74
Britain	11.7	11.9	0.98	8.4	11.6	0.72	6.3	8.7	0.72
France	4.1	5.9	0.69	5.9	6.0	0.98	5.0	5.2	0.96
Local procurements	26.5			22.6			35.1		
Total ($ billion)	13.3	5.4		43.7	23.5		102.0	46.4	

Members	By Mid 1991			By Mid 1999		
	Procure. % (A)	Contrib. % (B)	A/B	Procure. % (A)	Contrib. % (B)	A/B
United States	11.1	25.4	0.44	8.2	23.6	0.35
Japan	8.7	18.9	0.46	5.8	20.1	0.29
Germany	6.8	11.1	0.61	5.1	10.7	0.48
Britain	5.7	7.9	0.72	4.4	7.0	0.63
France	4.6	6.5	0.71	4.0	6.8	0.60
Local procurements	36.0			41.9		
Total ($ billion)	181.4	78.3		334.7	107.7	

Source: World Bank Annual Report, various years.

However, Japan was still largely passive despite its growing economic power. Its passivity stood out when the rise of oil-producing states, European consolidation, and increased developing country solidarity eroded the U.S. monopoly on power, creating a more balanced bargaining situation.[9] Over the debate with Americans over settlement system and adjustment mechanism, as recalled by Robert Solomon, a senior participant in the negotiations, Europeans were only "supported in a low key by those from Japan."[10] Contemporary Japanese media shared this assessment.[11] In addition, while Japan's voting power in the Bank increased slightly, from 4.02 percent in July 1970 to 4.94 percent in January 1981, its quota in the Fund remained around 4.25 percent in the 1970s.

Japan had to be cautious in the complex bargaining situation, first of all, to maintain its crucial ties with the United States for military protection and market access, and with the OPEC members and less developed countries (LDCs) for resources and markets. After all, Japan's increasing surplus power was also the reason for the heavy criticism it received at the 1977 annual meeting, called "concentrated fire" in the Japanese media.[12] Matsugawa Michiya, deputy finance minister, who was present, noted that Japan was like a "sacrificial lamb." This was the first time Japan was so severely criticized.[13] Such criticism highlighted the fact that Japan was largely on its own in the 1970s.

A second explanation for Japan's behavior is that the country remained institutionally disadvantaged in the Fund and the Bank. Japan had little impact on policy making. In contrast, Washington possessed institutional advantages that compensated for its declining power. Among other advantages, as recognized by the U.S. Treasury Department, the fact that the Bank is located in Washington made it easier for the U.S. government to deal directly with the Bank and with other members.[14] More important, the Bank adopted top-down decision-making under Bank president Robert McNamara (1968–81). Japan appointed an executive director, but its influence was limited because the Bank was "very much a management-run institution" and the approval by the directors of the Bank's management decisions was "more or less a formality."[15]

Another reason was that Japan remained focused on economic earning and was simply not that interested in sharing leadership responsibilities that entail high economic costs.[16] Japan actually received its money's worth in this period, scoring 0.94 in the ratio of its voting share by its share of financial contributions, compared to 0.81 for France, 0.67 for Britain, 0.66 for Germany, and 0.64 for the United States (Table

4.3). In addition, Japan continued to gain economically from the World Bank. As Table 4.5 indicates, the ratio of Japan's share of procurements to its share of financial contributions was 1.28 by 1980, larger than the ratios for the other four major financial powers.

One-Dimensional Power in the 1980s

Japan was a one-dimensional power in the 1980s in that it pursued greater voting shares while showing little interest in policy orientation or commercial interests.

Seeking Higher Status

Japan's main goal in the 1980s was to raise its status by increasing its voting shares. In the case of the World Bank, Tokyo adopted a strategy of "harmonization," linking its IDA contributions with its World Bank voting power. During the negotiation for IDA-6 for 1981–83, Japanese suggested to McNamara that Japan's ranking be raised as a price for more contribution. At the 1982 Bank–Fund annual meeting, Foreign Minister Watanabe Michio stated that Japan's position in the Bank should reflect its economic strength. While aiming at a number three position in the early 1980s, Japan started lobbying for number two after 1983 when Britain was no longer willing to increase its subscriptions.[17] Japan became more assertive after the mid 1980s. In 1986 Japan made known its wish for a share of 8 percent from General Capital Increase (GCI). One Ministry of Finance (MOF) official was quoted as saying that, "We want more voice in the IBRD. It's as simple as that." Executive Director Yamaguchi Kenji complained that the United States "wants a big voice, but pays less."[18]

Tokyo also made similar moves in the Fund. In particular, GoJ made a stronger demand for a larger quota in the late 1980s, especially before the Ninth General Review. Alternate Governor Sumita Satoshi pointed out in 1987 that the Fund should enhance its financial resources and Japan was willing to "contribute to the forthcoming Ninth Quota increase commensurate with its economic abilities."[19] Governor Hashimoto Ryutaro complained in 1989 that, "I cannot believe that Japan's relative position within the Fund—4.7 percent—accurately reflects the realities of the Japanese economy."[20]

Japan's increasing assertiveness in acquiring larger voting shares was based on its financial clout. Japan's share of paid-in contributions to the Bank increased rapidly, especially after 1986. As discussed in Chapter 2, the Japanese government announced three recycling programs between 1986 and 1989, totaling $65 billion of ODA, other official flows, and private flows, which were designed to encourage Japanese surpluses to flow to developing nations. Half of these $65 billion were to be channeled through multilateral financial institutions such as the World Bank, the IMF, and the ADB.[21] While using this infusion of funds for the IMF, the World Bank, and other multilateral development banks (MDBs) as its contributions to the international community, Japan's increasing financial contributions to the international financial institutions also enhanced its prestige in these institutions.

By mid 1991 Japan had contributed $703.5 million in paid-in subscriptions for the World Bank and $14,049.2 million in subscriptions and contributions for the IDA. In particular, Japan achieved influence through its IDA contributions. In this period, paid-in capital to the World Bank was only a small portion of overall financial contributions to the Bank: $68.9 billion for the IDA versus $9.4 billion paid-in subscriptions for the World Bank as of June 30, 1991. Japan committed 20.4 percent of the total IDA subscriptions and contributions by mid 1991, compared to 26.3 percent from the United States. The World Bank also received about one-fifth of its borrowings from the Tokyo market in the 1980s. In addition, Japan was the largest source of cofinancing for the bank through OECF and JExIm. The two Japanese agencies provided $1,405 million in 1991 out of a total of $7,057 million in cofinancing from official bilateral or other multilateral institutions.[22]

Japan was able and willing to increase its voting share, while the United States became reluctant to accept capital increases. During the negotiations for IDA-8, when the United States indicated that other nations had to make up for the $500 million gap between the $11.5 billion proposed by the United States and the $12 billion targeted by the Bank, Japan offered to make an additional contribution of $350 million on top of its $2,150 million allocation on the condition that its World Bank share be increased.[23]

Japan also made financial contributions to the Fund. After all, its recycling programs also included the IMF as a conduit. In the $10 billion recycling program announced in the fall of 1986, Japan committed $3.6 billion in government loans to the IMF over four years. Japan was the largest contributor to the original Enhanced Structural Adjustment Facility (ESAF) created in 1987 and its enlargement in 1994. The ESAF provides concessional loans to low-income countries to facilitate structural reforms necessary for sustainable growth and external payments viability. Japan committed 447 million of SDRs in grant (18.3 percent of the total) and 2,200 million SDRs in loans (42.8 percent) to the ESAF prior to enlargement.[24]

Japan achieved a number two position in the World Bank in 1984, a share of 5.19 percent, slightly larger than Germany's 5.17 percent. Its share increased to 6.81 percent after the 1988 GCI. As Japan paid its total increased subscription up front and the United States paid its share incrementally (completing payment in 1996), Japan's share went over 9 percent in 1989, while the U.S. share decreased to about 16 percent. Tokyo's status in the Fund rose more slowly than in the Bank. The Eighth Review of 1983 allowed an almost 70 percent increase for Japan's quota, only after 207.89 percent for Saudi Arabia. But Japan remained number five throughout the 1980s—less than 5 percent of quota as compared to around 20 percent for the United States. After difficult negotiations over the Ninth Quota review—which went well beyond the original closing date of March 1988 and were concluded only in June 1990—Japan increased the share to 6.10 percent, a number two position shared with West Germany, after the United States (19.62 percent). Japan had achieved this position in the World Bank six years earlier.

Japan's success in raising its ranking shows that adjustment of power in the World Bank and the IMF is possible, difficult, and slow, as it is. The two institutions have built-in mechanisms—periodic quota reviews and capital increases—that allow adjustment and prevent chaotic power struggle, a useful adaptability function that facilitates their existence. This arrangement allows slow but predictable adjustment of power and prestige.

While Japan gained a desirable rank-ordering, its gains were still limited if measured by its relative shares. As Tables 4.1 and 4.2 show, the distance between Japan's share and that of the United States was much larger than the gross national product (GNP) gap, while the gap between Japan's share and those of Germany, Britain, and France was much smaller than the gap between them in terms of GNP. In fact, Japan shared the same spot with Germany in the IMF. In addition, Japan contributed more for less formal power, its share of the total contributions far exceeding its voting share in the World Bank, with a ratio of 0.42 by 1991, compared to 0.68 for the United States and 0.55 for Germany (Table 4.3). Since the figures are cumulative, Japan's ratio in 1981–91 was even lower.

Japan's slow progress in increasing voting weight was due to the power structure within the institutions. As Sadako Ogata observed, burden sharing does not translate automatically into power sharing.[25] Japan's increase in voting shares means a decrease in others' shares. To start with, Tokyo's desire to increase voting shares through increased contributions conflicted with Washington's wish of holding on to its control of the institutions while decreasing its real-term contributions.[26] Japan generally finds it more difficult to assert itself when the United States takes a high-profile and public position. Unlike in the 1970s, Japan was less concerned in the 1980s about isolation in the Fund–Bank, thanks to increasing support from LDCs, which needed its economic assistance.[27] In the World Bank negotiation for Special Capital Increase (SCI) in the early 1980s, the LDCs supported Japan's request for a larger voting share. However, Germany, Britain, and France adopted the strategy of encouraging Japan to increase its contribution without increasing its share, arguing that the Bank's selective capital increase did not have to follow the IMF quota increase. Europeans had good reasons to be concerned: Japan could raise its ranking only at their expense. In the end, the United States gave some of its own shares to Japan and other nations on the condition that it maintain its veto power.[28]

Japan had more difficulties increasing its voting share in the Fund than in the Bank because advanced nations pay more attention to the Fund, which affects macroeconomic policies, while the Bank is involved in development issues. Britain and France were reluctant to allow Japan to surpass them in voting shares. The United States was unenthusiastic about changes initially but accommodated Japan's wish for a larger quota in exchange for support for Treasury Secretary Nicholas Brady's debt initiative.[29] The United States agreed to adjust the voting power distribution only after a new rule was adopted that lowered veto power from 20 percent to 15 percent, thus allowing it to maintain its control.

Limited Policy Influence

My discussion above leads to an important question: What did Japan need greater voting powers for, other than prestige? Japan's behavior in the 1980s gave little indication of what its ultimate objectives were. Ogata observed that "aside from concentrating efforts on the efficient management of the banks, it is not certain what influence it [Japan] will exert on the substantive policy of the operations of the Bank."[30] It is puzzling that Japan sought voting shares corresponding to its financial contributions but failed to achieve policy influence corresponding to its voting power. In fact, Japan was not particularly concerned about policy influence until 1988, when Finance Minister Miyazawa Kiichi introduced a policy initiative at the IMF–Bank annual meeting calling for debt reduction for middle income debtor countries.[31] Washington did not approve the Miyazawa plan, although part of it was incorporated in the Brady initiative several months later.[32]

Japan's limited influence in the Fund–Bank could be explained by institutional constraints. Voting share does not translate neatly into voting power. The weighted voting system adopted by the World Bank and the IMF means that to achieve a desired policy outcome a country needs to be in a winning coalition. An increase in one member's weighted vote by several percentage points "will not drastically affect the decisionmaking patterns of an international organization, where formal votes may be relatively rare," as Stephen Zamora pointed out .[33] This is especially the case for Japan, which does not have veto power on its own like the United States or find itself in a permanent voting coalition like Europeans. It is thus harder to translate financial power into policy influence than voting shares. "Expert knowledge in the operations, leadership posts in the secretariat, relevant policy proposals, the will to impose—these are factors that altogether contribute to building a country's power base in multilateral organizations," Ogata observes. "It is not only the financial resources that bring influence to the multilateral development banks."[34] All these factors favor the United States, which as the founder enjoys entrenched institutional advantages. Besides its voting power and control of the presidency, the United States also received influence through the headquarters of the Bank in Washington, the strength of the U.S. Executive Director's office, English as the working language, and more than a quarter of the senior professional staff as Americans.[35] An additional reason is that the Fund and the Bank have a clear print of American decision-making style, a different and difficult institutional environment for Japanese to exercise policy influence.[36]

Neglecting Commercial Interests

What is striking about Japan's relations with the Fund–Bank in this period was not only what it did but also what it did not do. While increasing contributions to the Bank, Japanese received fewer tangible commercial gains. Table 4.5 shows that the ratio of Japan's share of the Bank's total procurements to its share of the bank's total financial contributions decreased from 1.28 in 1980 to 0.64 in 1986 and 0.46 in 1991.[37] Japan's ratio was also low compared to other major developed nations. Given Japan's reputation as "an economic animal," this is puzzling.

Institutional constraints limited Japan's policy influence in the World Bank and the IMF, but we should also recognize Tokyo's own preference. Japan's institutional disadvantages do not explain why Japan did not try to be more efficient in using its financial resources, using less contribution for the same result in voting share increase and procurements. Tables 4.3 and 4.5 display Japan's increasing "inefficiency" in converting its contributions into voting shares and procurements. Japan's one-dimensional strategy reflected, to a large extent, its own choice for seeking a higher status but not policy influence and tangible commercial interests.

This choice was, first of all, a prominent prong of Japan's overall approach to accommodate the United States, as discussed in Chapter 2. This general policy constrained where and how far Japan wanted to confront the United States in the two global institutions. In fact, Japan used the World Bank and the IMF as conduits for its recycling plans, which were designed to demonstrate international contributions in the face of international criticism of huge trade and current account surpluses. It follows then that Japanese were not that interested in using the two institutions for achieving immediate policy objectives.

Second, given such a policy mandate favorable for cooperative policy, Japanese officials, who were interested in maintaining the stability of the international monetary system and promoting the development of Third World countries, were left to take charge of Tokyo's policy toward the Fund and the Bank. These people were concerned that Japan's cooperation would be compromised by tangible Japanese gains. In fact, there was greater emphasis on multilateral aid in the decade precisely because Japan could avoid foreign criticism of its use of bilateral aid as a policy tool to advance its self-interests.[38]

Attempt at Policy and Intellectual Influence in the 1990s

Japan remained accommodating toward the World Bank and the IMF in financial contributions in the 1990s. Japan had a share of 18.70 percent for IDA-11 (1997–99) and IDA-12 (2000–02), a decrease from 21.28

percent for IDA-10, but still a close second to the United States (20.86 percent) (Table 4.4).[39] Table 4.3 shows that Japan's share of cumulative financial contributions to the World Bank increased from 18.85 percent by mid 1991 to 20.13 percent by mid 1999, compared with 23.62 percent for the United States and 10.73 percent for Germany.

Japan's voting share remained low at 7.9 percent in mid 1999, compared to 16.5 percent for the United States. Japan's ratio of voting share to share of cumulative financial contributions was merely 0.39 by mid 1999, compared with 0.70 for the United States and 0.42 for Germany. In addition, Japan's ratio of share of procurements to share of financial contributions was 0.29 by mid 1999, the lowest among the five leading nations in the Bank (Table 4.5).

GoJ also continues to support the IMF. As of April 30, 1998, Japan committed 200 million of SDRs in grants (18.6 percent of the total) and 2,150 million SDRs in loans (47.6 percent) to the ESAF after the facility's enlargement in 1994.[40] It also committed financial resources to the Fund when extra money was needed to stabilize the international monetary system. In the new arrangements to borrow 34 billion SDRs decided in April 1997, Japan and Germany were the second largest contributors, with 3,557 million SDRs, next only to the U.S. share of 6,712 million SDRs.[41]

Japan paid greater attention to policy influence and intellectual contributions in the early 1990s. Tokyo became more interested in administrative and personnel issues in the World Bank.[42] More significant, GoJ began articulating a critique of the World Bank's approach to reform in developing nations and to point to a Japanese alternative. Shiratori Masaki, Japan's executive director to the World Bank in the late 1980s, urged the bank to study the Japanese and Asian development experience. The first public salvo by the Japanese aid community to voice their views abroad was the "Issues Relating to the World Bank's Approach to Structural Adjustment" (OECF Occasional Paper No. 1). The October 1991 report challenged the World Bank's universal, efficiency-oriented neoclassical approach to development and advocated positive government involvement in investment and industrial development, subsidized interest rates, and cautious privatization. At the Fund–Bank annual meeting in the same month, Mieno Yasushi, then governor of the Bank of Japan, called upon the World Bank and the IMF to conduct "a wide-ranging study" of Asian development experience.

Japan's efforts at greater policy input were related to its rising status in the institutions. As the number two power, Japan felt greater expectations of its own influence, especially after criticism of its checkbook diplomacy. More important, by the late 1980s differences between Japan and the United States in development philosophy came to the fore, prompted by the Reagan administration's commitment to the market mechanism, the Latin American debt crisis, and East Asia's stunning economic success. Japanese officials came to realize that silent support for the U.S. policy agenda did not serve their interests. GoJ did not criticize the World Bank neoclassical orthodoxy in the 1980s because they understood it poorly. In fact, Japan became the leading source of financial support for structural adjustment loans, the controversial conditional lending that was the chief mechanism for the World Bank to transfer its market-driven reform model to developing countries. But once they started studying the World Bank orthodoxy, they increasingly realized what they saw as serious flaws in the thinking and practice of the "Anglo-Saxon" development philosophy: over-reliance on as-yet-undeveloped markets to shape Third World economies. Scholars and officials began articulating a Japanese development model, which recognizes positive government intervention and emphasizes a long-term approach tailored to stages of development.[43]

Responding to Japanese concerns, World Bank chief economist Lawrence Summers launched a study of the East Asian development experience conducted by World Bank scholars with financing from the Japanese government. The study resulted in the publication of *The East Asia Miracle* in 1993, which largely attributed the region's stellar economic performance to compliance with the neoclassical orthodoxy. The report did acknowledge that directed credit worked in Japan and South Korea and that government intervention in export promotion might work under certain conditions but asserted that industrial policy did not work in East Asia. Although Japan did not succeed in changing the Bank's view on development, it was significant that Japan openly advocated its own development views and was taken seriously by the Bank.[44]

Japan's advocacy for an Asian development model suffered a major setback in 1997 when the miracle economies of Asia sank into a major economic crisis. Japan itself experienced seven years of economic stagnation before the government announced in June 1998 that Japan had entered economic recession—the first time since 1975. As discussed in the previous two chapters, Japan's performance in the crisis lowered its standing in the region and the world.

In the IMF and the World Bank, the Asian crisis offered Japan an opportunity to play a leading role in helping a region in its backyard.

After all, Japan had forged close economic ties with the region. It would suffer the most if its Asian neighbors failed. Tokyo initially tried. It took the lead in putting together the $17 billion Thailand rescue package in August 1997. In potentially its most significant initiative in the international monetary system, in August 1997 Japan proposed creating an Asian Monetary Fund (AMF) and secured pledges of $100 billion from itself and some key Asian nations, which would have independent funds and a permanent secretariat—and noticeably, without U.S. membership. However, the AMF did not materialize because Americans did not want to weaken the IMF and its strict conditionality and wanted to maintain their leadership position in the region (the original AMF proposal did not include the United States). After this setback, Japan retreated and resumed its supporter role for the West.

The IMF played the most prominent role in bailing out failing Asian economies, organizing three major packages for Thailand, Indonesia, and South Korea, totaling over $120 billion.[45] Behind the IMF, the United States took the leadership role, starting with the Indonesian package after refusing to participate directly in the Thailand package. In collaboration with the IMF, the World Bank also played a high-profile role in assisting Asia in adjusting its lending programs and advisory services. Japan was on the defensive as the IMF became more critical of Japan, rightly arguing that the country's failure to revive its own economy was hindering revival in Asia as a whole.

However, Japan remains the second most powerful player in the IMF and the World Bank, and its support is crucial for any important decisions. To illustrate, Japan's approval was crucial for the United States to gather the necessary support for suspension of multilateral lending to India and Pakistan after the South Asian rivals conducted nuclear tests in 1998. The World Bank suspended six Indian loan applications by June 2, 1998, totaling more than $1 billion, after the United States, Japan, and Canada had urged the bank to take no action on them.[46]

Furthermore, the IMF approach came under attack from Asians, the U.S. Congress, and some prominent economists in the West, charging that the IMF had failed to understand the cause of the crisis and provided ineffective policy prescriptions. Privately, Japanese believe it is too early to blame the Asian development model for the region's current problems and the jury is still out about whether the Asian model has failed.[47] Japanese finance minister Miyazawa Kiichi has voiced his criticism of the outdated IMF approach to financial crisis caused by a global-

ized capital market.[48] U.S. Treasury secretary Lawrence Summers proposed in December 1999 to reduce the IMF's long-term lending program
and focus instead on short-term assistance when financial crises take place.
Miyazawa opposed the idea and argued that the IMF should continue long-
term lending to deal with balance-of-payments adjustment.[49]

Ironically, while the Japanese face greater budget constraints, they
appear to be more interested in receiving status and influence in the
World Bank and the IMF that are consistent with their financial contributions. In a recent example, Tokyo challenged the unwritten IMF practice to have Europeans taking the top job and fielded its own candidate,
former vice finance minister Sakakibara Eisuke, when Michel
Camdessus announced his decision to resign in November 1999. Tokyo
formally nominated Sakakibara on February 23, 2000. Facing a controversial German candidate, Caio Koch-Weser of Germany (43 percent),
and another candidate, American Stanley Fischer (17 percent), who was
supported by Africans, Sakakibara received 9 percent of the votes in an
unofficial poll on March 2, 2000.[50] The outcome was not surprising, as
Japan stood little chance because Sakakibara received little support even
among Asians, but Tokyo was sending a message to the international
financial community and positioning itself for the next round.

Japan's Relations with the ADB

Establishing Leadership in 1962–72

Japan played a crucial role in creating the ADB in 1966. Its objective
was to create a regional institution to enhance its international prestige
and serve its economic interests at acceptable political and financial
costs, concerned that its interests in Asia were not well served by the
World Bank. Japan wanted to create "its own" development bank. The
idea for a regional development bank first emerged among a group of
influential Japanese in 1962. The group envisioned an Asian bank institutionally advantageous to Japan. To reduce Japan's financial and political costs, they adopted a strategy to work behind the scenes to avoid
suspicion of the developing countries and to invite the United States and
other developed nations to join. This "private" plan was later endorsed
by the government and became Japan's official policy. Watanabe Takeshi,
the chair of the Ohashi group, played a crucial role in the creation of the
ADB and was elected the first ADB president.[51]

Japan's strategy was largely successful. The Economic Commission for Asia and the Far East of the UN (ECAFE) made the first public move and invited Japan to participate in creating a regional bank. Japan's private plan entered the ECAFE project in a discreet fashion at the preparatory stage of an expert meeting held in 1964.[52] The major points in the Ohashi plan were later adopted in the Bank Charter. Washington was initially cool to the idea of an Asian bank but changed its mind in mid 1965 because of its own strategic interests. The Johnson administration now saw the ADB as part of a strategy for Vietnam.[53] Europeans were persuaded to join because of a moral obligation to assist LDCs and commercial opportunities offered by the bank. The LDCs welcomed the bank because it would provide additional capital and they saw it as a symbol of Asian unity.[54] This common interest provided a solid basis for the ADB, making the founding of the bank a success for everyone involved, especially Japan. Japan was awarded the presidency of the bank. Most significantly, Japan received as large a voting share as the United States, the only country that accomplished this feat in any international economic institution. Japan accomplished all this without much suspicion from other Asian nations. Japan also limited its financial burden by successfully soliciting significant contributions from the United States and other developed nations.

Despite common interests in creating a regional development bank, the participants were divided two ways: one between the donors and borrowers, and the other between the regional and nonregional members. The LDCs desired an "Asian" bank controlled by Asians, while the developed countries wanted to avoid a "borrowers' club." Japan was well positioned as the only Asian creditor nation (as ECAFE members, Australia and New Zealand are also regional members). As the United States and Europe did not wish to appear too powerful in an "Asian" bank, they wanted Japan to play a prominent role to safeguard the interests of the donors.[55]

Japan did not achieve all its objectives, failing in particular in its highly publicized bid for the headquarters. The head office site was such a high priority that the MOF was ready to give up the presidency for it.[56] However, the headquarters was awarded to Manila over Tokyo by a 9–8 vote in the third round of voting.[57] Japan's loss highlighted its limited economic leverage in this stage. Although a well-organized campaign and some "tricks" might have helped,[58] the crucial reason for Manila's success was that the Philippines treated its bid as a political issue and conducted high-level bargaining. Manila's campaign was greatly facilitated by a general feeling among the Asian LDCs that the ADB should be located in a developing nation. Although not involved in the secret voting, which was restricted to regional members, the United States helped Manila's cause by making known its preference for a Japanese president and a Manila location.[59]

In the period 1966–72, which overlapped with Watanabe's tenure as president, the ADB was transformed from a design on paper to a concrete multilateral bank. Japan had three goals: to build a reputable international institution, to establish its leadership, and to promote its economic and commercial interests.

The first objective reflected Japan's anxiety about making the first international institution financed and headed by Japanese a success. To accomplish this goal, Japan made generous contributions to assure a solid financial basis for the bank. Japan provided $173.7 million in paid-in subscriptions to Ordinary Capital Resources (OCR) and $122.6 million to special funds by the end of 1972, which amounted to 30 percent of the total for the bank, compared to 11.3 percent from the United States and 14.2 percent from Europe (Table 4.6). In addition, the bank borrowed $77 million in bonds and loans from Japan's budding capital market, which accounted for 39.2 percent of the total in 1966–72, larger than those of Europe (35.3 percent) and the United States (25.5 percent).[60] The bank launched the first issue of a foreign bond in Tokyo in 1970, supported by Japanese officials because "Mr. Watanabe is the president."[61] In addition to financing, Japan made sure that the bank management under a Japanese president enjoyed autonomy and that no members constrained bank operations. Japan succeeded in defining what matters could be subject to the review of the member states.[62] Japan also tried to separate economics from politics to avoid sensitive political issues, which would involve interference from member states and prevent the management from exercising effective control over bank operations.

The strategies mentioned above were designed also to help realize Japan's second objective: assuring its leadership role in the ADB. In this period, Japan's leadership in the bank became institutionalized. First, an informal practice was established for electing Japanese presidents—both a symbol of and a means for maintaining Japan's influence in the bank. Japan's grip on the presidency was reinforced by the rule that a new president should be elected in case of incapacity or resignation of the president. Second, Japan's leadership was placed on a firm

Table 4.6

Voting Powers Versus Contributions in the ADB of Key Members

	By end of 1972			By end of 1981			By End of 1986		
	Voting Share (A)	Contrib. Share (B)	A/B	Voting Share (A)	Contrib. Share (B)	A/B	Voting Share (A)	Contrib. Share (B)	A/B
Members									
Japan	20.2	30.4	0.66	13.6	35.5	0.38	12.5	41.9	0.30
United States	8.4	11.3	0.74	13.2	19.3	0.68	12.4	16.0	0.78
Europe	15.0	14.2	1.06	17.3	20.9	0.83	17.6	21.5	0.82
Other DCs	14.7	16.0	0.92	13.5	12.9	1.05	12.4	10.7	1.16
LDCs	41.7	28.1	1.48	42.4	11.4	3.72	45.1	10.0	4.51
Total ($ million)		974.2			5,359.9			9,864.4	

	By End of 1991			By End of 1998		
	Voting Share (A)	Contrib. Share (B)	A/B	Voting Share (A)	Contrib. Share (B)	A/B
Members						
Japan	12.3	44.5	0.27	13.2	48.3	0.27
United States	12.3	13.0	0.74	13.2	13.3	0.99
Europe	18.2	24.5	0.95	16.9	22.6	0.75
Other DCs	12.2	10.7	1.14	11.4	9.5	1.20
LDCs	45.0	7.2	6.25	45.3	6.3	7.19
Total ($ million)		16,154.2			23,218.0	

Source: Calculated from *ADB Annual Report*, various years.

Note: Contributions here include paid-in portions of subscriptions for Ordinary Capital and donations to the Asian Development Fund and other special funds. Other developed nations include Australia, Canada, and New Zealand. LDCs include Hong Kong, South Korea, Singapore, and Taiwan, which have graduated from being aid recipients.

transgovernmental basis as institutional ties developed between MOF and certain "reserved posts" within the bank. Six of the seven ADB presidents to date have been MOF officials. Chino Tadao, the current president, is also from MOF. This close linkage explains Japan's keen interest in the sound financial basis for the bank, a traditional concern for the conservative MOF. MOF also provided officers for a number of other key positions, notably the Administration Department.[63]

Japan's success in establishing its leadership in the bank could be explained by both its financial leverage and initial institutional advantages. Tokyo guaranteed its control of the presidency, because, to others, "it seemed preferable to have a Japanese president in order to induce more financial support from Japan."[64] Through the president and the director of the Administration Department, Japan influenced the shaping of the organization and procedures of the bank.

Japan's institutional advantages and financial dominance contributed to the realization of its third goal. Although willing to provide necessary funds for the bank, MOF was interested in economic returns to compensate Japan's costs. There was a high correlation between the ADB lending and Japanese foreign aid. In contrast, there was a negative correlation between the ADB loans and U.S. development assistance.[65] In sectoral distribution of loans, Japan advocated a focus on increasing agricultural production, as it was concerned about food security. Japan later focused on infrastructure and energy. In addition, Japan received 41.67 percent of the total procurements of goods in 1967–76, compared to 6.27 percent for the United States and 21.33 percent for the LDCs (Table 4.7). Japan accomplished all this by tying its special contributions to sectors and geographical areas it preferred and to the procurement of goods and services from Japanese firms, a practice common among donor nations, though Japan was sharply criticized for it.

Japan's success in employing its financial leverage to realize its objectives in this stage was made possible, to a large extent, by a convergence of interests, particularly with the United States. In addition, the ADB was not a simple story of Japan controlling the bank through the officials it had "planted" in these strategic locations. Rather, it was a story of Japan trying to shape the new institution in its image and itself being reshaped in the process. Its close ties with the bank served as a two-way track. The ADB was a project envisioned by a core group of Japanese, most associated with MOF, who were seeking a constructive

Table 4.7

Procurements and Consultancy Services in the ADB of Select Members

	1967–1976		1977–1986		1987–1996		1997–1998	
	(1) (%)	(2) (%)	(1) (%)	(2) (%)	(1) (%)	(2) (%)	(1) (%)	(2) (%)
Developed	78.77	93.63	51.69	79.79	35.22	63.98	19.52	68.12
Japan	41.67	11.44	23.65	13.41	9.51	5.78	5.46	3.89
United States	6.27	31.13	7.66	19.55	6.46	10.54	6.53	15.01
Germany	8.87	14.00	4.89	3.49	4.98	5.86	2.59	5.23
France	3.11	4.25	1.80	2.85	1.98	4.24	1.39	8.79
Britain	4.57	3.38	3.97	14.31	1.70	11.35	1.60	7.07
Developing*	21.23	6.37	48.31	20.21	64.78	36.02	80.48**	31.88
Indonesia	0.00	0.00	5.93	7.09	12.60	19.15	9.19	8.42
India	2.00	2.84	2.52	3.22	7.33	1.51	7.52	0.12
Pakistan	0.01	0.00	1.95	0.18	7.32	4.26	3.00	2.18
South Korea	8.93	1.46	13.32	3.40	6.53	1.16	19.28	0.00
Total ($ million)*	1,412.65	93.27	7,454.33	482.83	27,069.04	1,393.46	11,391.01	348.26

Source: Based on *ADB Annual Report 1998*, p. 278. The table includes both ordinary capital and ADF.
Note: (1) goods, related services, and civil works; (2) consulting services; total values for 1977–1986 and 1987–1992 are calculated from pp. 188–189.
* developing members include South Korea; Singapore; and Taipei, China, which have graduated from being aid recipients.
** including 7.14 percent for regional.

role for Japan in a broader international context. While hoping to achieve a major Japanese role, they also recognized Japan's responsibilities as a member of the international community. They helped to broaden Japan's national interests to include the necessity of contributing to the economic development of the region.[66]

Consolidation and Adjustment in 1972–86

Based on increased surplus capital, Japan was able and willing to provide contributions in this period. Its cumulative paid-in contributions reached $1.9 billion by the end of 1981 and $4.1 billion by the end of 1986. Japan's share of the bank's cumulative total increased from 30.4 percent in 1972 to 35.5 percent in 1981 and 41.9 percent in 1986 (Table 4.6). Since these figures are cumulative, Japan's relative share in this period was over 43 percent. Japan also lent $663.5 million (27.4 percent of the total) to the bank in 1973–81 and $1,316.9 million (30.6 percent) in 1982–86.

With its increased financial leverage, one would expect Japan to be more active and successful. However, we observe three puzzling phenomena in this period: Japan was paying more but talking less, receiving less, and weighing less. Japan's main objective was to consolidate the ADB into a well-managed bank based on its ongoing concern for national prestige in the 1970s and make the ADB a high-impact development agency in the 1980s. The most noticeable change in this period was that Japanese directors adopted a low-profile stance in bank affairs and did not initiate new programs. Yoshida Taroichi, the third president, recalled that Japanese directors never interfered with his decisions. "Looking back at my presidency," he noted, "the Japanese government had a very good attitude to provide money without interference."[67] In fact, Japanese directors were instructed not to differ openly from the management.[68]

While Japanese directors retreated to the backstage, Japanese presidents Inoue Shiro (1972–76), Yoshida (1976–81), and Fujioka Masao (1981–90) took the spotlight. All three presidents faced tough tests. Inoue encountered the oil crisis and its serious impact on the regional economy. Japan's hold on the presidency was challenged for the first time in late 1974, when Iran informally requested—with no success—an Iranian president as its condition for joining the ADB.[69] Yoshida faced the new aid policy of the Carter administration, which stressed poverty alleviation and human rights. He avoided using human rights as a criterion for loans but he remained sensitive to U.S. political interests. Although interested in assisting the reconstruction of Indochina, bank management was careful not to provoke the United States, freezing operations in Vietnam after Hanoi invaded Cambodia in 1979.

Different from his predecessors, Fujioka, nicknamed "the shogun" by his staff, exercised an "un-Japanese" style of firm leadership.[70] He came to Manila with a determination to open "a second chapter" for the bank after the growing pains of 1966–81. Based on projected new resources from a general capital increase, Asian Development Fund (ADF) replenishment, and bank borrowings, Fujioka announced an ambitious plan to lend $13 billion in 1983–87. In comparison, the bank lent a total of $13.4 billion during 1967–82.[71] Fujioka did not quite realize his plan despite initial success, in part because dropping commodity prices and the "graduation" of some major borrowers led to declining demand for loans after the mid 1980s. The bank lent $10.5 billion in 1983–87.

Fujioka's expansion plan was not well received by the Americans. The Reagan administration pressed the multilateral development banks to use stricter conditionality to push privatization and free market while cutting U.S. financial contributions. In the ADB, the Americans wanted zero paid-in capital and a drastic reduction in donations to ADF, but they eventually softened their position and the bank settled on a 105 percent increase with a 5 percent paid-in ratio for the third general capital increase. Japan and the United States also had differences over graduation, lending targets, and policy intervention. MOF did not want rigid standards for graduation, and held that there was a strong need for soft loans in the region.[72] The Americans criticized "the impulse to lend ever-increasing amounts of money in order simply to show institutional growth." But Fujioka stuck with his plan and threatened, in an "un-Japanese way," to dismiss department directors who would not meet his lending quotas.[73]

Washington was confrontational in this period. U.S. executive directors shifted strategies "from reliance on behind-the-scenes pressures to abstention on or voting against loans on specific policy grounds." In fact, while the ADB normally approves projects through consensus, "the U.S. stands out as the one member that has systematically used voting against projects as an instrument of policy."[74] With instructions from the Treasury, U.S. directors pushed for loans to countries they considered strategically important and lobbied for procurements for U.S. businessmen.[75] The disputes between Fujioka and the Americans emerged in 1983–84 and developed into an unprecedented open confrontation at the 1985 annual meeting. U.S. Director Joe Rogers sharply criticized the bank. Although other Americans tried to tone down his criticism, his charge became the central topic at the meeting. Fujioka and the management did not respond openly and effectively to Rogers's attacks.[76] In 1986 tension between Japan and the United States eased somewhat.[77] But Washington kept bringing pressure to bear on Fujioka. Fujioka reportedly yielded to most American demands behind closed doors.[78]

In sharp contrast to U.S. directors, Japanese directors virtually vanished from public view. Japan was stronger but more passive, while the United States was weaker but more assertive. As Table 4.6 shows, U.S. financial contributions were much smaller than Japan's, with 19.3 percent of the total versus 35.5 percent by 1981 and 16.0 percent versus 41.9 percent by 1986.

Balance of power arguments do not explain Japan's passive behavior in this period. It is true that the consensus crucial for a successful multilateral institution had eroded since the U.S. actions politicized the ADB. But Japan's position was not weakened. Compared to the early days, Asian developing members had become more sympathetic to Japan, which had been injecting huge funds into the bank with virtually no strings attached since 1974. In fact, they were resentful of the policy intervention by the United States. Europe, as a group, had outstripped the United States in contributions, with 21.5 percent versus 16 percent by 1986 (Table 4.6). As for lending to the bank, Europe was more important than both Japan and the United States, with 43.7 percent of the total in 1973–81 and 45.9 percent in 1982–86. This, however, did not suggest a tripolar structure between Japan, the United States, and Europe. Less interested in the region, Europeans did not act as a coherent group. Far from being isolated, Japan was often supported in controversial issues.

Two reasons explain Japan's reluctance to confront the United States in the bank. First, although the United States spent far less than Japan on the bank, it was able to exercise influence based on its overall power. Even though the United States did not make a clear linkage between the ADB and other issues in this period, Japan had to balance its policy toward the ADB with overall relations with its key ally. MOF officials admitted that they did not want to bargain with Americans over the ADB since they were already engaged in too many disputes with Washington.[79] As discussed in Chapter 2, Japan was busy trying to prove itself as a reliable and constructive ally for the United States in the 1980s. An open clash with the United States in the bank would have compromised that key objective. On politically sensitive issues, Japanese presidents had to take into serious consideration U.S. concerns and the concerns of other member nations. One of Fujioka's achievements was to accept the People's Republic of China into the bank while accommodating Washington's objection to expelling Taiwan and Taiwan's interest in remaining in the institution.[80]

Second, Japan could afford to be low key because it could accomplish its policy objectives from within the ADB. Bank operations were more in line with Japan's preferences than with those of others. In the 1970s, the United States influenced the bank's decisions over some sensitive political issues, such as Taiwan's membership and aid to Indochina.[81] But the Japanese presidents were in firm control on other issues. The bank responded to U.S. pressure with some highly publicized but token programs, while maintaining its traditional focus. The truth of the matter is that with Japanese in top management posts Japan could have its influence felt within the system without shouting at board meetings. In contrast, the United States had to take a high-profile stance from outside—an indicator of its lack of leverage within the bank.

While U.S. hegemony and Japan's institutional advantages combine to explain Tokyo's choice of passive strategy in the bank, they do not explain its decreased benefits in procurements and its shrinking voting shares. If the realist theory is right, nations like Japan should be concerned about their relative gains, not just their absolute gains. It is puzzling that Japan did not seem to be concerned even about its absolute gains in this period.

Japan was spending more but receiving less. Its share of procurements decreased from 41.67 percent in 1967–76 to 23.65 percent in 1977–86 (Table 4.7). If we divide Japan's share of cumulative procurements by its share of cumulative financial contributions, its ratio decreased from 1.47 by 1974 to 0.61 by 1986, the sharpest drop among major developed nation members (Table 4.8). In addition, Japan supported the ADF, which provided soft loans to low-income nations, with which Japan did not have crucial trade ties. Most soft loans were given to countries like Pakistan, Bangladesh, and Sri Lanka, which accounted for nearly 60 percent of total ADF lending by 1981 and 69 percent by 1986. And soft loans increased from 26.8 percent of Ordinary Capital Resources

Table 4.8

Procurements Versus Contributions in the ADB of Key Members

Members	By End of 1974 Procure. % (A)	Contrib. % (B)	A/B	By End of 1979 Procure. % (A)	Contrib. % (B)	A/B	By End of 1986 Procure. % (A)	Contrib. % (B)	A/B
Japan	44.3	30.2	1.47	35.4	36.4	0.97	25.7	41.9	0.61
United States	9.1	10.1	0.90	6.8	11.9	0.57	8.3	16.0	0.52
Germany	6.9	5.0	1.38	8.6	8.5	1.01	5.5	6.4	0.86
Britain	6.3	3.6	1.75	6.1	5.3	1.15	4.6	2.9	1.59
France	1.9	2.0	0.95	3.0	3.2	0.94	2.1	2.9	0.72
Australia	2.1	7.8	0.27	2.2	5.7	0.39	1.4	4.0	0.35
Canada	1.9	4.3	0.44	1.4	4.4	0.32	1.3	6.2	0.21
LDCs	10.0	28.6	0.35	10.9	14.7	0.74	13.2	10.0	1.32
Undetermined	7.5			14.5			29.2		
Total ($billion)							9.3	9.9	

Members	By End of 1991			By End of 1998		
	Procure. %	Contrib. %	A/B	Procure. %	Contrib. %	A/B
	(A)	(B)		(A)	(B)	
Japan	17.6	44.5	0.40	10.6	48.3	0.22
United States	8.1	13.0	0.62	6.2	13.3	0.47
Germany	4.5	6.6	0.68	4.2	5.8	0.81
Britain	3.6	3.2	1.13	2.1	3.0	0.70
France	2.4	3.6	0.67	1.8	3.5	0.51
Australia	1.6	4.2	0.38	1.5	4.1	0.37
Canada	0.9	6.1	0.15	0.7	4.9	0.14
LDCs	49.6	7.2	6.89	66.8	6.3	10.60
Undetermined						
Total ($billion)	20.5	16.2		47.3	23.2	

Source: Calculated from Robert Wihtol, *The Asian Development Bank and Rural Development* (Oxford: Macmillan, 1988), pp. 108–109; *ADB Annual Report*, various years. The table combines procurements for both ordinary and ADF. This table does not include consultancy.

(OCR) loans by the end of 1972 to 43.7 percent by 1981 and 46.4 percent by 1986. In terms of geographic distribution of ADB loans, the share of ASEAN and Northeast Asian nations, with which Japan had closer economic ties, decreased from 78.5 percent in 1967–72 to 64.8 percent in 1973–81 and 54.6 percent in 1982–86.

Another puzzle is that Japan was spending more for less weight in formal decision-making. Japan's voting share decreased from 20.2 percent in 1972 to 12.5 percent in 1986 (Table 4.6) due to increased membership and special increases for some members. There was an increased discrepancy between formal voting shares based on ordinary capital subscriptions and special funds donations. Japan had the lowest ratio of voting share by total contribution share in the bank, 0.38 in 1981 and 0.30 in 1986. Curiously, Japan did not voice any open concern about this trend until after the mid 1980s.

Japan's relative decline in voting share could be explained in part by its institutional advantages. Since Japan was powerful, it was able to control the bank, which in turn served its interests, and since Japan had the bank presidency securely at its disposal, it did not need to have a dominant voting position. But we still need to explain Japan's apparent neglect of its absolute gains or concrete benefits from the bank. The simple answer is that Japanese presidents and officials adopted a broad definition of national interests, which excluded taking advantage of the ADB for Japan's narrow interests. This definition was more conducive to international cooperation. But why did the Japanese adopt broader national interests? One may speculate that as Japan had hegemonic interests in this particular case, it was willing to provide public goods. This leads, however, to two more questions: Why did Japan not behave like a hegemon if it had hegemonic interests? And why was Japan willing to compromise its economic values in this case, contrary to its reputation for actively seeking economic gains around the world?

I argue that Japan adopted an accommodating strategy in this period, aimed at strengthening the bank at the expense of its immediate benefits. There was a strong tendency in this period for Japanese executives in Manila to identify their national interests with those of the ADB, a tendency reinforced by Japan's strong position in the bank. This high degree of parallel institutionalization was the crucial reason for Japan's cooperative strategies, providing common interests for Japan and other nations.

The Japanese presidents, in particular, played a crucial role in shaping Japan's policy toward the ADB. As former senior government officials, they were involved in high-level decision-making within the Japanese government with regard to the ADB.[82] In general, they wanted Japan to avoid a conspicuous presence and receive few concrete benefits. They saw Japan's interests differently, from their perspective as "frontline" commanders and senior "old boys" assigned for special missions, who knew better than headquarters. They were willing to sacrifice short-term victories on policy issues, procurement, or voting shares in order to further the "higher order" they believed to be the best course for Japan. Their perspectives were largely internationalist, with a different understanding of Japan's policy choices than more traditional officials at home.

In addition to the prominent role of the ADB presidents, there emerged a strong parallel institutional tie between the ADB and the MOF, especially the ministry's International Finance Bureau (IFB).[83] This strong linkage provided MOF officials with behind-the-scenes influence and led Japanese officials to identify strongly with the bank. The ADB had a strong constituency within MOF. Many IFB officials had some involvement with ADB affairs, facilitated by the MOF practice of sending officials to the bank on a short-term basis.[84] As ADB policy became routinized under IFB control, Japan was more cooperative based on broadly defined national interests.

Tentative Attempt at Hegemony in the Late 1980s

After the mid 1980s Japan made a tentative attempt to achieve a de jure hegemonic status in the ADB by raising its voting share above that of the United States. It also used the bank as a conduit for recycling surplus capital to the region, thus integrating its obligation to assist other Asian states with its strategic interest in securing a prosperous manufacturing base. This was a highly contentious period between Japan and the United States, which ended when Fujioka resigned in November 1990.

Japan made explicit demands for a larger voting share and initiated new programs. At the 1986 annual meeting Finance Minister Takeshita Noboru suggested a "harmonization" between voting powers for OCR and ADF contributions, which normally determine only voting powers for ADF. He argued that Japan's share needed to be raised to ensure domestic support for continued contributions.[85] Americans objected to the Japanese proposal. At the 1987 annual meeting held in Tokyo, Finance Minister Miyazawa announced a plan to increase funding for the

ADB and establish the Japan Special Fund (JSF) in the ADB modeled after a similar fund for the World Bank, as part of Japan's plan to recycle its surplus capital to the LDCs. The JSF was the first major Japanese initiative since the early 1970s.

Japan became assertive based on its massive financial contributions. At the 1987 annual meeting, Miyazawa announced Japan's plan to increase its overseas development flows by $30 billion in 1987–90, part of which would be allocated to the ADB. Japan's share of the cumulative contributions to OCR and special fund resources (SFRs) increased from 41.9 percent by 1986 to 44.5 percent by 1991. In contrast, the U.S. share decreased from 16.0 percent to 13.0 percent (Table 4.6). In addition, Japan was the largest lender to the bank, with $1,227.2 million, or 32.6 percent of the total in 1987–91, compared with 18.6 percent for the United States and 27.7 percent for Europe. With such a huge commitment of financial resources, the Japanese felt that it was only fair for them to have a larger share than the Americans. Although Japan was willing "to front-up considerable sums of money without prior concessions over its voting power," it was hoping to surpass the United States eventually.[86] However, despite much effort, Japan and the United States remained tied in voting powers, 12.3 percent each by the end of 1991 (Table 4.6).

Japan was not successful in achieving a dominant voting share, mainly due to strong U.S. resistance. The United States wanted to prevent Japan from achieving a special capital increase and preserve its parity with Japan.[87] It sought leadership at minimal expense: providing guidance while reducing contributions. Fujioka saw the U.S. strategy as "maintaining its voice without paying the bill."[88] In response to Japan's harmonization principle, Americans argued that voluntary ADF contributions have no legal implications for ADB's voting shares. A senior U.S. official dismissed the proposed JSF as a "side issue" and argued that the "real issue is where the bank is going to go in the 1990s."[89] During a trying period in the U.S.–Japan relationship, Japan did not want to challenge the United States. Washington linked its ADB voting share and its overall contributions to the region and argued that equal partnership with Japan in the bank should be maintained to prevent the impression that Washington was "drawing away from the region."[90]

Furthermore, the power distribution in the bank was not favorable for a drastic change in voting shares. Japan's harmonization principle was supported by some members, but often because they wanted a special increase in their shares as well. The LDCs had ambiguous feelings toward Japan. Although critical of U.S. pressure and sympathetic to Japan, they did not want a bank monopolized by Japan, a sentiment that strengthened the U.S. bargaining position.[91]

Japan made explicit use of the ADB as a diplomatic instrument in this period. As discussed previously, Japan used the ADB, along with the World Bank and the IMF, as important multilateral conduits for its recycling plans to demonstrate its international contributions and to alleviate international criticism of its chronic foreign trade and current account surpluses. Because the Japanese development finance bureaucracy is small compared with the volume of capital flows, MDBs offer Japan an attractive option to channel its surplus efficiently and quickly and compensate for its lack of expertise.

Equally important, Japan sought to advance its diplomatic agenda toward individual Asian countries through the bank. While Japan suspended bilateral aid to Hanoi in 1979 after the Vietnamese invasion of Cambodia in 1979, it supported a Vietnamese membership in the ADB and resumption of bank loans to that country. Japan was interested in reconstruction of Indochina for its own commercial interests and for the regional stability that would result from improved relations between Indochina and Association of Southeast Asian Nations (ASEAN). After China indicated interest in joining the ADB in the early 1980s, Fujioka engaged in intense shuttle diplomacy between Beijing and Taipei, with constant stops in Tokyo for consultation with the Japanese foreign and finance ministers. At one point, he requested that a China expert be seconded to the bank from the foreign ministry. He succeeded in admitting China in 1986 without expelling Taiwan, one of his major accomplishments as judged by Tokyo. In addition, the ADB supported the Corazon Aquino government after the collapse of the Ferdinand Marcos regime in 1986.[92]

Japan was also deferential to U.S. concerns on politically sensitive issues such as Vietnam and China. Japan was hoping to use its special fund in the ADB to lend to Vietnam. After all, Japan resumed bilateral aid to Vietnam in November 1992. But due to strong U.S. opposition, the ADB opted not to do so until the Clinton administration relaxed restrictions on MDB lending to Vietnam in 1994.

Fujioka was less deferential to Americans over bank operations than political issues. Washington wanted the bank to change lending modalities from project-based to program- and sector-based, with the belief that program and sectoral lending could assist the LDCs in market-oriented reforms. But Japan believed that the U.S. approach was too simplistic for Asian nations. Fujioka argued that there should not be "an arbitrary difference between the public and private sectors."[93] The ADB remained a project bank in 1986–91, with more than half its lending going to projects over this period. Program lending increased slowly. Furthermore, the bank maintained its cautious approach to private sector operations so as not to damage its credit rating in capital markets. The bank private sector lending increased slowly, from $19.7 million in 1986 (1 percent of the total lending of the year) to $214.8 million in 1991 (4.3 percent). All this shows that Japan was able to control bank operations despite some concessions to the United States.

Japan's ability to shape the policy orientation of the bank was due to its institutional advantages and financial leverage. GoJ controlled the presidency and crucial reserved posts, which allowed it to run the bank in a way similar to American dominance in the World Bank. The ADB operates like a Japanese institution, emphasizing painstaking consensus formation and seniority.[94] This style of management naturally suits the Japanese. Also, as the largest stockholder, Japan could influence the decision on how its money should be spent. In addition, Asians were now generally sympathetic to Japan, which had made generous financial contributions with few strings since early 1974.[95] They were also resentful of what they saw as Washington's ideological intrusion.[96] Fujioka observed in 1988 that some Asian nations were now "welcoming Japan's larger leadership role as an indication of the strengthened Asian character of the bank."[97]

The dispute between Japan and the United States in the ADB was exacerbated by strong personalities. Fujioka was independent, assertive, and competent—qualities that led him to confront the Americans head on. His strong personality put the Japanese ministry of finance in a bind. On the one hand, MOF supported him, as an "old boy," in financial contributions and board discussions, consistent with its traditional policy of supporting the Japanese presidents of the bank. In fact, starting in the mid 1980s MOF began sending "young turk" directors to the ADB. These directors—young, proficient in English, and familiar with bank operations—confronted the Americans at board meetings and voiced Japan's opinions about specific policy agendas. On the other hand, MOF officials were not always happy with Fujioka's independence. More important, they also worried that tension with the

United States in the bank was getting out of hand. Cooperation with the United States had been a pillar in the ADB even when Tokyo did not fully concur with U.S. policy positions. In the end, MOF eased Fujioka out to smooth relations with Washington. Fujioka was elected for a second five-year term in 1986 but resigned with two years remaining in his contract.[98] Fujioka possessed the leadership qualities and "Western management style" lacking among many Japanese sent to international organizations, but his style came to conflict with broader MOF objectives in the bank.

Cautious Leadership in the 1990s

Japan accepted co-leadership with the United States in the 1990s. MOF wanted to avoid further straining relations with the United States and chose a new president, Tarumizu Kimimasa, who, unlike Fujioka, adopted the Japanese management style—consensus building. Tarumizu was not very knowledgeable about international finance and Asian development. His authority was undercut from the beginning when he was not backed by MOF to oppose the only American candidate for vice presidency, who was pushed hard by the Americans. His indecisive leadership style created problems for both the bank and MOF. His performance prompted MOF to search for someone between Fujioka and Tarumizu when Tarumizu announced his decision to retire before his term expired.[99]

One major issue Tarumizu encountered was China. After the Tiananmen incident in June 1989, China was banned from borrowing for the second half of 1989. Tarumizu was in favor of full resumption of lending to China in spite of protests from the United States. "I don't think the American concept of basic human needs is universally accepted," he argued. "Human needs can be interpreted many ways."[100] Finance Minister Hashimoto also expressed willingness to resume full bank operations in China. Due to opposition of the United States and Canada, the Board did not make any decision at the 1991 annual meeting.[101] But after 1991, with support from a significant number of Asian members, Japan was able to resume ADB lending to China despite U.S. abstention from voting.[102] The decision did not cause much rift between Japan and the United States since Japan had already resumed yen loans to China with acceptance from President Bush and the World Bank had also resumed basic human needs and humanitarian aid to Beijing.

In the next few years, the Clinton administration did not pay as much attention to the bank as had the previous administrations, contributing to relative peace between Japan and the United States in the bank. Japan continued to use the ADB as a diplomatic instrument. Japan played a central role in admitting five new Central Asian republics (Kazakhstan, Uzbekistan, Tajikistan, Kyrgyzstan, and Turkmenistan) as regional members of the ADB even though they were already regional members of the European Bank for Reconstruction and Development. Japan also paid special attention to Mongolia and Turkey, which became ADB members in 1991. Mongolia became a Japanese favorite for economic and political reform, while Turkey was considered a moderate Islamic counterweight to fundamental Islamic influence from Iran. Tokyo's territorial claims over the Northern Territories and its wariness of Russia's borrowing needs explained its reluctance to accept that country as a regional (and thus borrowing) member.[103]

Japan continues to support the ADB with generous financial resources, thus creating a continuous (albeit less publicized than before) friction with the United States. Tokyo pushed for the Fourth General Capital Increase. Although it was hoped that the new Clinton administration would change the harsh policy adopted by the Republican administrations in 1980–92, U.S. representative Jeffrey Shafer, at the 1993 ADB annual meeting, opposed the proposed capital increase. He urged the bank to improve the quality rather than the quantity of its loans. The ADB and Japanese made adjustments in response to U.S. criticism. At the 1994 annual meeting, the ADB adopted a new lending strategy of "social linkage" in exchange for American support for the capital increase. Most Asian members resented this new policy, which requires at least 40 percent of loans to go to health, education, and environmental projects. They were also disappointed that Japan did not act assertively in Asia's interest in putting priority on infrastructure.[104] In the end, Sato Mitsuo, who became ADB president in November 1993, secured the 75 percent needed for approving the capital increase in May 1994.

Sato then turned attention to a new replenishment of the ADF, but his plan was frustrated at the 1995 annual meeting by lack of support from both Western donors and newly industrializing Asian economies. Washington did not want to discuss a new replenishment while it was $437 million in arrears on its pledge to the previous replenishment.[105] Negotiations were held throughout 1996. In May 1997, donors formalized a recommendation to replenish the ADF (ADF VII) for a total of $6.3 billion for the four-year period 1997–2000, but new contributions by donors amounted to only $3 billion. Japan committed $1,019 million, or 34.0 percent of the total donations, compared with $400 million for the United States, which also had to pay off its arrears of $237 million. Chino Tadao, who succeeded Sato in January 1999, asked for another four-year replenishment (ADF VIII) at the May 1999 annual meeting. The formal discussion will start in October. The ADB hopes to raise another $6 billion or so from donors, although it expects difficulties in persuading Washington to support the new replenishment.[106]

Japan's behavior in the bank in this period shows that it carefully balances its relations with the United States and its Asian neighbors. How Japan acts in the bank is also affected by the power balance in the bank and the strength of resistance of key member states to its policy. However, its policy is facilitated by its entrenched institutional advantages in the bank. In fact, MOF strengthened its institutional hold on the bank in the early 1990s, regaining the directorship of the Budget, Personnel, and Management Systems Department, which it lost in the late 1980s.

As in the 1980s, Japan's institutional strength and connection have made MOF officials more accommodating to the bank. The same officials who want to be more assertive vis-à-vis the United States feel that Japan should assist the Asian nations, whose economic development will be beneficial for Japan in the long term. They insist that Japan does not want to have any return from its foreign aid.[107] Japan's share of cumulative procurements keep decreasing, from 23.65 percent in 1977–86 to 9.51 percent in 1987–96 and 5.46 percent in 1997–98 (Table 4.7). Japan is also willing to contribute more to ADF for soft loans, which do not correlate well with its economic interests. After all, most ADF soft loans have gone to South Asia rather than East Asia—50.7 percent to Bangladesh and Pakistan alone by the end of 1998.[108]

The ADB faced a serious challenge to help resolve the Asian economic crisis in 1997. The ADB contributed considerable financial resources to the three IMF-sponsored rescue packages: $1.2 billion to Thailand, $3.5 billion for Indonesia, and a $4 billion loan to South Korea. As a result, ADB loans increased by 76.6 percent to $9.4 billion in 1997.[109] But the ADB was criticized as failing to predict the crisis and take the lead in dealing with it. The bank has played a supporting role for the IMF. "The IMF snatched the lead from our hands," commented a senior ADB official.[110] Sato defended the ADB approach, citing ADB's heavy involvement in designing rescue packages for Thailand, Indonesia, and South Korea.[111] Nevertheless, compared with the United States, the IMF, and the World Bank, the ADB was virtually invisible in its own backyard.

Conclusion

Japan has pursued a variety of goals in the IMF, the World Bank, and the ADB: international acceptance and economic and commercial benefits in the early years and status and policy influence in the later years. It is striking that Japan has sought to achieve its self-interests in the three institutions mainly through cooperation rather than confrontation—namely, facilitating the realization of their missions and objectives. As member states often dispute the very missions of the institutions, how cooperative Japan is depends on what one considers the central purposes of the institutions to be. Furthermore, one's evaluation of Japan's policy toward an international financial organization is colored by the implications of Japanese actions for one's own country.

Japan itself has tried to balance its policy toward the three financial institutions with its bilateral policies. Its two-track foreign policy is reflected in its policy toward the IMF, the World Bank, and the ADB. On the one hand, Japan uses global and regional institutions to serve different purposes: the World Bank and the IMF for demonstrating Japan's international contributions to the United States and the international community, and the ADB for promoting economic development in Asia. On the other hand, Japan tries to balance between its global and regional interests. Tokyo defends what it perceives to be Asia's interests in the World Bank and the IMF while maintaining cordial relations with the United States in the ADB. This has not been easy. Although the United States and Asian developing nations often have common interests, there is a rough dichotomy in the purpose for which each prefers the institutions to be used. Asia wants more development funding with few conditions, while the United States treats the institutions as catalysts for reforms in recipient countries. As a result, what is accommodating to Asia may not be as accommodating to the United States.

Japan has been cooperative in the three institutions. First, Japan has been largely a status quo power in these institutions, satisfied with their basic mission while trying to increase its own voting power in the 1980s and acquire greater policy influence and contribute ideas in the 1990s. Even in its most vocal challenge to the World Bank so far, namely its push for *The East Asia Miracle* report, Japan did not really challenge the dominant neoclassical orthodoxy of the bank but instead urged the bank to adjust its lending policy at the margins to accommodate Japan's own approach.[112] Japan is satisfied with its number two position in the World Bank and the IMF. Even in the ADB Japan has seen cooperation with the United States as a high priority.

Second, compared to other nations, Japan has spent more for less in both the ADB and the World Bank, judging by the ratio of voting shares to shares of cumulative financial contributions, which include paid-in portions of capital subscriptions and contributions to special funds. Japan's ratio in the ADB was 0.66 at the end of 1972, 0.30 in 1986, and 0.27 in 1998. Japan paid far more than other donor nations for the same proportion of voting powers. The ratios for the United States and European members in 1998 were 3.7 times and 2.8 times that of Japan (Table 4.6). Similarly, Japan's ratio at the World Bank was 0.94 in 1981 and 0.39 in mid 1999. In contrast, the ratios for the United States, Germany, and Britain in 1999 were 0.70, 0.42 and 0.61 (Table 4.3).

Third, Japan has contributed generously to the World Bank and the ADB without receiving proportionate economic gains. And it has become more cooperative over time. Japan's ratio of cumulative procurement share to cumulative contribution share in the ADB decreased from 1.47 at the end of 1974 to 0.61 in 1986 and 0.22 in 1998 (Table 4.8). Its ratio in 1998 was lower than all major developed nations except Canada (0.14). Table 4.5 shows that Japan's ratio in the World Bank decreased from 1.29 in 1971 to 0.64 in 1986 and 0.29 in mid 1999, compared with the ratios for other major powers (0.35 for the United States, 0.48 for Germany, 0.63 for Britain, and 0.60 for France).

Japan's strategies in this case can be explained, in part, by its economic power, the power distribution within the institutions, and the impact of the overall power balance. Japan's increasing financial power relative to other players in the three institutions explains why it has become more assertive and influential. Power does affect one's interests. Financial power gave Japan the confidence to openly campaign for larger voting shares in the 1980s and prompted its attempt at policy influence in the 1990s. A country's overall power is also important. U.S. influence in the three institutions has decreased because of its decreased financial contributions relative to other major industrial nations, but this decline has been offset to some extent by U.S. world leadership. Washington links its overall leadership burden with its voting power in the institutions. In sharp contrast, Japan is strong in financial support for the institutions but weak in world political capital.

However, the realist theory does not explain why Japan has not really adopted an assertive strategy in line with its increased financial power and why it focused on raising its voting shares rather than policy influence until recently. In addition, realist arguments are insufficient to explain some puzzling Japanese behavior. Japan is more cooperative in the ADB, where it has more bargaining power, than in the World Bank. Tables 4.3 and 4.6 show that Japan has spent more but weighed less in the ADB, compared to the World Bank, judging by the ratio of voting shares to shares of contributions. Japan had a ratio of 0.87 in the World Bank in 1971, 0.94 in 1981, and 0.39 in 1999. In contrast, its ratio in the ADB was 0.66 in 1972, 0.38 in 1981, and 0.27 in 1991 and 1998. If the realist theory is right, we should also observe a more active Japan competing for greater benefits in the ADB than in the World Bank. But Tables 4.5 and 4.8 show that Japan has received less tangible reward from the ADB than from the World Bank, although it has enjoyed a leadership position in the former and economic supremacy in the region. Japan had a ratio of procurements to contributions of 1.28 in 1980, 0.44 in 1991, and 0.29 in 1999 in the World Bank. In contrast, its ratio in the ADB was 0.97 in 1979, 0.40 in 1991, and 0.22 in 1998. To explain these puzzles, we need to examine the institutions, norms, and ideas involved.

The institutionalist approach provides a good explanation for Japan's strategies. First, any country that joins an international institution presumably finds it in its interest to be a member. Japan initially sought international acceptance, prestige, and tangible and intangible economic and commercial benefits. Since the late 1970s, Japan has also used the institutions to demonstrate its international contributions and advance its diplomatic agenda. Different from its bilateral ODA, its multilateral assistance could lessen Japan's commercial reputation, thus allowing it to score more diplomatic points. In addition, given the limited manpower and the dearth of regional expertise of the Japanese foreign aid bureaucracy, Tokyo could rely on these international financial institutions to disburse its surplus capital more rapidly and efficiently to developing countries.[113] At the same time, multilateral assistance provides cover for sensitive bilateral issues. For example, the international financial institutions may impose financial discipline on recipient countries in a way that Japan finds hard to do bilaterally. In addition, these institutions pool resources for projects that may be important for Japan's interests, as illustrated in the three IMF rescue packages for Asia.

Second, Japan's position in the three institutions and its institutional connection with them are different, which partially explains why the country has behaved differently in them. Japan enjoys clear institutional advantages in the ADB, unlike the World Bank and the IMF, in which the United States dominates. Japan controls the presidency and a number of important reserve posts in the ADB. Japanese are also more at ease in the ADB as an Asian institution. As a result, unlike the World Bank and the IMF, the ADB sees a larger presence for Japanese nationals on staff. A good number of career MOF officers have served in the ADB, giving them exposure to Asian development experience and a tilt toward Asia. This discrepancy explains in part why Japan is more successful in controlling the agenda in the ADB than in the World Bank and the IMF, even though it has not been that vocal in the bank. Japan's close institutional linkage with the ADB also explains why Tokyo has been even more accommodating in the ADB than in the two global institutions. It appears that an institutionally advantaged country is favored for setting the agenda but is also inclined to take the institution's interests as its own.

This leads to the question of how national interests are defined. For sustainable cooperation, countries involved need to move to more enlightened ones. Such a redefinition is as much a reflection of social interaction within the institutions as it is of changing domestic and international circumstances. The fact that Japanese officials sent to the institutions often return to be in charge of Japan's policy toward these very institutions facilitates Japan's cooperation because these officials are familiar with the institutional missions and concerns and are sometimes emotionally attached to them. Japan's policy toward these institutions is informed by its ideas about their role in promoting development in recipient countries, and these ideas are products of learning of past experiences. Tokyo did not challenge the World Bank in the 1980s partly because Japanese did not fully understand the implications of their reliance on the World Bank for its own bilateral aid program. And to affect the World Bank approach to development, Japanese had to make conscious efforts to reflect on Japan and Asia's development experience and to articulate their development theories. By contrast, Japan's management of the ADB certainly reflects its own ideas about how to achieve development in Asia.

Notes

1. The World Bank initially referred to only the IBRD established in 1945 but it came to be called the World Bank Group when the International Finance Corporation was added in 1956, the International Development Association in 1960, the International Center for Settlement of Investment Disputes in 1966, and the Multilateral Investment Guarantee Agency in 1988.

2. Ishida Tadashi, "Kokusai tsuka kikin oyobi kokusai fukko kaihatsu ginko e no kanyu ni tsuite" [Joining the IMF and the IBRD], *Keizai renko* (May 1952), pp. 5–8; Kase Shoichi, "Kokusai tsuka kikin no genjo o nihon no kaniu" [The present situation of the IMF and Japan's application], *Sekai shuho* 32, no. 25 (September 11, 1951), pp. 14–17. Note that Ishida was head of the Bureau of Finance of the MOF.

3. Paul Volcker and Toyoo Gyohten, *Changing Fortunes: The World's Money and the Threat to American Leadership* (New York: Random House, 1992), p. 51.

4. The largest borrower was India. Japan made the final repayment in February 1990.

5. *Ekonomisuto,* September 1, 1952, p. 36.

6. Tanaka Kakuei's statement to the Fund, *IMF Summary Proceedings,* 1964, p. 34.

7. Joseph Gold, "Amendments," in J. Keith Horsefield, ed., *International Monetary Fund, 1945–1965: Twenty Years of International Monetary Fund,* vol. 2 (Washington: IMF, 1969), pp. 595–600.

8. *World Bank Annual Report,* 1971, pp. 37–38.

9. "One or more of the other significant actors—management, other major donors, or borrowers—must support, or at least not oppose, the United States" in order for Washington to exercise influence, admitted a U.S. Treasury Department report. *United States Participation in the Multilateral Development Banks in the 1980s,* p. 64.

10. Robert Solomon, *The International Monetary System, 1945–81* (New York: Harper & Row, 1982), p. 239.

11. Nishida Yuichiro, "Kokusai tsuka seido kaikaku e zenshin" [Moving toward the reform of the international monetary system], *Seikai shuho* 54, no. 43 (October 23, 1973), p. 3.

12. Yata Takeichi, "IMF sokai o shuzai shite" [Covering the IMF annual meeting], *Fainansu* 13, no. 9 (December 1977), p. 20.

13. Matsugawa Michiya, "Segin-IMF sokai kara kaette" [Return from the Bank–Fund annual meeting], *Fainansu* 13, no. 9 (December, 1977), pp. 6–9.

14. *U.S. Participation in the Multilateral Development Banks in the 1980s,* p. 59.

15. A report by the Staff Association complained about "a selective one-way communication process from the top down" and believed that "middle managers play little more than a foreman's role." Quoted in Robert L. Ayres, *Banking on the Poor: The World Bank and World Poverty* (Cambridge: MIT Press, 1983), p. 65. Ayres did not find even one project being turned down by the directors during his research in 1975–80. There was also little evidence that the opinions of the directors were considered for future projects (p. 66).

16. "Like Germany, Japan is relatively unconcerned about prestige in international monetary affairs; also like the Germans, the Japanese have long struggled (with somewhat greater success) to prevent their currency from becoming an international reserve asset." Benjamin Cohen, *Organizing the World's Money:*

The Political economy of International Monetary Relations (New York: Basic Books, 1977), p. 149.

17. Sadako Ogata, "Shifting Power Relations in Multilateral Development Banks," *The Journal of International Studies* (Institute of International Relations, Sophia University, Tokyo), no. 22 (January 1989), pp. 11–14.

18. Amitabha Chowdhury, "The Grand Alliance Gives the Bank a New Lustre," *Asian Finance,* September 15, 1986, p. 60.

19. Sumita Satoshi's statement to the Fund, *IMF Summary Proceedings,* 1987, pp. 49–50. He made similar demands the next year. *IMF Summary Proceedings,* 1988, p. 40.

20. Hashimoto Ryutaro's statement to the Fund, *IMF Summary Proceedings,* 1989, pp. 28–29.

21. Toru Yanagihara and Anne L. Emig, "An Overview of Japan's Foreign Aid," in Shafiqul Islam, ed., *Yen for Development: Japanese Foreign Aid and the Politics of Burden-Sharing* (New York: Council on Foreign Relations Press, 1991), pp. 62–68.

22. Data in this paragraph are from *World Bank Annual Report,* 1991.

23. Utsumi Makoto, "Dai yonjuikkai IMF-segin sokai ni shussekishite" [Attending the 41st IMF–World Bank annual meeting], *Kokusai kinyu,* December 1, 1986, p. 8.

24. *IMF Annual Report,* 1997, p. 173.

25. Ogata, "Shifting Power Relations in MDBs," p. 18.

26. Oshiba Ryo, "Nihon gaiko to kokusai kinyu soshiki" [Japan's diplomacy and international financial institutions], *Kokusai mondai* 408 (March 1994), pp. 53–65.

27. As an important exception, India was against the idea because it was concerned that it might lose its 3 percent share, which gave it a seat on the Executive Board.

28. Ogata, "Shifting Power Relations in MDBs," pp. 17–18.

29. Susumu Awanohara, "Fairer Shares," *Far Eastern Economic Review,* September 7, 1989, p. 7.

30. Ogata, "Shifting Power Relations in MDBs," p. 19.

31. Murata Akio, "Ruiseki saimu mondai" [The problem of accumulated debts], *Ekonomisuto,* October 4, 1988, pp. 18–19; Kuroda Haruhiko, "Chushotoku saimukoku mondai ni kansuru nihon tean" [Japan's proposal regarding middle-income debtor nations], *Kinyu zaisei jijo,* November 7, 1988, pp. 42–45.

32. Yanagihara Toru, "Miyazawa koso o torikonda bureiditean" [The Brady Plan that incorporates the Miyazawa Plan], *Ekonomisuto* 67, no. 15 (April 11, 1989), pp. 37–48. At the joint annual meeting of the IMF and the World Bank in September 1988, Nicholas F. Brady, then U.S. Secretary of the Treasury, criticized the "alternative proposals" as "appear[ing] to conform to the basic principles of the debt strategy, but which in practice will produce only an illusion of progress." *Treasury News,* September 27, 1988.

33. Stephen Zamora, "Voting in International Economic Organization," *American Journal of International Law* 74, no. 3 (July 1980), p. 569.

34. Ogata, "Shifting Power Relations in MDBs," pp. 19–20.

35. Richard Feinberg, "An Open Letter to the World Bank's New President," in Feinberg and contributors, *Between Two Worlds: The World Bank's Next Decade* (New Brunswick: Transaction Books, 1986), p. 27.

36. For a comparison made by the Japanese who used to work or are currently working in the Fund and the Bank, see Masaya Hattori, former Bank vice president,

"'Yumi no sekai' ni ikiru hokoritakai rironka tachi" [The proud theorists who live in a "dream world"], *Toyo Keizai,* August 4, 1984, pp. 84–87; Kenichi Ohno and Izumi Ohno, *IMF to sekai ginko: uchi gawa kara mita kaihatsu kinyu kikan* [IMF and World Bank: the financial development institutions seen from inside] (Tokyo: Nihon hyoron sha, 1993).

37. Since data are cumulative, Japan's share of total procurements decreased even faster in this period, 9.1 percent in 1981–85 and 7.1 percent in 1986–91, compared to 14.3 percent in 1971–80. Calculated from *World Bank Annual Report,* various years.

38. Interviews with MOF officials, Tokyo, August 1992.

39. In fact, because the United States failed to contribute to IDA-11 until fiscal 1998, pending fulfillment of its commitments to IDA-10, all IDA donors except the United States created the Interim Trust Fund (ITF) in March 1996, which only allowed ITF donors to participate in decision-making and provide procurement for ITF projects. IDA-11 became effective in February 1998 when the United States submitted its Instrument of Commitment for IDA-11. *World Bank Annual Report,* 1998, p. 113.

40. *IMF Annual Report,* 1998, p. 125.

41. *IMF Annual Report,* 1997, p. 206.

42. Dennis T. Yasutomo, *The New Multilateralism in Japan's Foreign Policy* (New York: St. Martin's Press, 1995), pp. 67–69.

43. For a volume of important papers on the Japanese development philosophy and Japanese reservations about the World Bank approach, see Ohno and Ohno, *Japanese Views on Economic Development.* Also see Emig, "Japan's Challenge."

44. Not fully content with the outcome of the World Bank study, the Japanese continued to be vocal about the relevance of the Asian development experience and conducted further studies of the flaws of the World Bank orthodoxy, particularly in transition economies such as China, the former Soviet Union, and Vietnam.

45. In addition, the Fund provided a $1.1 billion package for the Philippines on July 18, 1997.

46. *Washington Post,* June 3, 1998, p. A18.

47. Based on my discussions with some leading Japanese development experts in 1997–98.

48. Todd Zaun, "Japanese Offers Advice to IMF," Associated Press, March 1, 1999.

49. Marc Castellano, "Sakakibara Officially Nominated to Head IMF," *JEI Report,* no. 9B (March 3, 2000), p. 7.

50. John Burgess, "German Falls Short in IMF Vote," *Washington Post,* March 3, 2000, p. E9. In the end, another German, Horst Kohler, was chosen.

51. Po-wen Huang, Jr., *The Asian Development Bank: Diplomacy and Development in Asia* (New York: Vantage, 1975), pp. 19–23; Takeshi Watanabe, *Towards a New Asia* (Singapore: ADB, 1977), pp. 1–8.

52. R. Krishnamurti, who was in charge of the ADB project as the head of the International Trade Division of the ECAFE, was not aware of the Japanese plan. Krishnamurti, *ADB: The Seeding Days* (Manila: ADB, 1977), fn. 1, p. 15.

53. Eugene Black, *Alternative in Southeast Asia* (New York: Praeger, 1969), pp. ix, 97–98; Watanabe, "Ajia kaigin ni kitai suru" [Looking forward to the Asian Development Bank], *Ekonomisuto,* October 19, 1965, p. 55.

54. Krishnamurti, *ADB,* p. 31.

55. Ibid., pp. 23–24.

56. Watanabe, *Towards a New Asia,* pp. 13–14.

57. Nakagawa Koji, *Ajia kaihatsu ginko: junen no jissekito tomen suru kadai* [The ADB: ten years of accomplishments and the tasks ahead] (Tokyo: Kyoiku sha, 1979), pp. 61–62.

58. There is some suspicion on the Japanese side about the result. Watanabe recalls that Japan's calculation indicated that Tokyo should have won by one vote, but Manila won by one vote, "something which will never be understood." "Ajia kaihatsu ginko nijune no ayumi to osaka sokai" [The twenty years of the Asian Development Bank and the annual meeting at Osaka], *Fainansu* 22, no. 12 (March 1987), p. 17.

59. Dennis T. Yasutomo, *Japan and the Asian Development Bank* (New York: Praeger, 1983), pp. 77–82.

60. *ADB Annual Report,* various years. Data on the ADB in this section are from *ADB Annual Report* unless specified otherwise.

61. Watanabe commented that Japan's attitude was very different from that of other capital markets, "where the credit of the bank was evaluated by the amount of the unpaid portion of the subscribed capital and not by the nationality of its president." Watanabe, *Towards a New Asia,* p. 70. Also, the ADB issued both the 100th and 200th bond issues in Japan, celebrated occasions for the bank and for Japan.

62. Yasutomo, *Japan and ADB,* pp. 92–93.

63. The Administration Department was later divided into the Budget, Personnel, and Management Systems Department and the Office of Administrative Services.

64. Commented by Watanabe about why he was succeeded by another Japanese when he resigned due to sickness. The Charter specifies only that the president should be from a regional member country, not necessarily Japanese. Watanabe, *Towards a New Asia,* p. 91.

65. Stephen D. Krasner, "Power Structures and Regional Development Banks," *International Organization* 35, no. 2 (Spring 1981), pp. 314, 319. By comparing the country allocation of the ADB loans and those of the bilateral loans of the major donors as of December 1983, Wihtol also concludes that the country allocation of the ADB was closest to Japan's preference. Robert Wihtol, *ADB and Rural Development* (Oxford: Macmillan, 1988), pp. 102–103.

66. For studies on the involvement and thinking of MOF officials, Japanese presidents of the ADB and other Japanese working in the bank, see Yasutomo, *Japan and ADB;* Watanabe, *Towards a New Asia;* Watanabe, "Ajia kaigin no yakuwari" [The role of the Asian Development Bank], *Ekonomisuto,* November 29, 1966, p. 43.

67. An interview with Yoshida, "Sokuko omoto meizu jikkurishita torikumio" [The game that requires caution, and not immediate results], *Ekonomisuto,* March 30, 1982, p. 47.

68. Yasutomo, *Japan and ADB,* p. 153.

69. Dick Wilson, *A Bank for Half the World: The Story of the Asian Development Bank, 1966–86* (Manila: Asian Development Bank, 1987), pp. 79–80.

70. Barun Roy, "Market Forces Give ADB a New Look," *Asian Finance,* April 15, 1983, p. 39; "New Issues for Fujioka as He Solves Most of the Old," *Asian Finance,* April 15, 1986, p. 62.

71. Rodney Tasker, "Lender of First Resort," *Far Eastern Economic Review,* May 17, 1984, p. 64.

72. "The Japanese View: The Hardy Annual of ADF Replenishment," *Asian Finance,* April 15, 1986, pp. 74–75. This view was shared by Watanabe in an interview with an *Asian Finance* correspondent in 1982. "Founding President Watanabe Speaks to *Asian Finance:* The Gentle Art of Compromise," *Asian Finance,* April 15, 1982, p. 84. Yoshida voiced a similar view in an interview in 1982, "Sokuko omoto meizu jikkurishita torikumio," p. 47.

73. Tasker, "Lender of First Resort," p. 64.

74. Wihtol, *ADB and Rural Development,* p. 46.

75. Jonathan Sanford and Margaret Goodman, "Congressional Oversight and the Multilateral Development Banks," *International Organization* 29, no. 4 (Autumn 1975), p. 1058.

76. Anthony Rowley, "Full-Frontal Attack," *Far Eastern Economic Review,* May 16, 1985, p. 63; Barun Roy, "New Issues for Fujioka as He Solves Most of the Old," *Asian Finance,* April 15, 1986, p. 63.

77. One crucial reason is that Rogers resigned effective September 1, 1986.

78. J. Clad, "Last-Resort Lender," *Far Eastern Economic Review,* May 15, 1986, p. 64.

79. "Japanese View," p. 74.

80. China indicated its intention to join the ADB in November 1982 and formally submitted its application in February 1983. Fujioka engaged in intense shuttle diplomacy among Tokyo, Beijing, and Taiwan, while respecting the U.S. position. China joined the ADB in early 1986. Fujioka Masao, *Ajia kaigin sosai nikki: manira e no sato-gaeri* [ADB president's diary: return to Manila] (Tokyo: Toyo keizai shimposha, 1986), pp. 152–168.

81. Congress's opposition to the expulsion of Taiwan partly explained why the PRC was accepted as a member only in 1986. Washington prevailed on the Indochina issue, the concern for which provided the initial motivation for its participation in the bank. Japan's interest in helping Indochina after 1975 was frustrated. Aware of U.S. opposition to communist Indochina, the ADB provided little lending to that region in the late 1970s.

82. This observation was confirmed in an interview with an MOF official in March 1992.

83. MOF also allowed other Japanese institutions to send one or two employees to the bank on secondment for one or two years, since most Japanese organizations were unwilling to lose people to the bank. This practice allowed these organizations to have their own "reserved posts."

84. Dennis T. Yasutomo, "Japan and the Asian Development Bank: Multilateral Aid Policy in Transition," in Bruce M. Koppel and Robert M. Orr, Jr., eds., *Japan's Foreign Aid: Power and Policy in a New Era* (Boulder: Westview Press, 1993), p. 324.

85. Wilson, *A Bank for Half the World,* p. 134.

86. Anthony Rowley, "The Tokyo Initiative," *Far Eastern Economic Review,* May 7, 1987, p. 140.

87. Yano Toru, "'Nihonka' senryakuni tsuyoi keikai" [Be very watchful of "Japanization" strategy], *Ekonomisuto,* April 28, 1987, p. 33. It was reported in 1991 that the United States was not enthusiastic about the Fourth General Capital

Increase because it was afraid that Japan would be alone on top in terms of voting power. *Nikkei*, November 4, 1991, p. 9.

88. Fujioka, "Enjo o seicho sokushin no teko ni" [Assistance as the lever that promotes growth], *Nihon keizai kenkyu senta kaiho*, November 1, 1987, p. 22.

89. South Korea sided with the United States because it did not want Japan's influence to be too strong. Anthony Rowley, "We'll Do It Our Way," *Far Eastern Economic Review*, May 14, 1987, p. 68.

90. Rowley, "Tokyo Initiative," p. 140.

91. Philip Bowring, "Waiting for Wisdom," *Far Eastern Economic Review*, May 12, 1988, p. 62.

92. Yasutomo, "Japan and the ADB," pp. 316–319.

93. "Interview," *Asian Finance*, April 15, 1988, p. 34.

94. A non-Japanese ADB official who later moved to the World Bank commented that the ADB's management style is very different from the World Bank's. He left the ADB because the bank emphasizes seniority, which is unappealing for young professionals. But he allows that the ADB is more predictable than the World Bank. Discussion, November 1, 1998.

95. Fujioka, "Ajia ni takamaru nihon no hyoban" [Japan's higher reputation in Asia], *Kinzai Weekly*, August 1, 1988, p. 82.

96. Rowley, "We'll Do It Our Way," p. 70.

97. He also pointed out that Europeans were concerned about their role in Asia when they saw Japan's prestige rising. The United States was trying to have a larger voice while reducing its financial contributions. Compared to twenty-two years ago, the international relations have changed greatly. Fujioka, "Ajia ni takamaru nihon no hyoban," p. 83.

98. See Yasutomo, "Japan and the ADB," pp. 324–330.

99. Yasutomo, *Multilateralism in Japan's Foreign Policy*, pp. 97–98.

100. Jonathan Friedland, "Enter Mr. Nice Guy," *Far Eastern Economic Review*, March 29, 1990, p. 58.

101. This dispute frustrated MOF officials. One MOF official commented that the MOF failed to resume aid to China due to the "incompetence" of Tarumizu in carrying out the mission. He resented the fact that the United States had too much influence in the bank while paying far less than Japan. Interview with a MOF official in March 1992 in Tokyo.

102. Anthony Rowley, "Nice to Be Needed," *Far Eastern Economic Review*, May 7, 1992, pp. 42–43.

103. Yasutomo, *Multilateralism in Japan's Foreign Policy*, pp. 90–91.

104. Shada Islam, "Loan Words," *Far Eastern Economic Review*, May 19, 1994, p. 47.

105. Wendy Cooper et al., "Sato Cold-Shouldered by Asians," *Institutional Investor*, June 1995; Kevin Murphy, "In Search of a New ADB," *International Herald Tribune*, May 6, 1995; Chan Sue Meng, "ADB Trips on Hard Issue of Soft Loan," *The Straits Times*, May 6, 1995, p. 6.

106. Discussion with an official at the ADB's North American Representative Office, Washington, DC, July 26, 1999.

107. Interview with an MOF official in March 1992. Japan's more broadly defined national interests might still be out of joint with those of the United States.

"We don't care about Africa or Eastern Europe. We are only concerned about Asia," the official said.

108. *ADB Annual Report,* 1998, p. 214.

109. *ADB Annual Report,* 1998, p. 7. ADB loans for 1998 dropped to $6 billion, which is only slightly above the 1990s average.

110. Salil Tripathi, "Strategic Shift," *Far Eastern Economic Review,* September 17, 1998, p. 44.

111. Justin Marozzi, "ADB: Chief Defends His Corner," *Financial Times,* April 7, 1998. For ADB self-defense, see Ian Gill, "Battling the Asian Contagion," *ADB Review* (ADB Online) 1, no. 1 (May/June 1998).

112. Emig, "Japan's Challenge to the World Bank."

113. The Japanese foreign ministry reasoned that multilateral aid monies "make use of the specialized knowledge of the various international organizations," "secure the political neutrality of aid," "establish new relations with countries such as in Africa, with which Japan has had little human interchange," and "bring about improvements in the tying status and quality of ODA." MFA, *Japan's ODA 1988,* p. 57.

5

Japan Between the United States and East Asia

This chapter integrates the explanations for Japan's relations with the United States, East Asia, and the three international financial institutions provided in the previous chapters. By resorting mainly to economic means—and mostly cooperative at that—Japan behaves "strangely" compared with normal major powers, which augment cooperative economic statecraft with military threats, military force, and punitive economic measures. At the same time, Japan's unique domestic and international circumstances make its behavior more understandable. Section 1 discusses whether Japan has been strategic. Section 2 illustrates Japan's balancing between Asia and the West. Section 3 highlights the theoretical implications of my discussions and what remains uncertain. Section 4 discusses Japan's current foreign relations and contemplates its future foreign orientations.

How Strategic Is Japan Anyway? What Does Strategy Mean?

Japan has been strategic. First, a strategic country has focused and shared objectives. Japan's shared mission is maintenance of a stable international environment in which the country can survive and prosper and it should focus on acquisition of wealth. Second, a strategic country pursues its goals by maximizing gains given the incentive structure it faces. Japan has done that consistently. Its balance between competition and cooperation and between the United States and Asia illustrates its strategic calculations.

The Japanese strategic behavior is unique not in its goals but in the way Japan implements them. Rather than seeking discrete goals and measuring success accordingly, the Government of Japan (GoJ) has adopted a process-oriented strategic approach, aiming mainly at creating a dynamic situation that favors its interests. People often fail to see Japan as strategic because of its highly decentralized decision-making mechanism. But even countries such as the United States do not always have consistent strategies. The Yoshida doctrine is as strategic as the U.S. cold war strategy.[1]

Competition and Cooperation

Japan's use of economic power in the world shows that competition and cooperation are not incompatible. In fact, Japanese policy elites are aware of this important point. For example, Kuriyama Takakazu, Japan's ambassador to the United States in 1992–95 and former vice foreign minister, observed that "the central issue in our [Japan–United States] economic relations was how to make cooperation and competition compatible."[2] Japan has been a competitor in creating wealth but a cooperator in the use of economic power, which ultimately helps it achieve competitive aims.[3] Japan is a competitor and supporter for the United States, a unique leader in Asia, and a financier of multilateral financial organizations. It often cooperates just enough to accomplish its competitive objectives, well short of the expectation of its partners. But it has rarely challenged the United States, threatened Asia, or pushed hard in the institutions.

Cooperation requires, first of all, clear intention and efforts. Japan has indeed made purposeful efforts aimed at cooperation. Second, cooperation has to be appreciated as such by target countries or international organizations, which explains their different assessment of Japan's cooperation. Perceptions aside, Japan is highly selective about where and by how much it cooperates. It has, most notably, tried to substitute its lack of cooperation in trade with contributions in other areas.

Assessing Japan's Approach

Japan, on the one hand, has achieved what it really wants. It has become fabulously rich while improving its position between Asia and the West.

Looking at its record, Japan's gains from its foreign relations are substantial, its competition intense, and its conflicts constant but low in intensity. In shaping relations with the West, Asia, and international organizations, Japan's use of economic resources has been central to its success. For Japan, economic tools entail lower costs than military statecraft overseas, which is forbidden by its constitution in any case.

On the other hand, this approach has also restricted the extent of Japan's diplomatic gains. It is difficult to deal with conventional security concerns with economic means alone, particularly during crises. By the late 1980s Japanese showed considerable confidence in assuring security with economic tools, particularly their technological clout. But the Persian Gulf War changed that. As Kosaka Masataka observed, the "suggestion that we were entering an age of economic power has clearly lost its credibility in the wake of the Iraqi invasion of Kuwait."[4] China's rise and its military exercises in 1995–96 also weakened that Japanese conviction. North Korea's failed missile test over Japan in August 1998 shocked the Japanese nation and facilitated a swing of public mood for enhancing Japan's defense capabilities. It is also difficult to achieve discrete objectives with economic statecraft alone. A good example was the failed effort by Ozawa Ichiro in 1991 to offer Moscow $26 billion of aid in exchange for its concession in the territorial issue.[5] Furthermore, substitution of economic cooperation for defense cooperation can go only so far. The United States adopted a much harsher economics-centered strategy toward Japan after the end of the cold war. Besides the inherent problems of economic statecraft, the reputation for shrewd calculation Tokyo has gained means that even its friends often question its intentions.

Japan Between the United States and East Asia

Japan straddles Asia and the West. "Japan's modernization process has been like the swing of a pendulum, first swinging toward the West, then back to indigenous and culturally familiar Asia," pointed out Yoichi Funabashi.[6] Samuel P. Huntington called Japan "a civilization unique to itself," whose cultural differences from other East Asian countries "preclude it from creating a Japanese-led regional economic group" and whose cultural differences with the West "exacerbate misunderstanding and antagonism in its economic relations with the United States and Europe."[7] In a less flattering tone, a senior Japan specialist in the Chinese foreign ministry sees Japan as "a strange creature between Asia and the West," with features from both, and asserts that "Japan's true interest should be in Asia," since "Japan is not accepted by the West as a Western nation."[8]

GoJ has expressed its intention to balance between Asia and the West and has taken actions accordingly.[9] Japan's use of economic power illustrates its balancing, which means making sure what is cooperative for one party will not be seen as uncooperative by a third party. As Table 5.1 shows, Japan has employed economic power differently vis-à-vis the United States, East Asia, and the three international financial organizations. Japan has used defense contributions, participation in sanctions, financial contributions to the World Bank, the International Monetary Fund (IMF), and the Asian Development Bank (ADB), official development assistance (ODA), foreign direct investment (FDI), and portfolio investments in the West to alleviate Western criticism of its foreign economic practices and ensure its security arrangements with the United States and access to the U.S. market and technologies. For East Asia, Tokyo has concentrated on economic cooperation, which essentially means ODA, other official flows (OOF), and private capital flow. Japan has used economic ties with Asia to enhance its competitiveness against the West while relying on security arrangements with the United States to ensure its security in Asia and to avoid confrontation with key Asian nations. For the international financial institutions, Tokyo commits massive financial resources to demonstrate its international contributions, to raise its international status, and to influence, tentatively, its policy and orientation.

Serious asymmetries in what Americans and Asians want at any given time make Japan's balancing challenging. Japan's economic relations are competitive with the West and complementary with Asia despite increased competition in recent years. In contrast, its security interests converge with those of the United States while conflicting with those of key Asian nations such as China. The following paragraphs elaborate on these asymmetries and the growing importance of a strategic triangular dynamic among China, Japan, and the United States.

Economic Cooperation

Two features stand out in Japan's economic relations with Asia and the West. First, in Asia Japan's behavior has been conditioned in important

Table 5.1

Japan's Cooperation with the United States, Asia, and International Financial Organizations

	Japan and the United States	Japan and Asia	Japan and Institutions
I. Nature of Relations			
1. Gains	Security, market, technology, stable international system	Market, resources, labor, industrial base	Capital, technology, acceptance, contribution, status, information, financial stability
2. Competition	Trade, FDI, high technology, competitive edge in Asia	Exports, low technology	Voting shares, policy influence, and development models
3. Conflict	Serious trade disputes	Territorial disputes with China, Korea, Taiwan, and Russia, possible conflict	The World Bank Miracle Report, ADB management disputes with United States with North Korea and China
II. Use of Economic Power			
1. Security spending	Gradual increase in defense spending, payment for U.S. troops in Japan, payments for the Gulf War	Slow increase in defense spending, gradual expansion of regional security role	Not relevant
2. Imports	Increase, but still far less than exports	Increase, but still less than exports	Not relevant
3. Investment	Portfolio investments, FDI, domestic stimulation	Direct investment	FDI in developing nations
4. Economic statecraft			
1) Sanctions	Limited support for the United States	Rare use	Avoidance of conditionality
2) Assistance	ODA and debt relief	Massive ODA and OOF, recent financial bailout	Financing
III. Japan's Role	Competitor and supporter	Unique and selective leader	Financier

ways by U.S. interests in the region. In contrast, Japan's East Asian neighbors have to adapt to the consequences of Japan's economic cooperation or tension with the United States without having any significant direct input into the management of that crucial bilateral relationship. Second, Japan needs also to balance between different countries in the region, particularly between Association of Southeast Asian Nations (ASEAN) members and China.

The United States has had an important impact on the dynamic of Japan's economic relations with East Asian nations even though it has not always succeeded in dictating its ally's actions in the region. Through the 1960s Japan offered economic assistance to Taiwan and South Korea in Northeast Asia and noncommunist countries in Southeast Asia, encouraged by the United States in support of its cold war strategy. And Japan maintained only limited trade with Asian communist countries. It offered aid to China in 1979, something the U.S. government could not do by law. To alleviate the U.S. concern about Japan using ODA to gain an economic edge in China, the Ohira government declared policy guidelines pledging to coordinate its China policy with Western nations and not to sacrifice the ASEAN members in dealing with China.

Japan found it more difficult to balance between Asia and the United States after the late 1980s. What was cooperative to one party was no longer cooperative to the other party. Americans increasingly worried that Japan was using its ODA, foreign direct investment, and trade to advance its long-term economic interests at the expense of its Western competitors. As Ezra F. Vogel noted, "by the late 1980s Japan's lead [over the United States in Asia] was indisputable."[10] Dennis J. Encarnation maintained that "East Asia represents . . . a new arena for America and Japan to play out their rivalry."[11] By the early 1990s the newly industrializing countries in East Asia exported manufactured goods to the United States while importing technology, capital, and intermediate goods from Japan. Obviously, this resulted in trade surpluses for Japan and deficits for the United States.[12]

However, Japan did contribute to the economic success in the region. Japan was also cooperative from an Asian perspective because it largely avoided using economic power punitively against Asian nations. It was thus not in Asia's interest to see a worsening U.S.–Japan economic relationship. ASEAN members were concerned that greater U.S.–Japan economic tensions would mean greater U.S. pressure on them since they had received heavy Japanese investments. But they also welcomed U.S.

pressure on Japan to open its domestic market, a move that would also benefit ASEAN exports to Japan, with rice from Thailand as a prominent example.[13] China, in contrast, was mainly a curious observer of U.S.–Japan economic tensions, although somewhat more sympathetic to Japan.[14] Few Asian nations could influence the management of U.S.–Japan economic relations, nor did they complain about Japan's economic contributions to the international community. After all, those contributions went principally to Asia. Similarly, massive Japanese capital flows to the United States were watched in Asia with amazement rather than resentment, partly because Japanese money also flowed into Asia.[15]

In the immediate aftermath of the Thai currency crisis in the summer of 1997, it appeared that Japan's efforts at economic cooperation in the region over the years had paved the way for Tokyo to emerge as the natural leader. But the United States, collaborating with the IMF, assumed the lead, given the magnitude of the crisis and Japan's inability to lead. The United States shared a common interest with most East Asian nations in pressuring Japan to revive its economy to serve as a locomotive for the whole region. However, Japan has recovered from its setback as the region has recovered from the crisis and is promoting regional economic integration and enhancing its influence in the process.

Political and Security Cooperation

Compared to the economic arena, Japan finds it harder to balance between Asia and the West in the sensitive political and security areas. This book focuses on the use of economic power. But the anticipation, demand, or fear of Japan's translation of economic power into political and security power shape in important ways its relations with Asia and the West and make it difficult for Tokyo to balance between the two regions. Also, how Japan uses economic power between the two regions has important political and security implications. Furthermore, the country has used economic cooperation to substitute for political and security cooperation or compensate political and military damages.

Japan has attempted to balance between Asia and the West politically by acting as a bridge between the two regions. On the one hand, Tokyo hopes to represent Asia's interests in international forums when other Asian nations are absent, particularly in the Group of Seven (G-7)/Group of Eight (G-8) summits. Tokyo made serious diplomatic efforts to represent Asia when it hosted the G-8 summit in July 2000.[16] On the other hand, Japan wants to include the United States in any regional political arrangements in Asia. For example, Japan wanted to include the United States in the Asia-Pacific Economic Cooperation (APEC) forum and opposed the East Asian Economic Caucus (originally East Asian Economic Group)—which excludes the United States—proposed by Malaysian prime minister Mahathir Mohamad. As my discussion of the ADB shows, Japan also does not want to exclude the United States from the regional bank. Interestingly, when Japan was perceived to be rising at the expense of the United States in the late 1980s and early 1990s, the country talked about becoming "a global leadership partner" with the United States but avoided any appearance of becoming a conventional leader in East Asia, where its relative power was far greater. Tokyo has mainly used financial contributions to enhance its political influence in the region and the world while avoiding confrontation and high-pressure tactics. This book confirms the conventional wisdom that Japan has been a one-dimensional power. Japan mainly pursues wealth and employs economic instruments in its foreign policy.

Japan's Asian neighbors have different views about its political ambitions in the region from Americans. From the U.S. perspective, Japan has been timid politically despite its economic strength, depending mainly on "checkbook diplomacy." Asians, in contrast, see a more politically active Japan in both the global and regional context. Chinese analysts and officials, in particular, share a common conviction that Japan has been trying to graduate from "economic diplomacy" to "political diplomacy" in the 1990s.[17] While based on some Japanese rhetoric and actions, this view reflects more Chinese worries than Japanese realities in East Asia. In reality, GoJ has been cautious in its approach toward Asia.

Japan has been extra cautious in security issues. Through the early 1970s Japan could balance between Asia and the West in the security arena only by taking an extremely low profile. In the 1970s, due to a growing Soviet threat, neither Japan's financial backing of the United States nor its greater defense efforts caused tension with Asia. Chinese premier Zhou Enlai even suggested in 1975 that Japan should deepen its security ties with the United States and maintain its self-defense force.[18] The Chinese position shifted after the mid 1980s when the Soviet threat diminished. Japan now found it difficult to balance. While the United States judged Japan's cooperation by how much its ally increased defense expenditure, Asian nations generally wanted Japan to restrain its defense efforts. Paying attention to Japan's military and civilian technological capabilities, China and other Asian nations felt alarmed about the revival of Japanese militarism. Asians generally supported the U.S.–Japan security treaty, which would keep Japan in check. "Without the U.S.–Japan security arrangement," as Prasert Chittiwatanapong of Thailand noticed, "the ASEAN countries would find Japan's role in regional conflicts more a source of instability than a contribution to the region's peace and stability."[19]

Japan's transfer of financial resources and technologies certainly may have security implications. Chapter 2 examined Washington's interest in obtaining dual-use technologies from the Japanese and its anger when Toshiba transferred to Soviets equipment that improved the capacity of Soviet submarines. Nevertheless, Japan's technology transfer did not become an issue for either the United States or Asian nations, thanks to its well-established reputation of unwillingness to share technologies with foreign countries. Of East Asian nations, China's Japan specialists paid great attention to the strategic implications of Japan's high-tech cooperation with the United States.[20] But this was not an official bilateral issue between China and Japan. Conversely, Washington has virtually never accused the GoJ of helping to improve the military capacity of Asian nations—China in particular—that may threaten U.S. interests. The GoJ has been careful to avoid publicity on these sensitive issues. It also helps when Tokyo compensates those that may potentially be hurt by its cooperative relations with a third party.

Asian nations' attitudes toward Japan's defense policy have diverged since the mid-1990s. China alone is critical of Japan's security partnership with the United States. Noticing Japan's increased defense spending, two Chinese scholars argued that "Japan would quicken its pace to seek a big-nation status within the framework of the new U.S.–Japan security-safeguarding structure."[21] A Chinese foreign ministry spokesman announced on April 10, 1997, China's opposition to the presence of U.S. troops in Asia and the expansion of the U.S.–Japan Security Treaty into regional issues, causing much concern to other Asian nations that support the presence of U.S. troops in the region.[22] China's rising power is the main concern for other countries in the region.[23] However, the support by Asian nations—now excluding China—for the presence of the U.S. military in the region and the continuation of the U.S.–Japan Security Treaty does not equate with support for an expanded Japanese military role in the region.

Developments in the 1990s show that Japan's balancing between the

West and East Asia has increasingly become balancing between the United States and China. It is a major challenge for Japan to balance between the United States and China. U.S. demands and expectations have increased. If Sino–U.S. relations become strained, whether Japan backs up the United States will become a litmus test for cooperation, and no substitutes for direct support for the United States will be sufficient. China will also increase pressure on Japan, its adamant opposition to the U.S.–Japan defense guidelines and the Theater Missile Defense (TMD) system being a case in point. While refusing to accommodate Beijing over these issues, Tokyo has extended economic cooperation as compensation. During President Jiang Zemin's November 1998 visit, Japan offered China $3.2 billion of yen loans for 1999–2000. When Prime Minister Obuchi Keizo visited Beijing in July 1999, to prevent a further deterioration of the bilateral relationship, the Japanese government reached an agreement with the Chinese government on China's entry into the World Trade Organization (WTO). By endorsing China's WTO bid, Tokyo hoped to demonstrate to Beijing its difference from the United States while not offending the United States.[24] However, economic cooperation will not be a sufficient substitution for addressing China's security concerns and strong sense of historical wrong by Japanese.

Power, Institutions, and Ideas

Three factors explain how Japan has used its economic power, namely its bargaining position, its participation in international institutions, and its changing norms. Based on variation of Japan's behavior toward Asia and the West, the book shows how each approach matters in the Japanese case. A crucial theoretical implication of the book is that to understand Japanese behavior it is essential to study what Japanese want and how they define their interests, which are not automatically derived from Japan's structural position or institutional participation. One would make wrong predictions about Japan's foreign policy at crucial junctions by relying solely on international power structure, interdependence, and institutions without considering Japanese ideas and norms learned from past success and failure and dealings with other countries and institutions.

Realist Arguments

Power matters in Japan's foreign policy. First, power shapes Japan's goals and provides it with policy instruments. Japan wants power, indicated by its obsession with gross national product (GNP) growth rates and ranking in the world. When its power grew, Japan became more active in all three cases discussed in the book. Increased power affected Japanese strategies by multiplying options. And everyone else wanted a piece of the enlarging Japanese pie. Conversely, due to its declining economic power, which started with 1990's bursting bubble but became apparent after the mid 1990s, Japan has begun a gradual retreat from global responsibilities, with a reduction of ODA and continued reticence to liberalize trade. Second, international power structure matters in Japan's strategic calculations. The cold war imperative conditioned Japan's relations with the United States and Asia and its end has led to a serious debate in Japan about where the country is headed. Changing power distribution also matters in that a triangular relationship among Japan, China, and the United States is now more important than other combinations. And U.S. pressure has been an important factor influencing Japanese foreign policy.

However, this book shows that structural arguments provide only imprecise explanations for Japan's competitive cooperation. For Japan–U.S. relations, structural arguments do not explain why Japan has found it necessary to make more contributions rather than challenge the United States.[25] And U.S. *gaiatsu* (foreign pressure) does not explain why Japan is least accommodating in areas such as trade and defense where American pressure is greatest. For Japan–Asia relations, structural arguments do not explain why Japan has failed to balance against a rising China. For the three international financial institutions, structural arguments do not explain why Japan is not very sensitive to relative gain concerns or why it is more cooperative in the ADB, where it enjoys greater structural power, than in the World Bank and the IMF.

Japan's bargaining position provides a better explanation than does the structural position for its behavior. Different from structural position, the country's bargaining position varies between regions and issue areas, contingent on the relative position and interests of Japan's partners or adversaries as much as on those of Tokyo itself. Japan is in a stronger bargaining position vis-à-vis the United States than its structural position would suggest. The two countries are allies in security but rivals in trade. Until the end of the cold war, Washington held a prevailing view that trade problems should not compromise security cooperation. This U.S. preference enhanced Japan's ability to bargain in trade areas, which it considered to be more important. Japan's security concern about China grew after the mid 1990s, but the U.S. security concerns also grew, which denied the United States an enhanced bargaining position. While Japan has greater needs for U.S. protection, the United States also needs greater Japanese cooperation. Japan is in a weaker bargaining position in Asia than its structural position would suggest. The distribution of preferences in Asia does not favor Japan. Asian nations have less resistance to Japan becoming a global power than a regional leader and they prefer a balance of power system to a Japanese hegemony. And Asian nations as well as Japan (now excluding China) want the U.S. presence in the region.

Bargaining position also fails to explain why Japan cooperates in the first place. It leaves unanswered the question of why Japan is less concerned about its gains from the ADB, where it has a stronger bargaining position, than from the World Bank and the IMF. More important, bargaining position involves more factors than just raw power. As Tanaka Akihiko noted, only the United States and China exert *gaiatsu* that affects Japanese domestic politics. China's ability to exert pressure derives from Japanese guilt about the war and respect for Chinese civilization. In contrast, the United States has tangible power resources, pro-U.S. feelings among Japanese, extensive government and business networks between the two countries, and the security treaty. U.S. *gaiatsu* also enjoys a certain degree of "legitimacy."[26] All these point to the importance of interdependence, norms, and ideas. Japan's calculations only partially derive from its power position.

Liberalist Arguments

Interdependence and institutionalization explain partially why Japan has chosen to be a supporter rather than a challenger in its foreign policy. Interdependence offers incentives for cooperation, and institutions facilitate cooperation by reducing transaction costs, sharing information, and changing the incentive structures for countries involved.

Japan's dependence on foreign supplies of resources and markets is well-known. As a creditor nation, Japan also has high stakes in the global economy. But interdependence does not make Japan forgo its competitive interests. Japan has competed with the United States on the economic front since the early 1970s and its economic relations with East Asia have also become more competitive in recent years. On the other hand, interdependence does make it necessary for Japan to demonstrate its willingness to contribute to the international system and to convince others of the "beneficial" nature of its tremendous earnings. "As interdependence of nations deepens," the Japanese foreign ministry reasons, "Japan alone would not be able to enjoy prosperity."[27] Japan's greater interdependence with the United States than with East Asia makes it more important to accommodate the United States than Asia. Interdependence also makes it easier for other countries to accept Japan, implying a non–zero sum game among nations.

Japan has tried to constrain its East Asian neighbors through economic interdependence the way it has constrained itself by its close economic ties with the United States. It has helped to shape an emerging loose and open Asian regionalism. But the United States is also in an interdependent relationship with most countries in the region, albeit with a lower degree of vulnerability than Japan. And, as T.J. Pempel argues, while Japan was at the center in the first stage of regional economic integration based on trade and aid, the second stage, based on FDI, involved "a much more complicated criss-crossing and interpenetration of economic forces than the earlier pattern."[28]

Interdependence, as a general trend, does not explain specific policy well. For that, we need to examine international institutions. International institutions provide both incentives and constraints on Japanese foreign policy. Not surprisingly, Japan's participation in the three institutions discussed in the book help to shape its policy toward them. But institutions also affect its relations with the United States and Asia. Japan has been more enmeshed in formal institutions with the United States than with East Asian nations. Japan is firmly linked with the United States in a bilateral security treaty, while not having formal security arrangements with any other Asian nations. Like any other institution, the alliance needs constant maintenance as well as the justification of perceived external threat. The alliance has been strengthened in the past few years not solely by China's rise. Equally important have been a multitude of formal and informal channels between the security policy communities in the two countries.

In nonsecurity issues, Japan is also an important member of multilateral institutions, such as the G-7 summit, the Organization for Economic Cooperation and Development (OECD), the IMF, and the World Bank. Japan's participation in these U.S.-dominated institutions offers both opportunities and constraints for its foreign policy. On the positive side, multilateral institutions soften the one-on-one focus between the United

States and Japan over trade disputes and sometimes work in Japan's favor. For example, the WTO made a preliminary ruling in November 1997 against the claims by an American film maker, Eastman Kodak, that Fuji Film of Japan had used unfair rules to discourage Japanese wholesalers and retailers from selling Kodak products in Japan. Institutions serve other useful functions. In the early days, the World Bank and the IMF were important for Japan's economic recovery and subsequent growth. In the 1980s they offered expertise and implementation capabilities for Japan's rapidly expanding ODA program. It is also harder to criticize a country's multilateral aid as commercially driven than to criticize its bilateral aid for that reason. The Asian financial crisis also demonstrated the importance of the IMF/World Bank, imperfect as they are, for assisting the region crucial for Japan's own interests.

On the constraint side, international institutions condition how cooperative Japan has to be. In particular, Japan is more constrained in the U.S.-dominated global institutions than the regional institution because its institutional weaknesses in the former seriously constrain its attempt at leadership. The United States enjoys institutional advantages as a host country for most of these important institutions and in terms of the working language, institutional culture and ideology, and appointment of senior executives. In contrast, Japan enjoys certain institutional advantages in the ADB, forcing the United States to operate within an institutional structure and culture largely dominated by Japan.

In addition to opportunities and restraints, institutions also educate and socialize member states, affecting their definition and calculations of national interests. This factor is a key to explaining why Japan is more cooperative with the ADB than with the World Bank. Japan has identified more with the ADB as its own bank, meshing its self-interests and bank interests together. In fact, as Ministry of Finance (MOF) officials who have served in the ADB take charge of Japan's ADB policy, one may make a reasonable case that they formulate favorable policy toward the bank because of their familiarity with its institutional culture and needs.

Similar to its participation in global international institutions, Japan also benefits from its membership in regional ones. In particular, Japan believes that it can play a more active role safely in multilateral forums. Interestingly, Japan sees gains from regional institutions precisely because they constrain its actions, thus easing its neighbors' concerns. However, except for the ADB, Asian regional institutions are loose and informal. Unlike Europe and North America, the region lacks a security community. Japan's institutional linkage with Asia is characterized as "networking," as contrasted with the more legalistic arrangements with the West.[29]

The institutionalist arguments do not fully explain Japan's choice. Interdependence and institutions serve as external catalysts for change, similar to direct pressures from the United States. Such external pressure is effective only when there is a convergence of interests between domestic and external players. In addition, Japan's interests are much more complicated than what the institutionalist arguments would assume. This leads to a discussion of ideas and norms.

Ideationalist Arguments

One cannot simply assume Japanese interests from a structural or institutional theory. Ideas and norms—Japan's and those of its partners—shape Japan's strategic considerations. I discuss instrumental ideas and norms, which are different from fundamental beliefs about what is right and wrong, and refer to those ideas and norms that concern what is the best way to accomplish goals, thus offering immediate guidance for actions. Japan is a changed power in its instrumental ideas and norms. First, Japan has developed a comprehensive and nonconfrontational approach to security, which is different from that of the United States.[30] Japan has avoided militarization in part because of its disastrous war experience. The Yoshida doctrine used the alliance with the United States to realize the goal of catching up with and surpassing the West.[31] Japan became a trading nation by choice as well as by necessity.[32] Proven wise by later developments, the Yoshida doctrine has continued to characterize Japan's postwar policy making, with little change to its essential ideas.

Japan's pacifist tendency has also been reinforced by its understanding of the "spirit of time." "In the global competition among states," Kitaoka Shinichi points out, "the rules of behavior and the meaning of victory vary from one age to the next." Learning from Japan's World War II defeat and the Soviet demise, he argues that "in today's world, a nonmilitaristic development strategy seems to offer the most advantage. It is revealing that Japan and Germany, the two countries that have made the fastest progress in growth, are both lightly armed and have put economic considerations first."[33] This is not just a scholar's musing. The Higuchi report, which reviewed Japan's defense policy for the post-cold war era, concluded that a possible intensified economic competition among industrialized nations seems unlikely to "trigger an arms race in the classic sense of the term."[34] This pacifist conviction limits how much Japan wants to cooperate with the United States in security.

Second, Japan sees science and technology as central to national power. This notion is related to the previous point. Similar to many Japanese, Kitaoka is thinking mainly of technological trends when talking about the spirit of time. Richard J. Samuels labels this entrenched Japanese thinking and behavior as "techno-nationalism."[35] Chinese scholars also see acquisition and advancement of science and technology as central to the Japanese conception of national power.[36] In fact, some Japanese believe that technology is by itself a strong military deterrent. Atsushi Oi, director of the procurement division of the Japan Defense Agency, commented that "strength in military technology and the defense industry means a stronger military capability; it is a deterrent [against attack]; and it gives us more bargaining power in negotiating over imports of equipment or licensed production."[37]

Third, Japanese have developed some basic ideas about the most appropriate and effective way to behave in the world. Takashi Inoguchi argues that it is "unwise" for Japan to seek preeminence and wise to present itself as a supporter rather than a challenger.[38] Simply put, Japan does not want the kinds of goals and roles the United States seeks. Yoichi Funabashi calls on Japan to "search for various avenues of enhancing political power based on economic might, not on military power, in order to stimulate a new perception of the changing nature of power and the recognition that Japan, in these new terms, is a power in its own right."[39] Moreover, as Susan J. Pharr observes, Japan adopts an approach that can be characterized as "defensive driving"—namely, choosing a "low-cost, low-risk, benefit-maximizing strategy."[40]

Japan's dealings with the United States and Asia have reinforced its cautious approach. Japan generally fares better when it is cooperative, thus increasing the incentive for further cooperation.[41] Learning has also enhanced its determination to balance between Asia and the West and helps to explain why Japan has behaved differently vis-à-vis Asia and the West.[42] Saito Shiro recognizes that "Americans are not ready to be followers; nor, for different reasons, are Asians." As a result, "Japan will not be able to assume leadership by a quick initiative."[43] Learning explains why Japan has been more a one-dimensional power in Asia, where it has greater bargaining power. As Asians generally have a stron-

ger memory of Japan's aggression than Americans, they keep remind-
ing Japan of its past, creating incidents to constrain its actions.

It is also important to recognize that due to mutual learning between
Japan and its partners, it is not just Japan's ideas and norms that matter.
Other countries' entrenched ideas or new thinking are also important.
To cite two examples, China's changing views toward Japan and the
revisionist thinking in the United States in the late 1980s and the early
1990s set different parameters for Japanese response. This book shows
that all parties involved are adjusting what they construe as cooperation
from Japan.

Fourth, Japan has its own development philosophy, which influences
its formulation and implementation of ODA policy, the most cooperative ingredient in its use of economic power. At philosophical and operational levels, Japan's ideas of development, embedded in its
development institutions, originated from the experience of its own development and the Asian development. While not articulated through
the 1980s, these ideas guided Japan's choice of development projects.
Partly in response to international criticism of Japan's lack of development philosophy, some Japanese aid specialists tried to articulate a Japanese development philosophy in the early 1990s. They maintain that
Japan supports self-help and manages aid with a small government.[44]
And they argue that the model works. As Nakasone Yasuhiko notes,
"Japan's creation of an internationally applicable economic development model . . . is a significant postwar accomplishment."[45]

At a strategic level, Japan's idea about its role in Asian development
is best summarized in the notion of "flying geese formation." First developed by Kaname Akamatsu, the basic idea of flying geese is that
Japan leads a pack of Asian nations to prosperity in an orderly fashion,
with technologies and skills passing from Japan to the second tier countries and then the third tier and so on and so forth.[46] While other countries benefit from its economic cooperation, Japan remains in a
competitive command in the dynamic process of economic development and transformation.

The Japanese ideas and norms discussed above relate specifically to
why and how Japan cooperates in using its economic power vis-à-vis
Asia and the West, explaining in important ways why Japan chooses
cooperation over confrontation and substitutes economic cooperation
for political and military cooperation. All these ideas and norms should
be balanced against the predominant neomercantilist thinking in Ja-

pan, which provides a strong competitive drive for the country and constrains the extent and arena of its cooperation. Japan's entrenched neomercantilism explains why it has been reluctant to change its trade practice, which is the root cause of its huge trade and current account surpluses. As T.J. Pempel points out, even though many policy tools serving Japan's "embedded mercantilism" in the 1960s were changed in the early 1990s, the Japanese market remained closed to high-value-added manufacturing goods and direct investments from foreign countries.[47] In comparison, Japan's use of economic power in selective areas, such as ODA, is more influenced by economic liberalism.

It is too difficult, and not particularly productive, to separate the two ideologies. The more important point is that there is a fit between economic nationalism and economic liberalism in Japan's use of economic power. Both realists and liberals want a cooperative approach for different reasons. Nationalists accept cooperative spending as a necessary price for keeping Japan's profitable economic relationship with the United States and the world, using its cooperative spending in exchange for its uncooperative earning patterns. In comparison, liberals see benefits in expanding ties with the United States, with whom Japan is in a close interdependent relationship. For East Asia, nationalists want to gain economic advantages through its commitment of economic resources. They are also realistic enough to know that Japan has little choice but to be supportive, given the existing strong resistance to an assertive Japanese leadership role in the region. Japan's economic interests will be enhanced if Japan is perceived by Asia as nonthreatening and helpful in East Asia's pursuit of economic success. Liberals want to transform East Asian nations into peaceful traders, enhancing prosperity and security of the region, and in turn making Japan more secure and prosperous.

Domestic Arguments

This book has not dealt with domestic politics. But I recognize that to fully explain Japan's foreign relations, realist, liberalist, and ideationalist explanations all have to be placed in its domestic context. The following paragraphs point to two areas where domestic politics may help to explain Japan's use of economic power.

First, Japan's domestic politics explains why economic nationalism dominates. The triangle of the Liberal Democratic Party (LDP), bureaucracy, and business offers a powerful domestic basis for the ideology, which favors certain sectors to compete in foreign markets and discriminates against foreign goods. Similar to its domestic practice of offering side payments to other sectors to assure social and political stability, Japan's cooperation in the use of economic power is essentially an international side payment to compensate those hurt by its relentless foreign economic practices.[48] As observed by Ozawa Ichiro, a long-time influential insider in LDP politics, in the postwar period "Japanese politics has had only one role: the supervision of the fair distribution of the wealth generated by the hard work of the citizenry. Politics, in other words, has been reduced to the task of apportioning the dividends of 'Japan Inc.'"[49] Similarly, the global role of the Japanese government is to spend its money cooperatively and distribute part of the earnings of the Japanese citizens to other countries.

Ironically, such a political system biased toward wealth creation and distribution impedes strong leadership. In fact, Ozawa argued that "strong leadership . . . was unsuitable to the fair distribution of wealth, which rested on mutual dependence and compromise.[50] Again, the same logic may be extended to Japan's foreign policy. Japan's weak domestic institutions have constrained its foreign policy. It should be recognized, however, that Japan's domestic constraints have not put its fundamental interests in jeopardy. After all, economic growth strategies and cooperative spending strategies have virtually never been divisive issues in Japanese domestic politics.

Second, in a two-level game, the Japanese government has to negotiate with both foreign governments and its own domestic constituencies. Thus, how willing Japan is to cooperate with foreign governments is constrained by its domestic politics as much as by its foreign partners. At the same time, the Japanese government has turned this game to its own advantage: It has used *gaiatsu* to force domestic change and domestic resistance to pressure foreign governments for concessions.

Japan at the Crossroads

Looking into the future, how will Japan use its economic power and balance between Asia and the West? The point of departure for answering these questions is Japan's declining power relative to the United States and China, a significant twist of fortune for the nation. Since the early 1990s Japan has been in economic stagnation and recession, while the United States has enjoyed an economic boom and China has continued to grow at a fast pace. This basic fact affects the challenges Japan faces.

The number one challenge for Japan is reviving its economy. To do so, Japan needs to reform its entrenched and once successful system.[51] The GoJ and the LDP have adopted some measures, such as stimulus packages and banking reform, and the Japanese economy is now showing signs of a slow recovery. But one cannot be overly optimistic about Japan's ability to reform, given its failed promises in the 1990s. The second challenge is trying to be effective with a shrinking economic base. Japan's status as a declining power has implications for its use of economic power. Tokyo, for example, has already reduced its ODA. Japan will also find it more difficult to rely on its checkbook diplomacy, based on lessons learned from the Persian Gulf War, China's military exercises to intimidate Taiwan in 1995–96, and India and Pakistan's nuclear tests in 1998. North Korea's missile program and testing over Japan led to a serious Japanese review of their basic assumptions about their security and the effect of economic diplomacy. Third, Japan's main challenge in the years ahead remains balancing between Asia and the West, particularly between the United States and China. As a declining power relative to a resurgent America and a rising China, Japan will have a decreasing capacity to influence the direction and terms of the regional international order.

However, it is wrong to write Japan off. After all, Japan remains the second-largest economy in the world and it is by far the largest one in East Asia. And Japan continues to provide financial resources for international institutions and projects. Ironically, Japan is becoming more assertive in foreign policy just when its economic power has stopped ascending because of the emergence of a new generation of Japanese leaders and growing anxiety over Japan's economic difficulties and security threats in the region. Tokyo has become more willing to use punitive economic means to advance its political and security interests. It is also more willing to shoulder a more expansive regional security role and strengthen its war-fighting capabilities, making it easier constitutionally and institutionally to employ military force overseas. Thus we are likely to see the following scenario. Japan will continue to seek a strong alliance with the United States, but will want more decision sharing. Japan will continue to seek cooperative relations with its East Asian neighbors, but will want to assert a greater leadership role in the region, even if such a move will create tensions with China. Japan will continue to contribute to international institutions, but will demand more policy influence and higher status. In short, Japan is likely to become a more "normal" diplomatic power in the near future. But Tokyo will continue to seek balance between Asia and the West, and economic tools will remain its most important foreign policy instrument.

Notes

1. In fact, Akira Iriye argued that "Japan may even be said to have defined a clearer approach to the Third World—at least insofar as Asia was concerned—than the United States during the 1950s and the 1960s." Akira Iriye, "The United States and Japan in Asia: A Historical Perspective," in Gerald L. Curtis, ed., *The United States, Japan, and Asia: Challenges for U.S. Policy* (New York: W.W. Norton, 1994), p. 46.

2. Takakazu Kuriyama, "Japan and the United States: Partnership in Need of Repair," The International House of Japan, *IHJ Bulletin* 19, no. 1 (Winter 1999), p. 2.

3. For a contrast between how Japan seeks wealth and how it spends its economic power, see Ming Wan, "Spending Strategies in World Politics: How Japan Has Used Its Economic Power in the Past Decade," *International Studies Quarterly* 39, no. 1 (March 1995), pp. 85–108.

4. Kosaka Masataka, "The Iraqi Challenge to the World Order," *Japan Echo* 18, no. 1 (1991), p. 8.

5. Robert Delfs, "Carrying the Can," *Far Eastern Economic Review,* July 18, 1991, p. 18.

6. Yoichi Funabashi, "Introduction: Japan's International Agenda for the 1990s," p. 11.

7. Samuel P. Huntington, *The Clash of Civilizations and the Remaking of World Orders* (New York: Simon & Schuster, 1996), pp. 134–35.

8. Discussion with the official, December 20, 1997.

9. See Shiro Saito, *Japan at the Summit.*

10. Ezra F. Vogel, "Japan as Number One in Asia," in Gerald L. Curtis, ed., *The United States, Japan, and Asia: Challenges for U.S. Policy* (New York: W.W. Norton, 1994), p. 159.

11. Dennis J. Encarnation, *Rival Beyond Trade,* p. 2.

12. Yung Chul Park and Won-Am Park, "Changing Japanese Trade Patterns and the East Asian NICs," in Paul Krugman, ed., *Trade with Japan: Has the Door Opened Wider?* (Chicago: University of Chicago Press, 1991), pp. 85–115.

13. Prasert Chittiwatanapong, "Japan's Roles in the Posthegemonic World," p. 219.

14. Wang Jisi, "Building a Constructive Relationship," in Morton I. Abramowitz, Funabashi Yoichi, and Wang Jisi, *China–Japan–U.S.: Managing the Trilateral Relationship* (Tokyo: Japan Center for International Exchange, 1998), p. 31.

15. For example, see Chen Jiyong, "Lun bashi niandai yilai Riben dui Meiguo zhijie touzi de fazhan yu tedian" [The trends and features in Japan's direct investment in the United States since the 1980s], *Riben xuekan* 2 (1992), pp. 19–32.

16. It should be noted that Beijing has never accepted Japan as Asia's representative. In fact, the West has not really accepted Japan as the Asian representative either. Japanese sometimes talk to Americans as if they know Asia better, much to

the annoyance of the latter. As a U.S. official commented, "there are times that the U.S. feels that we can talk for Asia with more credibility than Japan does" due to a history of heavy U.S. involvement in the region. Interview with an official of the Japan Desk of State Department, May 9, 1995.

17. Biqing Zhang, "Riben jiasu tuixing zhengzhi waijiao de xindongxiang"; Liu Jiangyong, ed., *Kua shiji de riben zhengzhi jingji waijiao xinqushi* [Japan to the year 2000: new trends in politics, economy and diplomacy] (Beijing: Shishi chubanshe, 1995), pp. 342–40; Ye Ruan, "Guoji xinzhixu de butong gouxiang" [Competing visions of international order], in Du Gong and Ni Liyu, eds., *Zhuanhuan zhong de shijie geju* [Global structure in transition] (Beijing: Shijie zhishi chubanshe, 1992), pp. 314–23; Sun Cheng, ed., *Riben yu yatai shiji zhijiao de fenxi yu zhanwang* [Japan and the Asia-Pacific region: analysis and outlook at the turn of the century] (Beijing: Shijie zhishi chubanshe, 1997); Jin Xide, *Rimei jizhou yu jingji waijiao riben waijiao de zhuanxing* [Japan–U.S. pillar and economic diplomacy: the transformation of Japanese diplomacy] (Beijing: Zhongguo shehui kexue chubanshe, 1998).

18. A. Doak Barnett, *China and the Major Powers in East Asia* (Washington: Brookings Institution, 1977), pp. 115–16.

19. Chittiwatanapong, "Japan's Roles in the Posthegemonic World," p. 220.

20. See Institute of Japanese Studies, *Gaojishu yu Riben de guojia zhanlue.*

21. Wang Zaibang and Yang Minjie, "World Political Outlook 1996," *Contemporary International Relations* 6, no. 1 (January 1996), p. 5. My interviews with over a dozen Chinese analysts in Beijing and Shanghai in May–June 1999 confirmed this view.

22. *World Journal,* April 11, 1997, A1, A2.

23. See Jonathan D. Pollack and Richard H. Yang, eds., *In China's Shadow: Regional Perspectives on Chinese Foreign Policy and Military Development* (Santa Monica: Rand, Conference Proceedings, 1998).

24. A Japanese diplomat calculated that Japan's overture would not receive negative U.S. reaction since the United States is also interested in China's entry. He also noted that Japan's endorsement does not mean that much since the U.S. decision is central. Tokyo wants to see China and the United States reach an agreement, which will improve their relationship and allow Japan to benefit from a more open China market. Discussion with the official, Washington, DC, July 1, 1999.

25. When the United States was perceived to be declining in the late 1980s, Japan's rational choice, in accordance with the hegemonic stability theory, was to seek relative gains by continuing to get a free ride on the hegemon or to take over the leadership for initial benefits. Richard Rosecrance and Jennifer Taw, "Japan and the Theory of International Leadership," *World Politics* 42, no. 2 (January 1990), pp. 186–90.

26. Tanaka Akihiko, "Nihon gaiko to kokunai seiji no renkan gaiatsu no seijigaku" [The connection between Japanese diplomacy and domestic politics: politics of external pressure], *Kokusai mondai* 348 (March 1989), pp. 23–36.

27. MFA, *Japan's ODA 1994,* p. 49.

28. T.J. Pempel, "Transpacific Torii: Japan and the Emerging Asian Regionalism," in Peter J. Katzenstein and Takashi Shiraishi, eds., *Network Power: Japan and Asia* (Ithaca: Cornell University Press, 1997), p. 51.

29. Peter J. Katzenstein and Takashi Shiraishi, eds., *Network Power: Japan and Asia* (Ithaca: Cornell University Press, 1997); Donald C. Hellmann and Kenneth B.

Pyle, eds., *From APEC to Xanadu: Creating a Viable Community in the Post–Cold War Pacific* (Armonk, NY: M.E. Sharpe, 1997); Vinod K. Aggarwal and Charles E. Morrison, eds., *Asia-Pacific Crossroads: Regime Creation and the Future of APEC* (New York: St. Martin's Press, 1998). For informal networks between China and Japan, see Quansheng Zhao, *Japanese Policymaking: The Politics Behind Politics— Informal Mechanisms and the Making of China Policy* (Hong Kong: Oxford University Press, 1996). For a comparison among the Asia Pacific and the Americas and Europe, see Jeffrey A. Frankel, *Regional Trading Blocs in the World Economy System* (Washington: Institute for International Economics, October 1997).

30. Peter J. Katzenstein, *Cultural Norms and National Security: Police and Military in Postwar Japan* (Ithaca: Cornell University Press, 1996).

31. Kosaka Masataka, *Saisho Yoshida Shigeru* [Prime Minister Yoshida Shigeru] (Tokyo: Chuo koronsha, 1968).

32. For discussion of trading nations, see Richard Rosecrance, *The Rise of the Trading State: Commerce and Conquest in the Modern World* (New York: Basic Books, 1986).

33. Kitaoka Shinichi, "Opting for Global Alliance," *Japan Echo* 19, special issue, 1992, pp. 27–28.

34. Advisory Group on Defense Issues, *The Modality of the Security and Defense Capability of Japan: The Outlook for the 21st Century,* August 1994, p. 3.

35. Richard J. Samuels, *Rich Nation Strong Army: National Security and Technological Transformation of Japan* (Ithaca: Cornell University Press, 1994).

36. Institute of Japanese Studies, *Gaojishu yu riben de guojia zhanlue.*

37. Quoted in "Home Alone," *Economist,* June 14, 1997, p. 14.

38. Takashi Inoguchi, "Japan's Images and Options: Not a Challenger, but a Supporter."

39. Funabashi, "Introduction: Japan's International Agenda for the 1990s," p. 16.

40. Susan J. Pharr, "Japan's Defensive Foreign Policy and the Politics of Burden Sharing."

41. As former prime minister Nakasone Yasuhiro sees it, in the past half century, "our country has enjoyed remarkable economic development and prosperity, and its social and cultural fabric has been enriched to an unprecedented degree." Yasuhiro Nakasone, "Reflections on Japan's Past," *Asia-Pacific Review* 2, no. 2 (Autumn/ Winter 1995), p. 61.

42. John W. Dower points out that in the postwar period, Yoshida held "a strain of thought" that he had cultivated before the war, "the thesis that Japan was as 'Western' as it was Asian, that its destiny was to be a global power, and that the expansion as well as security of the state was best guaranteed by close alliance with the dominant Western power in Asia and the Pacific." Dower, *Empire and Aftermath,* p. 307.

43. Shiro Saito, *Japan at the Summit,* p. 185.

44. See Nishigaki Akira and Simomura Yasutami, *Kaihatsu enjo no keizaigaku* [Economics of development assistance], 2d. ed. (Tokyo, Yuhikaku, 1997). For an excellent collection of some leading articles on the topic by Japanese authors, see Ohno and Ohno, *Japanese Views on Economic Development.*

45. Nakasone, "Reflections on Japan's Past," p. 62.

46. Kaname Akamatsu, *Sekai keizairon* [World economics] (Tokyo: Kunimoto shobo, 1965). However, the notion fails to capture the complex realities in the re-

gion. Bernard and Ravenhill, "Beyond Product Cycles and Flying Geese."

47. T.J. Pempel, *Regime Shift: Comparative Dynamics of the Japanese Political Economy* (Ithaca, NY: Cornell University Press, 1998), pp. 146–50.

48. For Japan's domestic practice of side payments, see Kent E. Calder, *Crisis and Compensation: Public Policy and Political Stability in Japan, 1949–1986* (Princeton: Princeton University Press, 1988).

49. Ichiro Ozawa, *Blueprint for a New Japan*, p. 22.

50. Ibid., p. 23.

51. For critique of the Japanese system, see Richard Katz, *Japan—The System that Soured: The Rise and Fall of the Japanese Economic Miracle* (Armonk, NY: M.E. Sharpe, 1998); Jon Woronoff, *The Japanese Economic Crisis* (New York: St. Martin's Press, 1993); Christopher Wood, *The End of Japan, Inc: And How the New Japan Will Look* (New York: Simon & Schuster, 1994).

Bibliography

Advisory Group on Defense Issues. *The Modality of the Security and Defense Capability of Japan: The Outlook for the 21st Century.* August 1994.

Aggarwal, Vinod K., and Charles E. Morrison, eds. *Asia–Pacific Crossroads: Regime Creation and the Future of APEC.* New York: St. Martin's Press, 1998.

Amako, Satoshi, ed. *Chugoku wa kyoika* [Is China a threat]. Tokyo: Keiso shobo, 1997.

Armacost, Michael H. *Friends or Rivals? The Insider's Account of U.S.–Japan Relations.* New York: Columbia University Press, 1996.

Asher, David L. "A U.S.–Japan Alliance for the Next Century." *Orbis* 41, no. 3 (Summer 1997), pp. 343–74.

Asian Development Bank. *Asian Development Bank Annual Report,* Various years.

Asia Yearbook. Hong Kong: *Far Eastern Economic Review.*

Ayres, Robert L. *Banking on the Poor: The World Bank and World Poverty.* Cambridge: MIT Press, 1983.

Bae, Ho Hahn. "Policy Toward Japan." In Youngnok Koo and Sung-joo Han, eds., *The Foreign Policy of the Republic of Korea.* New York: Columbia University Press, 1985, pp. 167–97.

Baldwin, David A. "Power Analysis and World Politics: New Trends Versus Old Tendencies." *World Politics* 31, no. 2 (January 1979), pp. 161–94.

———. *Economic Statecraft.* Princeton: Princeton University Press, 1985.

Baldwin, David, ed. *Neorealism and Neoliberalism: The Contemporary Debate.* New York: Columbia University Press, 1993.

Barnett, A. Doak. *China and the Major Powers in East Asia.* Washington: The Brookings Institution, 1977.

Berger, Thomas U. *Cultures of Antimilitarism: National Security in Germany and Japan.* Baltimore: Johns Hopkins University Press, 1998.

Bergsten, C. Fred. "Japan and the United States in the World Economy." Paper prepared for Conference on Wisconsin–U.S.–Japan Economic Development, Lake Geneva, Wisconsin, June 19, 1998.

Bergsten, C. Fred, and Marcus Noland. *Reconcilable Differences? United States–Japan Economic Conflict.* Washington: Institute for International Economics, 1993.

Bernard, Mitchell, and John Ravenhill. "Beyond Product Cycles and Flying Geese: Regionalization, Hierarchy, and the Industrialization of East Asia." *World Politics* 47, no. 2 (January 1995), pp. 171–209.

———. "The Pursuit of Competitiveness in East Asia: Regionalization of Production and Its Consequences." In David P. Rapkin and William P. Avery, eds., *National Competitiveness in a Global Economy.* Boulder: Lynne Rienner, 1995, pp. 103–31.

Black, Eugene R. *Alternative in Southeast Asia.* New York: Praeger, 1969.

Blaker, Michael. *Japanese International Negotiating Style.* New York: Columbia University Press, 1977.

———. "Evaluating Japanese Diplomatic Performance." In Gerald Curtis, ed., *Japan's Foreign Policy After the Cold War: Coping with Change.* Armonk, NY: M.E. Sharpe, 1993, pp. 1–42.

Bridges, Brian. *Japan and Korea in the 1990s: From Antagonism to Adjustment.* Aldershot, UK: Edward Elgar, 1993.

Calder, Kent E. *Crisis and Compensation: Public Policy and Political Stability in Japan, 1949–1986.* Princeton: Princeton University Press, 1988.

———. *Strategic Capitalism: Private Business and Public Purpose in Japanese Industrial Finance.* Princeton: Princeton University Press, 1993.

———. "Japanese Foreign Economic Policy Formation." *World Politics* 40, no. 4 (July 1988), pp. 517–41.

Campbell, John Creighton. "Japan and the United States: Games That Work." In Gerald L. Curtis, ed., *Japan's Foreign Policy After the Cold War: Coping with Change.* Armonk, NY: M.E. Sharpe, 1993, pp. 43–61.

Castellano, Marc. "Japan's Foreign Aid Program in the New Millennium: Rethinking 'Development.'" *JEI Report,* no. 6A (February 11, 2000).

———. "Rapid Recovery in Southeast Asia Strengthens Japan–ASEAN Economic Relations." *JEI Report,* no. 24A (June 23, 2000).

Cha, Victor D. *Alignment Despite Antagonism: The United States–Korea–Japan Security Triangle.* Stanford: Stanford University Press, 1999.

Chen, Jiyong. "Lun bashi niandai yilai Riben dui Meiguo zhijie touzi de fazhan yu tedian" [The trends and features in Japan's direct investment in the United States since the 1980s]. *Riben xuekan,* no. 2 (1992), pp. 19–32.

Chittiwatanapong, Prasert. "Japan's Roles in the Posthegemonic World: Perspectives from Southeast Asia." In Tsuneo Akaha and Frank Langdon, eds., *Japan in the Posthegemonic World.* Boulder: Lynne Rienner, 1993, pp. 201–31.

Choate, Pat. *Agents of Influence.* New York: Alfred A. Knopf, 1990.

Clawson, Patrick. "Iran." In Richard N. Haass, ed., *Economic Sanctions and American Diplomacy.* New York: Council on Foreign Relations, 1998, pp. 85–106.

Cohen, Benjamin J. *Organizing the World's Money: The Political Economy of International Monetary Relations.* New York: Basic Books, 1977.

Cooper, Richard N. "Economic Interdependence and Foreign Policies in the Seventies." *World Politics* 24, no. 2 (January 1972), pp. 159–81.

Cossa, Ralph A. "Asian Multilateralism: Dialogue on Two-Track." *Joint Force Quarterly* 7 (Spring 1995), pp. 32–36.

Cox, Robert W., and Harold K. Jacobson. "The Framework for Inquiry." In Robert W. Cox and Harold K. Jacobson, eds., *The Anatomy of Influence: Decision Making in International Organization.* New Haven: Yale University Press, 1974, pp. 1–36.

Cronin, Patrick M., and Michael J. Green, *Redefining the U.S.–Japan Alliance: Tokyo's National Defense Program,* McNair Paper 31. Washington: Institute for National Strategic Studies, National Defense University, November 1994.

Cunha, Derek Da. "Southeast Asian Perceptions of China's Future Security Role in its 'Backyard.'" In Jonathan D. Pollack and Richard H. Yang, eds., *In China's Shadow: Regional Perspectives on Chinese Foreign Policy and Military Development.* Santa Monica: Rand, conference proceedings, 1998, pp. 115–26.

Dam, Kenneth W., John Deutch, Joseph S. Nye, Jr., and David M. Rowe. "Harnessing Japan: A U.S. Strategy for Managing Japan's Rise as a Global Power." *Washington Quarterly* 16, no. 2 (Spring 1993), pp. 29–42.

Destler, I.M. "Has Conflict Passed Its Prime? Japanese and American Approaches to Trade and Economic Policy." *Maryland/Tsukuba Papers on U.S.–Japan Relations,* Center for International and Security Studies at Maryland, School of Public Affairs, University of Maryland at College Park and Graduate School of International Political Economy, University of Tsukuba, March 1997.

Destler, I.M., Haruhiro Fukui, and Hideo Sato. *The Textile Wrangle: Conflict in Japanese–American Relations, 1969–1971.* Ithaca: Cornell University Press, 1979.

Dore, Ronald, and Inoki Masamichi. "Reviewing the Structure of Japan–U.S. Relations." *Japan Echo* 19, special issue (1992), pp. 37–43.

Dower, John W. *Empire and Aftermath: Yoshida Shigeru and the Japanese Experience, 1878–1954.* Cambridge: Harvard East Asia Monographs, 1979.

———. *Embracing Defeat: Japan in the Wake of World War II.* New York: W.W. Norton, 1999.

Edwin O. Reischauer Center. *The United States and Japan in 2000: Seeking Focus.* Paul H. Nitze School of Advanced International Studies, Johns Hopkins University, 2000.

Emig, Anne L. "Activating the Export-Import Bank of Japan as a Development Lending Agency." Unpublished manuscript, Columbia University, 1998.

———. "Japan's Challenge to the World Bank: An Attempt at Intellectual Leadership." *The Japanese Economy* 27, no. 1 (January-February 1999), pp. 46–96.

Encarnation, Dennis J. *Rivals Beyond Trade: America Versus Japan in Global Competition.* Ithaca: Cornell University Press, 1992.

———, ed. *Japanese Multinationals in Asia: Regional Operations in Comparative Perspective.* New York: Oxford University Press, 1999.

Ensign, Margee. *Doing Good or Doing Well? Japan's Foreign Aid Program.* New York: Columbia University Press, 1992.

Fallows, James. "Containing Japan." *Atlantic Monthly,* May 1989, pp. 40–54.

Fearon, James D. "Counterfactuals and Hypothesis Testing in Political Science." *World Politics* 43, no. 2 (January 1991), pp. 169–95.

Feinberg, Richard E. "An Open Letter to the World Bank's New President." In Feinberg and contributors, eds., *Between Two Worlds: The World Bank's Next Decade.* New Brunswick: Transaction Books, 1986, pp. 3–44.

Finnemore, Martha. *National Interests in International Society.* Ithaca: Cornell University Press, 1996.

Foreign Economic Policy Study Group of the Policy Research Council. "Taigai keizai seisaku kenkyu gurupu hokkokusho" [Report by the Foreign Economic Policy Study Group]. *Sekai keizai hyoron* 24, no. 6 (June 1980), pp. 52–73.

Frankel, Jeffrey A. *Regional Trading Blocs in the World Economy System.* Washington: Institute for International Economics, October 1997.

Friedman, David. *The Misunderstood Miracle: Industrial Development and Political Change in Japan.* Ithaca: Cornell University Press, 1988.

Friedman, George, and Meredith LeBard. *The Coming War with Japan.* New York: St. Martin's Press, 1991.

Fujioka, Masao. *Ajia kaigin sosai nikki: manira e no sato-gaeri* [ADB president's diary: return to Manila]. Tokyo: Tokyo keizai shimposha, 1986.

Fukui, Haruhiro. "East Asian Perspectives on U.S.–Japan Leadership Sharing." Paper presented at the 37th ISA conference, San Diego, April 16–20, 1996.

Fukushima, Kiyohiko. "Japan's Real Trade Policy." *Foreign Policy* 59 (Summer 1985), pp. 22–39.

Fukuyama, Francis, and Kongdan Oh, *The U.S.–Japan Security Relationship After the Cold War.* Santa Monica: Rand, 1993.

Funabashi, Yoichi. "Tokyo's Depression Diplomacy." *Foreign Affairs* 77, no. 6 (November/December 1998), pp. 26–36.

———. "Introduction: Japan's International Agenda for the 1990s." In Yoichi Funabashi, ed., *Japan's International Agenda.* New York: New York University Press, 1994, pp. 1–27.

———. *Alliance Adrift.* New York: Council on Foreign Relations Press, 1999.

Garrett, Banning, and Bonnie Glaser. "Chinese Apprehensions About Revitalization of the U.S.–Japan Alliance." *Asian Survey* 37, no. 4 (April 1997), pp. 383–402.

Garten, Jeffrey E. *A Cold Peace: America, Japan, Germany, and the Struggle for Supremacy.* New York: Basic Books, 1992.

Gilpin, Robert. *The Political Economy of International Relations.* Princeton: Princeton University Press, 1987.

Gold, Joseph. "Amendments." In J. Keith Horsefield, ed., *International Monetary Fund, 1945–1965: Twenty Years of International Monetary Fund,* vol. 2. Washington: International Monetary Fund, 1969, pp. 595–605.

Goldstein, Judith, and Robert O. Keohane, eds. *Ideas and Foreign Policy: Beliefs, Institutions and Political Change.* Ithaca: Cornell University Press, 1993.

Gowa, Joanne. "Bipolarity, Multipolarity, and Free Trade." *American Political Science Review* 83, no. 4 (December 1989), pp. 1245–56.

Green, Michael J. *Arming Japan: Defense Production, Alliance Politics, and the Postwar Search for Autonomy.* New York: Columbia University Press, 1995.

Green, Michael J., and Benjamin L. Self. "Japan's Changing China Policy: From Commercial Liberalism to Reluctant Realism." *Survival* 38, no. 2 (Summer 1996), pp. 35–58.

Haas, Ernst B. *When Knowledge Is Power.* Berkeley: University of California Press, 1990.

Harwit, Eric. "Japanese Investment in China: Strategies in the Electronics and Automobile Sectors." *Asian Survey* 36, no. 10 (October 1996), pp. 978–94.

Hatch, Walter, and Kozo Yamamura. *Asia in Japan's Embrace: Building a Regional Production Alliance.* New York: Cambridge University Press, 1996.

Havens, Thomas R. *Fire Across the Sea: The Vietnam War and Japan, 1965–1975.* Princeton: Princeton University Press, 1987.

Heginbotham, Eric, and Richard J. Samuels. "Mercantile Realism and Japanese Foreign Policy." *International Security* 22, no. 4 (Spring 1998), pp. 171–203.

Hellmann, Donald C. "The United States and Asia in an Age of International Upheaval." *Current History* 91, no. 569 (December 1992), pp. 401–406.

Hellmann, Donald C., and Kenneth B. Pyle, eds. *From APEC to Xanadu: Creating a Viable Community in the Post-Cold War Pacific.* Armonk, NY: M.E. Sharpe, 1997.

Hiroshi, Yashiki. *Nichu boeki annai* [Information of Japan–China trade]. Tokyo: Nihon keizai shimbunsha, 1964.

Holsti, K.J. *International Politics: A Framework for Analysis,* 4th ed. Englewood Cliffs, NJ: Prentice-Hall, 1983.

Hosono, Akio. "The United States and Japan in Development Assistance and International Cooperation." In Hideo Sato and I.M. Destler, eds. *Leadership Sharing in the New International System: Japan and the United States,* Special Research Project on the New International System, University of Tsukuba, Japan, September 1996, pp. 114–15.

Huang, Po-wen, Jr. *The Asian Development Bank: Diplomacy and Development in Asia.* New York: Vantage, 1975.

Hufbauer, Gary Clyde, Jeffrey J. Schott, and Kimberly Ann Elliott. *Economic Sanctions Reconsidered: History and Current Policy,* vol. 1, 2d ed. Washington: Institute of International Economics, 1990.

Huntington, Samuel P. *The Clash of Civilizations and the Remaking of World Orders.* New York: Simon & Schuster, 1996.

Inada, Juichi. "Japan's Aid Diplomacy: Economic, Political or Strategic? *Millennium: Journal of International Studies* 18, no. 3 (1989), pp. 399–414.

———. "Stick or Carrot? Japanese Aid Policy and Vietnam." In Bruce M. Koppel and Robert M. Orr, Jr., eds., *Japan's Foreign Aid: Power and Policy in a New Era.* Boulder: Westview, 1993, pp. 111–34.

———. "Ajia josei no hendo to nihon no ODA" [The changes in Asia and Japan's ODA]. *Kokusai mondai* 360 (March 1990), pp. 45–59.

Inoguchi, Takashi. "Japan's Images and Options: Not a Challenger, but a Supporter." *Journal of Japanese Studies* 12, no. 1 (1986), pp. 95–119.

Institute of Japanese Studies, Chinese Academy of Social Sciences. "Gaojishu yu Riben de guojia zhanlue" [High-tech and Japan's state strategies]. Internal publication, 1991.

International Monetary Fund. *Annual Report.*

———. *Direction of Trade Statistics Yearbook.*

———. *International Financial Statistics Yearbook.*

———. *International Monetary Fund Annual Report.*

———. *Summary Proceedings.*

———. *World Economic Outlook.* May 1993.

Iriye, Akira. "The United States and Japan in Asia: A Historical Perspective." In Gerald L. Curtis, ed., *The United States, Japan, and Asia: Challenges for U.S. Policy.* New York: W.W. Norton, 1994, pp. 29–52.

Japan Defense Agency. *Defense of Japan.*

Japan Export-Import Bank. *Annual Report.*

Japan External Trade Organization. *JETRO White Paper on Foreign Direct Investment 1994.* March 1994.

Japan Ministry of Finance. *Financial Statistics of Japan.*

Japan Ministry of Foreign Affairs. *Japan's ODA.*

———. *Wagakuni no seifu kaihatsu enjo* [Japan's ODA].

Japan Ministry of International Trade and Industry. *Keizai kyoryoku no genjo to mondaiten* [Current conditions and issues of economic cooperation].

Jin, Xide. *Rimei jizhou yu jingji waijiao Riben waijiao de zhuanxing* [Japan–U.S. pillar and economic diplomacy: the transformation of Japanese diplomacy]. Beijing: Zhongguo shehui kexue chubanshe, 1998.

Johnson, Chalmers. "The State and Japanese Grand Strategy." In Richard Rosecrance and Arthur A. Stein, eds., *The Domestic Bases of Grand Strategy.* Ithaca: Cornell University Press, 1993, pp. 201–23.

———. *MITI and the Japanese Miracles.* Stanford: Stanford University Press, 1982.

———. "Trade, Revisionism, and the Future of Japanese–American Relations." In Kozo Yamamura, ed. *Japan's Economic Structure: Should It Change?* Seattle: Society for Japanese Studies, 1990, pp. 105–36.

Kaname, Akamatsu. *Sekai keizairon* [World economics]. Tokyo: Kunimoto shobo, 1965.

Kaplan, Morton. *System and Process in International Politics.* New York: Wiley, 1957.

Katada, Saori N. "Two Aid Hegemons: Japanese–U.S. Interaction and Aid Allocation to Latin America and the Caribbean." *World Development* 25, no. 6 (June 1997), pp. 931–45.

———. "The Japanese Government in Two Mexican Financial Crises: An Emerging International Lender-of-Last-Resort." *Pacific Affairs* 71, no. 1 (Spring 1998), pp. 61–79.

Katz, Richard. *Japan—The System That Soured: The Rise and Fall of the Japanese Economic Miracle.* Armonk, NY: M.E. Sharpe, 1998.

Katzenstein, Peter J., ed. *Cultural Norms and National Security: Police and Military in Postwar Japan.* Ithaca: Cornell University Press, 1996.

Katzenstein, Peter J., and Takashi Shiraishi, eds. *Network Power: Japan and Asia.* Ithaca: Cornell University Press, 1997.

Keddell, Joseph P., Jr. *The Politics of Defense in Japan: Managing Internal and External Pressures.* Armonk, NY: M.E. Sharpe, 1993.

Kennedy, Paul. *The Rise and Fall of the Great Power.* New York: Random House, 1987.

Keohane, Robert O. *After Hegemony: Cooperation and Discord in the World Political Economy.* Princeton: Princeton University Press, 1984.

———. *International Institutions and State Power: Essays in International Relations Theory.* Boulder: Westview Press, 1989.

Keohane, Robert O., ed. *Neorealism and Its Critics.* New York: Columbia University Press, 1986.

Keohane, Robert O., and Joseph S. Nye, Jr. *Power and Interdependence.* Boston: Little, Brown, 1977.

Kindleberger, Charles P. *The World in Depression, 1929–1939.* Berkeley: University of California Press, 1986.

King, Gary, Robert O. Keohane, and Sidney Verba. *Designing Social Inquiry: Sci-*

entific Inference in Qualitative Research. Princeton: Princeton University Press, 1994.

Kitaoka, Shinichi. "Opting for Global Alliance." *Japan Echo* 19, special issue (1992), pp. 26–36.

———. "Wangan senso to nihon no gaiko" [The Gulf War and Japan's diplomacy]. *Kokusai mondai* [International affairs] 377 (August 1991), pp. 2–13.

Kosaka, Masataka. *Saisho Yoshida Shigeru* [Prime Minister Yoshida Shigeru]. Tokyo: Chuo koronsha, 1968.

———. "The Iraqi Challenge to the World Order." *Japan Echo* 18, no. 1 (1991), pp. 8–13.

Krasner, Stephen D. "Power Structures and Regional Development Banks." *International Organization* 35, no. 2 (Spring 1981), 303–29.

———. "Structural Causes and Regime Consequences." In Krasner, ed., *International Regimes*. Ithaca: Cornell University Press, 1983, pp. 1–22.

———, ed. *International Regimes*. Ithaca: Cornell University Press, 1981.

———. "Global Communications and National Power." *World Politics* 43, no. 3 (April 1991), pp. 336–66.

———. "State Power and the Structure of International Trade." *World Politics* 28, no. 3 (April 1976), pp. 317–47.

Krishnamurti, R. *ADB: The Seeding Days*. Manila: ADB, 1977.

Krugman, Paul, ed. *Trade with Japan: Has the Door Opened Wider?* Chicago: University of Chicago Press, 1991.

Kuriyama Takakazu. "Gekidono 90 nendai to nihongaiko no shintenkai" [The great upheaval of the nineties and the new directions in Japanese diplomacy]. *Gaiko Forum*, May 1990, pp. 12–21.

———. "Japan and the United States: Partnership in Need of Repair." International House of Japan, *IHJ Bulletin* 19, no. 1 (Winter 1999), pp. 1–4.

Lee, Chae-Jin. *China and Japan: New Economic Diplomacy*. Stanford: Hoover Institution Press, 1984.

Lincoln, Edward J. *Japan's Unequal Trade*. Washington: Brookings Institution, 1990.

———. "Japan in the 1990s: A New Kind of World Power." *Brookings Review* (Spring 1992), pp. 12–17.

———. "Japan's Financial Mess," *Foreign Affairs* 77, no. 3 (May/June 1998), pp. 57–66.

Lindsey, Brink, and Aaron Lukas. "Revisiting the 'Revisionists': The Rise and Fall of the Japanese Economic Model." Cato Institute, Trade Policy Analysis No. 3, July 31, 1998.

Liu Jiangyong, ed. *Kua shiji de Riben zhengzhi jingji waijiao xinqushi* [Japan to the year 2000: new trends in politics, economy and diplomacy]. Beijing: Shishi chubanshe, 1995.

Lu, Zhongwei. *Xinjiu jiaoti de Dongya geju* [East Asia in transition]. Beijing: Shishi chubanshe, 1993.

Mason, Mark. *American Multinationals and Japan*. Cambridge: Council on East Asian Studies, Harvard University, 1992.

Mendl, Wolf. *Japan's Asia Policy: Regional Security and Global Interest*. London: Routledge, 1995.

Minami, Ryoshi. *The Economic Development of Japan: A Quantitative Study*, 2d ed. London: Macmillan Press, 1994.

Mochizuki, Mike M. "American and Japanese Strategic Debates: The Need for a New Synthesis." In Mike M. Mochizuki, ed., *Toward a True Alliance: Restructuring U.S.–Japan Security Relations.* Washington: Brookings Institution, 1997, pp. 43–82.

———. *Japan Reorients: The Quest for Wealth and Security in East Asia.* Washington: Brookings Institution, 1998.

Modelski, George. "Is World Politics Evolutionary Learning?" *International Organization* 44, 1 (Winter 1990), pp. 1–24.

Morgenthau, Hans J. *Politics Among Nations*, 5th ed., revised. New York: Alfred A. Knopf, 1978.

Morimoto, Satoshi. "Chinese Military Power in Asia: A Japanese Perspective." In Jonathan D. Pollack and Richard H. Yang, eds., *In China's Shadow: Regional Perspectives on Chinese Foreign Policy and Military Development.* Santa Monica: Rand, conference proceedings, 1998, pp. 37–49.

———. "Confronting the North Korean Threat." *Japan Echo* 26, no. 1 (February 1999), pp. 25–29.

Morita, Akio, and Ishihara Shintaro. *"No" to ieru Nihon* [The Japan that can say "no"]. Tokyo: Kobunsha, 1989.

Morrison, Charles E. "Japan and the ASEAN Countries: The Evolution of Japan's Regional Role." In Takashi Inoguchi and Daniel I. Okimoto, eds., *The Political Economy of Japan: The Changing International Context,* vol. 2. Stanford: Stanford University Press, 1988, pp. 414–45.

———. "Southeast Asia and U.S.–Japan Relations." In Gerald L. Curtis, ed., *The United States, Japan, and Asia: Challenges for U.S. Policy.* New York: W.W. Norton, 1994, pp. 140–58.

Nakagawa, Koji. *Ajia Kaihatsu Ginko: Junen no Jisseki to Tomen Suru Kadai* [The Asian Development Bank: 10 years of accomplishments and the tasks ahead]. Tokyo: Kyoikusha, 1979.

Nakasone, Yasuhiro. "Reflections on Japan's Past." *Asia-Pacific Review* 2, no. 2 (Autumn/Winter 1995), pp. 53–71.

Nau, Henry R. "Identity and International Politics: An Alternative to Neorealism." Paper presented at the annual meeting of the American Political Science Association, Washington, September 1993.

Nishigaki, Akira, and Yasutami Shimomura. *Japan's Aid: Historical Roots, Contemporary Issues and Future Agenda.* Tokyo: Overseas Economic Cooperation Fund, January 1996.

———. *Kaihatsu enjo no keizaigaku* [Economics of development assistance], 2d ed. Tokyo: Yuhikaku, 1997.

Nishihara, Masashi. "Japan's Receptivity to Conditional Engagement." In James Shinn, ed., *Weaving the Net: Conditional Engagement with China.* New York: Council on Foreign Relations Press, 1996, pp. 174–90.

Noda, Nobuo. "Japan in a World of Rival Empires." *Japan Echo* 26, no. 3 (June 1999), pp. 8–11.

Nye, Joseph S., Jr. "Neorealism and Neoliberalism." *World Politics* 40, no. 2 (January, 1988), pp. 237–51.

———. "Nuclear Learning and U.S.–Soviet Security Regimes." *International Organization* 41, no. 3 (Summer 1987), pp. 371–402.

———. "The Case for Deep Engagement." *Foreign Affairs* 74, no. 4 (July/August 1995), pp. 90–102.

Ogata, Sadako. "Japanese Attitudes Toward China." *Asian Survey* 5, no. 8 (August 1965), pp. 389–98.

———. "Shifting Power Relations in Multilateral Development Banks." *Journal of International Studies* [Institute of International Relations, Sophia University, Tokyo], 22 (January 1989), pp. 1–25.

Ohno, Kenichi, and Izumi Ohno, eds. *Japanese Views on Economic Development: Diverse Paths to the Market.* London: Routledge, 1998.

———. *IMF to sekai ginko: Uchi gawa kara mita kaihatsu kinyu kikan* [IMF and World Bank: the development of financial institutions seen from inside]. Tokyo: Nihon hyoronsha, 1993.

Okazaki, Hisahiko, and Sato Seizaburo. "Redefining the Role of Japanese Military Power." *Japan Echo* 18, no. 1 (1991), pp. 20–25.

Okimoto, Daniel I. *Between MITI and the Market: Japanese Industrial Policy for High Technology.* Stanford: Stanford University Press, 1989.

Okita, Saburo. *Japan's Challenging Years: Reflections on My Lifetime.* Sydney: George Allen & Unwin, 1983.

Organization for Economic Cooperation and Development. *Development Cooperation* (Washington, 1975).

Orr, Robert M., Jr. *The Emergence of Japan's Foreign Aid Power.* New York: Columbia University Press, 1990.

———. "The Rising Sun: Japan's Foreign Aid to ASEAN, the Pacific Basin and the Republic of Korea." *Journal of International Affairs* 41, no. 1 (Summer/Fall 1987), pp. 39–62.

———. "The Aid Factor in U.S.–Japan Relations." *Asian Survey* 28, no. 7 (July 1988), pp. 740–56.

———. "Collaboration or Conflict? Foreign Aid and U.S.–Japan Relations." *Pacific Affairs* 62, no. 4 (Winter 1989/90), pp. 476–89.

Oshiba, Ryo. "Nihon gaiko to kokusai kinyu soshiki" [Japan's diplomacy and international financial institutions]. *Kokusai mondai* 408 (March 1994), pp. 53–65.

Overseas Economic Cooperation Fund. *The Overseas Economic Cooperation Fund Annual Report,* 1988.

Ozawa, Ichiro. *Blueprint for a New Japan: The Rethinking of a Nation.* Tokyo: Kodansha International, 1994.

Park, Yung Chul, and Won-Am Park. "Changing Japanese Trade Patterns and the East Asian NICs." In Paul Krugman, ed., *Trade with Japan: Has the Door Opened Wider?* Chicago: University of Chicago Press, 1991, pp. 85–115.

Patrick, Hugh, and Henry Rosovsky, eds. *Asia's New Giant: How the Japanese Economy Works.* Washington: Brookings Institution, 1976.

Pempel, T.J. *Regime Shift: Comparative Dynamics of the Japanese Political Economy.* Ithaca: Cornell University Press, 1998.

———. "From Exporter to Investor: Japanese Foreign Economic Policy." In Gerald L. Curtis, ed., *Japan's Foreign Policy After the Cold War: Coping with Change.* Armonk, NY: M.E. Sharpe, 1993, pp. 105–36.

———. "Transpacific Torii: Japan and the Emerging Asian Regionalism." In Peter J. Katzenstein and Takashi Shiraishi, eds., *Network Power: Japan and Asia.* Ithaca: Cornell University Press, 1997, pp. 47–82.

Pharr, Susan J. "Japan's Defensive Foreign Policy and the Politics of Burden Sharing." In Gerald L. Curtis, ed., *Japan's Foreign Policy After the Cold War: Coping with Change.* Armonk, NY: M.E. Sharpe, 1993, pp. 235–62.

Pharr, Susan J., and Ming Wan. "Japan's Leadership: Shaping a New Asia." In Hideo Sato and I.M. Destler, eds., *Leadership Sharing in the New International System: Japan and the United States,* Special Research Project on the New International System, University of Tsukuba, Japan, September 1996, pp. 133–70.

———. "Yen for the Earth: Japan's Pro-Active China Environment Policy." In Michael B. McElroy, Chris P. Nielsen, and Peter Lydon, eds., *Energizing China: Reconciling Environmental Protection and Economic Growth.* Cambridge: Harvard University Committee on the Environment, Harvard University Press, 1998, pp. 601–38.

Policy Council of the Japan Forum on International Relations. *The Policy Recommendations on the Future of China in the Context of Asian Security.* January 1995.

Pollack, Jonathan D., and Richard H. Yang, eds. *In China's Shadow: Regional Perspectives on Chinese Foreign Policy and Military Development.* Santa Monica: Rand, Conference proceedings, 1998.

Porges, Amelia. "U.S.–Japan Trade Negotiations: Paradigms Lost." In Paul Krugman, ed., *Trade with Japan: Has the Door Opened Wider?* Chicago: University of Chicago Press, 1991, pp. 305–27.

Posen, Adam. *Restoring Japan's Economic Growth.* Washington: Institute for International Economics, September 1998.

Prestowitz, Clyde, Jr. *Trading Places: How We Allowed Japan to Take the Lead.* New York: Basic Books, 1988.

Putnam, Robert D., and Nicholas Bayne. *Hanging Together: Cooperation and Conflict in the Seven-Power Summits.* Cambridge: Harvard University Press, 1987.

Pyle, Kenneth B. "In Pursuit of a Grand Design: Nakasone Betwixt the Past and the Future." In Kenneth B. Pyle, ed., *The Trade Crisis: How Will Japan Respond?* Seattle: Society for Japanese Studies, 1987, pp. 5–32.

———. *The Japanese Question: Power and Purpose in a New Era,* 2d ed. Washington: AEI Press, 1996.

Ravenhill, John. "Japanese and U.S. Subsidiaries in East Asia: Host-Economy Effects." In Dennis J. Encarnation, ed., *Japanese Multinationals in Asia: Regional Operations in Comparative Perspective.* New York: Oxford University Press, 1999, pp. 261–84.

Research Institute for International Investment and Development (JExIm). *Kaigai toshi kenkyusho ho* [Journal of Research Institute for International Investment and Development].

Rix, Alan. *Japan's Economic Aid: Policy-Making and Politics.* New York: St. Martin's Press, 1980.

Rosecrance, Richard. *Action and Reaction in World Politics: International Systems in Perspective.* Boston: Little, Brown, 1963.

———. *The Rise of the Trading State: Commerce and Conquest in the Modern World.* New York: Basic Books, 1986.

Rosecrance, Richard, and Jennifer Taw. "Japan and the Theory of International Leadership." *World Politics* 42, no. 2 (January 1990), pp. 184–209.

Saito, Motohide. "Japan's 'Northward' Foreign Policy." In Gerald L. Curtis, ed. *Japan's Foreign Policy After the Cold War: Coping with Change.* Armonk, NY: M.E. Sharpe, 1993, pp. 274–302.

Saito, Shiro. *Japan at the Summit: Its Role in the Western Alliance and in Asian Pacific Cooperation.* London: Routledge, 1990.

Sakamoto, Masahiro. "Japan's Role in the International System." In John H. Makin and Donald C. Hellmann, eds., *Sharing World Leadership? A New Era for America and Japan.* Washington: American Enterprise Institute, 1989, pp. 175–202.

Samuels, Richard J. *The Business of the Japanese State: Energy Markets in Comparative and Historical Perspective.* Ithaca: Cornell University Press, 1987.

———. *"Rich Nation Strong Army": National Security and Technological Transformation of Japan.* Ithaca: Cornell University Press, 1994.

Sanford, Jonathan E., and Margaret Goodman. "Congressional Oversight and the Multilateral Development Banks." *International Organization* 29, no. 4 (Autumn 1975), pp. 1055–64.

Sato, Hideo. "Global Leadership Sharing: A Framework of Analysis." In Hideo Sato and I.M. Destler, eds., *Leadership Sharing in the New International System: Japan and the United States,* Special Research Project on the New International System, University of Tsukuba, Japan, September 1996, pp. 1–29.

Sato, Seizaburo, and Yuji Suzuki. "A New Stage of the United States–Japan Alliance." In John H. Makin and Donald C. Hellmann, eds., *Sharing World Leadership? A New Era for America and Japan.* Washington: American Enterprise Institute, 1989, pp. 153–74.

Schaller, Michael. *Altered States: The United States and Japan Since the Occupation.* New York: Oxford University Press, 1997.

Schoppa, Leonard J. *Bargaining with Japan: What American Pressure Can and Cannot Do.* New York: Columbia University Press, 1997.

Schwarzkopf, Norman H., with Peter Petre. *It Doesn't Take a Hero.* New York: Bantam Books, 1992.

Shih, Chih-yu. "National Role Conception as Foreign Policy Motivation." *Political Psychology* 9, no. 4 (December 1988), pp. 599–629.

Shimoda, Takeso. *Sengo nihon gaiko no sogen* [Testimony on postwar Japanese diplomacy], 2 vols. Tokyo: Gyosei mondai kenkyusho, 1984 and 1985.

Snitwongse, Kusuma. "Securing ASEAN's Future: An Overview of Security in Southeast Asia." *Harvard International Review* 14, no. 2 (Spring 1994), pp. 8–11, 60.

Snyder, Glenn. "The Security Dilemma in Alliance Politics." *World Politics* 36, no. 4 (July 1984), pp. 461–95.

Soeya, Yoshihide. "Japan: Normative Constraints Versus Structural Imperatives." In Muthiah Alagappa, ed., *Asian Security Practice.* Stanford: Stanford University Press, 1998, pp. 198–233.

Solomon, Robert. *The International Monetary System, 1945–81.* New York: Harper & Row, 1982.

St. John, Ronald Bruce. "Japan's Moment in Indochina: Washington Initiative . . . Tokyo Success." *Asian Survey* 35, no. 7 (July 1995), pp. 668–81.

Stockholm International Peace Research Institute. *SIPRI Yearbook.*

Sudo, Sueo. *The Fukuda Doctrine and ASEAN: New Dimensions in Japanese Foreign Policy.* Singapore: Institute of Southeast Asian Studies, 1992.

———. "Japan–ASEAN Relations: New Dimensions in Japanese Foreign Policy." *Asian Survey* 28, no. 5 (May 1988), pp. 509–25.

Sun, Cheng, ed. *Riben yu yatai shiji zhijiao de fenxi yu zhanwang* [Japan and the

Asia-Pacific region: Analysis and outlook at the turn of the century]. Beijing: Shijie zhishi chubanshe, 1997.

Suriyamongkol, Marjorie L. *Politics of ASEAN Economic Cooperation: The Case of ASEAN Industrial Projects.* Singapore: Oxford University Press, 1988.

Tanaka, Akihiko. *Nitchu kankei, 1945–1990* [Japan–China relations, 1945–1990]. Tokyo: Tokyo Daigaku shuppankai, 1991.

———. "Nihon gaiko to kokunai seiji no renkan gaiatsu no seijigaku" [The connection between Japanese diplomacy and domestic politics: politics of external pressure]. *Kokusai mondai* 348 (March 1989), pp. 23–36.

———. "Obuchi Diplomacy: How to Follow a Successful Start." *Japan Echo* 26, no. 2 (April 1999), pp. 8–12.

Thurow, Lester C. *Head to Head: The Coming Economic Battle Among Japan, Europe, and America.* New York: William Morrow, 1992.

Tokunaga, Shojiro. "Japan's FDI-Promoting Systems and Intra-Asia Networks: New Investment and Trade Systems Created by the Borderless Economy." In Shojiro Tokunaga, ed., *Japan's Foreign Investment and Asian Economic Interdependence: Production, Trade, and Financial Systems.* Tokyo: University of Tokyo Press, 1992, pp. 5–47.

Tyson, Laura D'Andrea. *Who's Bashing Whom? Trade Conflict in High-Technology Industries.* Washington: Institute for International Economics, 1992.

United States Department of Defense. *United States Security Strategy for the East Asia-Pacific Region.* Washington: Asia and Pacific Affairs, February 1995.

United States Department of the Treasury. *United States Participation in the Multilateral Development Banks in the 1980s.* Washington: Department of the Treasury, 1982.

van Wolferen, Karel. *The Enigma of Japanese Power.* New York: Vintage, 1990.

Vogel, Ezra F. "Japan as Number One in Asia." In Gerald L. Curtis, ed., *The United States, Japan, and Asia: Challenges for U.S. Policy.* New York: W.W. Norton, 1994, pp. 159–83.

Vogel, Steven K. "The Power Behind 'Spin-Ons': The Military Implications of Japan's Commercial Technology." In Wayne Sandholtz et al., *The Highest Stakes: The Economic Foundations of the Next Security System.* New York: Oxford University Press, 1992, pp. 55–80.

———. "The 'Inverse' Relationship: The United States and Japan at the End of the Century." In Robert J. Lieber, ed., *Eagle Adrift: American Foreign Policy at the End of the Century.* New York: Longman, 1997, pp. 193–214.

Volcker, Paul, and Toyoo Gyohten. *Changing Fortunes: The World's Money and the Threat to American Leadership.* New York: Random House, 1992.

Walker, Stephen G., ed. *Role Theory and Foreign Policy Analysis.* Durham: Duke University Press, 1987.

Walt, Stephen. *The Origins of Alliances.* Ithaca: Cornell University Press, 1987.

Waltz, Kenneth N. *Theory of International Politics.* Reading, MA: Addison-Wesley, 1979.

Wan, Ming. *Human Rights in Chinese Foreign Relations: Defining and Defending National Interests..* Philadelphia: University of Pennsylvania Press, 2001.

———. "Spending Strategies in World Politics: How Japan Has Used Its Economic Power in the Past Decade." *International Studies Quarterly* 39, no. 1 (March 1995), pp. 85–108.

———. "Human Rights and U.S.–Japan Relations in Asia: Divergent Allies." *East Asia: An International Quarterly* 16, nos. 3/4 (Autumn/Winter 1998), pp. 137–68.

Wanandi, Jusuf. "ASEAN's China Strategy: Towards Deeper Engagement." *Survival* 38, no. 3 (Autumn 1996), pp. 117–28.

Wang, Jisi. "Building a Constructive Relationship." In Morton I. Abramowitz, Funabashi Yoichi, and Wang Jisi, *China–Japan–U.S.: Managing the Trilateral Relationship.* Tokyo: Japan Center for International Exchange, 1998, pp. 21–36.

Wang, Qingxin Ken. "Recent Japanese Economic Diplomacy in China: Political Alignment in a Changing World Order." *Asian Survey* 33, no. 6 (June 1993), pp. 625–41.

Wang, Xinsheng. "Ji Zhonghua quanguo Riben jingjixuehui diwujie nianhui" [The fifth annual conference of All-China Association of Japanese Economy], *Riben wenti* 26, no. 4 (1989), pp. 61–63.

Wang, Yizhou. *Dangdai guoji zhengzhi xilun* [International politics]. Shanghai: Shanghai renmin chubanshe, 1995.

Wang, Zaibang, and Yang Minjie. "World Political Outlook 1996." *Contemporary International Relations* 6, no. 1 (January 1996), pp. 1–10.

Watanabe, Akio. "Sengo nihon no shuppatsuten" [The departure point of postwar Japan]. In Watanabe, ed., *Sengo nihon no taigai seisaku* [Postwar Japanese foreign policy]. Tokyo: Yuhikaku, 1985, pp. 1–15.

Watanabe, Takeshi. *Towards a New Asia.* Singapore: Asian Development Bank, 1977.

Watanabe, Toshio. "Drawing Communist Asia into the Free-World Economy." *Japan Echo* 18, no. 2 (1991), pp. 56–62.

Wendt, Alexander. "Collective Identity Formation and the International State." *American Political Science Review* 88, 2 (June 1994), pp. 384–96.

Whiting, Allen S. *China Eyes Japan.* Berkeley: University of California Press, 1989.

———. "ASEAN Eyes China: The Security Dimension." *Asian Survey* 37, no. 4 (April 1997), pp. 299–322.

Wihtol, Robert. *The Asian Development Bank and Rural Development.* Oxford: Macmillan, 1988.

Wilson, Dick. *A Bank for Half the World: The Story of the Asian Development Bank, 1966–86.* Manila: Asian Development Bank, 1987.

Wish, Naomi Bailin. "Foreign Policy Makers and Their National Role Conceptions." *International Studies Quarterly* 24, no. 4 (December 1980), pp. 532–54.

Wood, Christopher. *The End of Japan, Inc: And How the New Japan Will Look.* New York: Simon & Schuster, 1994.

World Bank. *Annual Report.* (Washington: World Bank, 1981).

———. *Summary Proceedings.* (Berlin: World Bank, 1988).

Woronoff, Jon. *The Japanese Economic Crisis.* New York: St. Martin's Press, 1993.

Wu, Xuewen, Lin Liande, and Xu Zhixian, *Zhongri guanxi* [Sino–Japanese relations, 1945–4]. Beijing: Shishi chubanshe, 1995.

Xi, Runchang. *Hehou shidai de jianglin: dazhanlui yu lieguo fenzheng* [The coming of the Post-Nuclear Age: the great strategy and the various countries' dispute]. Changsha: Hunan chubanshe, 1992.

Yamakage, Susumu. "Ajia taiheiyo to nihon" [Asian-Pacific region and Japan]. In Akio Watanabe, ed., *Sengo nihon no taigai seisaku* [Postwar Japanese foreign policy]. Tokyo: Yuhikaku, 1985, pp. 135–61.

————. "The Logic of U.S.–Japan Interdependence: Political Games of Market Access." *USJP Occasional Paper 89-09*, Program on U.S.–Japan Relations, Harvard University.

Yanagihara, Toru. "Miyazawa koso o torikonda bureiditeian" [The Brady Plan that incorporates the Miyazawa Plan]. *Ekonomisuto* 67, no. 15 (April 11, 1989), pp. 37–48.

Yanagihara, Toru, and Anne Emig. "An Overview of Japan's Foreign Aid." In Shafiqul Islam, ed., *Yen for Development: Japanese Foreign Aid and the Politics of Burden-Sharing.* New York: Council on Foreign Relations Press, 1991, pp. 37–69.

Yasutomo, Dennis T. *Japan and the Asian Development Bank.* New York: Praeger, 1983.

————. *The Manner of Giving: Strategic Aid and Japanese Foreign Policy.* Lexington, MA: Lexington Books, 1986.

————. *The New Multilateralism in Japan's Foreign Policy.* New York: St. Martin's Press, 1995.

————. "Japan and the Asian Development Bank: Multilateral Aid Policy in Transition." In Bruce M. Koppel and Robert M. Orr, Jr., eds., *Japan's Foreign Aid: Power and Policy in a New Era.* Boulder: Westview Press, 1993, pp. 305–40.

Ye, Ruan. "Guoji xinzhixu de butong gouxiang" [Competing visions of international order]. In Du Gong and Ni Liyu, eds., *Zhuanhuan zhong de shijie geju* [Global structure in transition]. Beijing: Shijie zhishi chubanshe, 1992, pp. 299–338.

Yee, Albert S. "The Effects of Ideas on Policies." *International Organization* 50, no. 1 (Winter 1996), pp. 69–108.

Yoshida, Shigeru. *The Yoshida Memoirs,* trans. Yoshida Kenichi. Cambridge: Riverside Press, 1962.

Zamora, Stephen. "Voting in International Economic Organization." *American Journal of International Law* 74, no. 3 (July 1980), pp. 566–608.

Zhang, Biqing. "Riben jiasu tuixing zhengzhi waijiao de xindongxiang" [The new trends in Japan's push for political diplomacy]. *Riben wenti* 6 (1990), pp. 9–16.

Zhao, Quansheng. "Japan's Aid Diplomacy with China." In Bruce M. Koppel and Robert M. Orr, Jr., eds., *Japan's Foreign Aid: Power and Policy in a New Era.* Boulder: Westview Press, 1993, pp. 163–87.

————. *Japanese Policymaking: The Politics Behind Politics-Informal Mechanisms and the Making of China Policy.* Hong Kong: Oxford University Press, 1996.

Index

Ming Wan is an assistant professor in the Department of Public and International Affairs, George Mason University. He received his Ph.D. from the Government Department, Harvard University, in 1993. He held postdoctoral fellowships at Harvard from the Program on U.S.–Japan Relations, the John M. Olin Institute for Strategic Studies, and the Pacific Basin Research Center, and was a visiting research scholar at Tsukuba University in Japan. He is the author of *Human Rights and Chinese Foreign Relations* (2001).